John Dewey and the Paradox of Liberal Reform

SUNY Series
Global Conflict and Peace Education
Betty Reardon, EDITOR

John Dewey and the Paradox of Liberal Reform

William Andrew Paringer

STATE UNIVERSITY OF NEW YORK PRESS

Published by
State University of New York Press, Albany

® 1990 State University of New York

Printed in the United States of America

For information, address State University of New York
Press, State University Plaza, Albany, NY 12246

Library of Congress Cataloging-in Publication Data
Paringer, William Andrew, 1948-
    John Dewey and the paradox of liberal reform / William
Andrew Paringer.
        p.   cm. — (SUNY series, global conflict and peace
    education)
    Includes bibliographical references.
    ISBN 0-7914-0253-3 (alk. paper). — ISBN 0-7914-0254-1 (pbk. :
alk. paper)
    1. Dewey, John, 1859-1952. 2. Education—Philosophy. I. Title.
II. Series.
LB875.D5P37   1990
370′.1′092—dc20
[B]

10   9   8   7   6   5   4   3   2   1

Contents

Acknowledgments

Where does one begin? Since a tour of duty in Vietnam in 1969, the many people I have known, the many places I have been, certainly the many books, have helped to shape this book. I began reading the world those twenty years ago and this project is a partial account of it.

Friends and colleagues have been helpful and supportive. I have appreciated their presence more than I can say. In particular, Gene Lieber has labored with his careful eye through several drafts.

Sheri Rosen is the alpha and omega. Time and time again she has set me on track; she goes on with me. From getting this book off the ground to getting my priorities before me she just gets better. I hope I can be the same for her.

Foreword

In this volume William Paringer illuminates what a number of
leading peace educators assert to be the central problem of peace
education, the way we think. In challenging the revival of
progressivism and the attempts to build a contemporary
pedagogy on the works of John Dewey, he comes to the heart
of a central debate in education and a fundamental question for
American and European educators seeking to derive a pedagogy
appropriate to the development of a just, global society. Is
traditional Western liberal education adequate to the task of
developing critical consciousness in a "post Auschwitz, post
Hiroshima" world? This is a voice which brings to the discourse
on the philosophy of education a new and original challenge, a
voice which resonates with those of feminists and Third World
scholars who have posed similar challenges to "the claims of a
few to control the many" (p. 226).

His critique of Dewey which rejects the notion of linear
progress, already challenged by history itself is grounded in a
thorough review of the philosophical underpinnings of contemporary educational discourse. And it arises from his assertion
that education should "situate learning in an agency of social
responsibility" (p. 229), an agency essential to global transformation sought by those who work to apply the fruits of research
and education to the issues and problems of global conflict and
peace. His challenges are those of one deeply concerned with
social justice and exposing the impediments education has
placed in the way of its realization through "the preservation
of unjust relations of power imbedded in school practice" (p. 54).

Paringer shares with the field of peace research a strong belief
that all problem analysis must take social structures and power
arrangements into account. One need not agree with his
conclusions on Dewey to attend to the significance of his critique
and the questions he raises. It is because of his fundamental and
essential questions about pedagogy and his argument that "we
require a transformational praxis which encourages us to look
through the nuclear terror" (p. 244) that his book is included in
this series.

Betty Reardon
Teachers College
Columbia University

Preface

The man who seeks knowledge must be able not only to love his enemies but also to hate his friends.
— Nietzsche, *Thus Spoke Zarathustra*

In a fundamental and personal way, this book has been a catharsis. Not only as a release from its actual production, but in the act of separation from a pedagogical parent. Feeling a certain amount of frustration, anger, and regret towards the current efforts to resuscitate the legend of John Dewey, I argue that his importance and relevancy for guiding contemporary educational theory and practice are severely limited. My critique should not imply an exorcism but a clarification of the ideological premises of his pedagogical praxis.

The distinction between "reform" and "radical," as I have interpreted each in their context of educational theory, shapes my first objection to Dewey and the discourse to which his ideas are so central. A framework which includes the ideological and structural aspects of theory and practice, therefore, is a central aspect of my analysis. In extracting a workable notion of ideology from the plethora of interpretation I argue that it can shed considerable light on the paradoxes of reform as well as assist a pedagogical alternative.

As an initial point of departure, the contrast between reform and radical may be located by determining into whose social footsteps each of us follow, Rousseau or Marx. Henry Giroux, a contemporary educational theorist, states an initial objection radical educators have with the former:

> While this group [who begin with Rousseau] attempts to restructure and reshape the social relations of students along lines conducive to democratic socialist values, they, in fact, end up by divorcing the social relations of the classroom from the kind of theoretically informed action that could link classroom social relations to a viable political perspective. By down-playing the role of content and the need for an overt political framework by which students can examine and come to an understanding of the ideological assumptions embedded in specific forms of classroom social relations [this group] depoliticizes the

1

function of methodology and ends up reproducing in their
pedagogy a limited subjectivist notion of freedom.[1]

In this passage Giroux alludes to what I will be arguing is the
origin of the paradoxes clouding the reform discourse. The
politics of social relations, for example, are explicitly ideological
in nature, but in Dewey we find a philosophical theory which
purposely avoids this terrain. In very general terms, I am
referring to a type of philosophical argument which seeks to
synthesize and/or dissolve the contradictory or *dialectical*
tensions of lived culture by a means of a "reconstruction" process
of the dominant system of practices, meanings, and values within
a culture.[2] My objection with the pragmatics to *unify the dialectic*
is with who and what are left out. I employ a contrasting notion
of dialectic, one which ontologically begins in a "dividing the
one"[3] (rather than Dewey's unification of reality), as the following
passage of Herbert Marcuse expresses:

> Dialectical thought starts with the experience that the
> world is unfree, that is to say, man [sic]* and nature exist
> in conditions of alienation, exist as "other than they are."
> Any mode of thought which excludes this contradiction
> from its logic is a faulty logic. Thought "corresponds" to
> reality only as it transforms reality by comprehending
> its contradictory structure.[4]

The notion of paradox with which I have painted Dewey,
then, is to be understood by a kind of distancing from the
concrete dialectic of human be-ing[5] as rooted in historical
conditions, configurations of social relations, and the structures
of power/domination. While Dewey, of course, was not entirely
unaware of such entanglements, the praxis (or course of action)
which could confront these tensions fundamentally consisted in
"getting rid, by means of thinking as exact and critical as
possible, of perpetuations of ... outworn attitudes which prevent
those engaged in philosophic reflection from seizing the
opportunities now open."[6] His social reform agenda, in my
opinion, too narrowly offered "intelligence as an alternative

*References to mankind as "man" and to an individual as "he" are
retained in direct quotations and are used by the author throughout
the body of this work. This choice was made, in the (regretable) absence
of a more universal term, to avoid for the reader the cumbersome use
of [sic], s/he or her/himself, etc.

method of social action."[7] In claiming the primacy of scientific thinking as this method, he sought a pedagogical theory which could "progressively" generate an educational praxis that situated the learner (individual) within a public sphere, instilling democratic awareness and creating social harmony.[8]

My objection, however, is not entirely *philosophical.* Significantly, it takes issue with the depoliticized nature of liberal reform and the limitations which this form of analysis poses for any educational praxis claiming to be progressive. Much more endemic than another of the "problems of men," the nuclearization of the planet during the past forty-five years provides a point from which to examine how far Dewey's social philosophy will grapple with structural reproduction. While Dewey cannot be rightly connected with a "situation of crisis" that has evolved largely after his time, it is my contention that "reform" has historically ignored how the more longstanding structural and ideological dimensions of human be-ing condition our everyday lives. The result is that reform claims only the more limited agenda of "humanizing inhumanity."[9]

When the recent prognosis of the Atomic Scientists calculates barely three minutes until space and time may be irrevocably ravaged, we seem to be up against a great deal more than Dewey's "philosophical dualisms." In the "Introduction" I expand this theme and the dialectic of optimism *and* pessimism, the hope *and* despair which a pedagogical theory must include. It is this important dialectical insight which begins to distinguish the contextual scope, inquiry, and results of a "radical" or "critical" praxis from Dewey's "scientific" method of investigating social reality. The deficiencies of the reform model, to which Giroux's remark refers, have been concealed in no small degree by the taken-for-granted legitimacy with which its scientific veiling of social reality has been the methodological imperative. At issue here, as Stanley Aronowitz recently spells out in magnificent detail, "is the claim of enlightenment science to certainty and its refusal to acknowledge its own discourse as a form of ideology."[10]

By means of an explicit ideological critique I undertake the deconstruction of the four pillars of Dewey's social theory, particularly as it touches educational practice. By these I mean "democracy," "science," "nature," and "experience." I refer to these with three broadly conceived chapters in which the dialectical tensions of scientific and transformational (Part One), natural and historical (Part Two), and personal and political (Part Three) are examined.

In Part One the particular associations which Dewey made between democracy and science are critiqued, as well as his concept of subjectivity, emergent in the "new individual" embedded within that matrix. The outcome of Dewey's socialization process (self and society), viz., his concept of the democratic, is contrasted with a notion of "social justice," a designation which better accounts for the "structurated" aspects in that process. I think that the difference between a scientific and a critical method points out certain ideological elements of Deweyan "democracy," as well as the preliminary framework for a notion of praxis and an educational agenda for exploring human be-ing.

The ideological foundation of Dewey's "democracy and education," the parameters of his "liberalism and social action," and the characteristics of the "public and its problems" have been intellectually fortified, and the validity of educational reform legitimated, by what I refer to as his "naturalist metaphysics." This intellectual subsoil to which his rendering of democracy and science were connected was spelled out in his organic and heavily biological reading of social reality.[11] He built an infrastructure for a pragmatic philosophy which took as "natural" the functional unity, evolutionary and developmental processes, and progressive teleological direction of the modern liberal worldview. In Part Two I reject the premise of the "natural" in Dewey's liberalism for three basic reasons: 1) it implicitly presumes an "escape" from ideological posturing; 2) on its own grounds, the "scientific approach" inherent to naturalism is incomplete for generating social change and challenging existing hegemonic structures; and 3) the focus tends to be both ahistorical and depoliticized.

In Part Three I try to address the relation of the personal and the political and its centrality for a theory of educational praxis. Here again the extensive historical articulation of the praxis is too large for a full analysis. However, in juxtaposing my understanding of it with Dewey's praxis, heretofore identified as "experience" — the fourth pillar — I believe the distinctiveness of the educational praxis I am advocating will be clear. The context as well as the promise of a praxis which recognizes both individual agency and structural transformation as elements in any process of change, it is argued, advance a powerful theoretical construct by which educators can ground their practices.

In a book published over a decade ago, *Pragmatism versus Marxism* (1975), George Novack asked, "If Dewey's procedures, ideas, and aims are so admirable — and they are — why after seventy-five years haven't they succeeded in accomplishing more in the spheres of educational and social reform? Why have they fallen so far short of expectations?"[12] *Schooling in Capitalist America* (1976) by Samuel Bowles and Herbert Gintis also seriously began a critical reappraisal of the liberal reform orientation in education. The reader may also detect some of my concern contained in C. Wright Mills' *Sociology and Pragmatism* (1964). There Mills implicitly challenged Dewey's unequivocal "celebration" of the "growth of power through science and technology." To have questioned the celebration, Mills goes on, "would have committed him to face squarely the political and legal problem of the present distribution of power as it exists within this social order. And this Dewey has never done."[13] Each work provides argument and research upon which my investigation is built and presses upon educators and citizens to find an answer to Novack's questions. Dewey's pedagogical insights and his stated concern for "the freedom of the learner" will remain stillborn unless the incredible complexity of the structures of domination in this country can also be challenged. I hope that this book renews the debate.

Introduction
Problem and Crisis

In philosophy, as in psychotherapy, what is not said, or what is
avoided, is often as significant as the manifest content of
thought.
— Jane Flax, "The Patriarchal Unconscious"

An admittedly overworked term, *crisis* has been used to
depict any number of situations where immediate, decisive, and
often extraordinary action must halt or reverse the existing
condition. When educators speak of crisis, they may be referring
to test scores, increased illiteracy, dropout rate, deteriorating
school buildings, rampant delinquency, or more profoundly, the
moral and spiritual vacuity in the schooling process.[1] While not
unmindful of such problems, the image of crisis I would have us
consider is the destabilizing and alienating conditions of
modernity itself symbolized most frighteningly by the mushroom
cloud. The educator who sees crisis from this perspective is
alarmed—*angst*—in the existential meaning of that term. Life has
been disrupted, our finitude stares us in the face.

In the reformist view, however, the recognizable
dysfunctioning of elements of our technologically sophisticated
economic and social organization "suggest their own remedies."[2]
In 1931 Dewey wrote that we were living in "a period of
depression," a social life of "disorder, confusion, and insecurity."[3]
Dewey's remedy was better planning and the greater use of
science. "The story of the achievement of science in physical
control is evidence of the possibility of control in social affairs."[4]
The "problems of men," then, referred not to a disease but to an
insufficient amount of medicine being prescribed.

My arguments in this book are framed by the distinction
between problem and crisis: are the issues of social reality (at
any historical moment) to be understood only as "problems" of
reconstruction, reassertion, and reapplication of scientific
method, or as symptomatic of a deeper malaise, a "crisis" and
a transformational agenda. The respective ground tilled by
reform and radical educational approaches[5] involves
fundamentally different *ways of seeing* the aberrational and the
paradoxical. How we perceive the situation of humanity, how

we address its conflicts, significantly conditions our praxis. This introductory chapter offers a broad context for defining an educational praxis which takes crisis as a transformational project for school and society.

Reform and Schooling

In general, the perspective of liberal reform in the discourse of American schooling and education historically has attempted to placate the paradoxes emergent in social reality. In large measure, as Walter Feinberg observes, reformers have addressed "the moral, social, emotional, and intellectual aspects of childhood," and "the injustices and hardships" wrought by "private industry and capitalism,"[6] without relinquishing "the process of capitalist growth"[7] itself. In the advance of modern industrial economy during the nineteenth century, technological innovation, the increasing dependence of political economy upon a labor force to work its complicated machines, and the need for greater regulation of both, school reformers set out to educate a population who, it was assumed, could progressively enter into and embrace the new capitalist order.[8]

An influential aspect of the reform movement today, of course, is propelled by the interests of big business who promulgate their own sense of crisis.[9] Well over a century ago, Horace Mann (1796–1859), a name normally linked with the early progressive education movement in America, recognized that a fuller institutionalization of schooling along a common set of beliefs would best hold the greatest opportunity of upward mobility while preserving the social functions and stability for a growing industrial nation:

> Education is not only a moral renovator and a multiplier of intellectual power, but . . . also the most prolific parent of material riches. . . . It is not only the most honest and honorable, but the surest means of amassing property.[10]

In *Schooling in Capitalist America*, the authors explain that the premise of early reform was that

> formal education, by extending to the masses what has been throughout human history the privilege of the few, opens the upper levels in the job hierarchy to all with the ability and willingness to attain such skills. Hence, the increasing economic importance of mental skills

enhances the power of a fundamentally egalitarian school system to equalize economic opportunity.[11]

In order to facilitate the transition from partial (youth) to full (adult) participation in the social occupations of an expanding, evolving economic order, the reform agenda has stressed two post-Revolution principles: the "conservative concern for order," and a "progressive interest in freedom."[12] A good deal of the reform rhetoric in educational discourse today remains similarly motivated by strong interests to stabilize economic functions and harmonize social relations while securing individual freedoms. The *material* contradictions this orientation produces are not being examined.

The context for reform, where universal schooling was to be "a balance wheel of the social machinery,"[13] draws upon several further assumptions that should also be scrutinized. I believe that these assumptions have been retained throughout the liberal discourse from Mann to Dewey to the present. John Dewey (1859–1952), the figure in American educational history most identifiable with this effort during the twentieth century, expounded upon these concerns during a lifetime of prodigious work.[14] In focusing most of my remarks upon Dewey, my intention is not to isolate the man but to identify his reform agenda within a certain ideological context. My argument claims that the philosophical foundations for reform cannot support a transformational pedagogy.

In the first place, the instrumental needs of a rapidly growing economy required the concomitant development of a citizenry who would either appreciate or acquiesce to those needs. A certain pragmatic outlook was promoted which could "look the other way" when means and ends were complex. Secondly, "thanks to science and technology, we now live in an age of potential plenty," Dewey wrote in 1935, an assumption that reflected the rationality, the means, and the spirit with which social reality would be explained. If the world is knowable because it reveals itself naturally through the senses and the mind, the continual effort to improve our "vision," or powers of observation, what Dewey associated with the function of science itself, offers the key to ever-increasing control and personal satisfaction. Thirdly, and this is a point with which I believe all education is concerned, schooling was claimed as the mechanism whereby consciousness was to be sown; in the case of reform, the ideology of liberal democracy. As Dewey put it in his

Liberalism and Social Action (1935), reformers must address the larger "problem of establishing an entire social order, possessed of a spiritual authority that would nurture and direct the inner as well as the outer life of individuals."[15]

It has always been quite clear that the context for reform begin pragmatically, as Dewey stated in *Individualism Old and New* (1929), with "the corporate and industrial world in which we live, and by thus fulfilling the precondition for interaction with it, we . . . create ourselves as we create an unknown future."[16] This functional relation between self and society, a union never completely understood by the great majority of people, was assumed to be "natural"; i.e., it was never contested by Dewey that the relations of that union which defined the socialization process might be malconstructed. However, in a political economy which requires that its pieces be available, replenishable, and functional to its needs, in a system, moreover, whose instrumental values infiltrate, if not dominate, the discourse and practices supervising the child's development (and the future citizen), subjects come to be increasingly controlled by a "system of surveillance." In Michel Foucault's words, such a system does not require

> arms, physical violence, material constraints. Just a gaze . . . a gaze which each individual under its weight will end by interiorising to the point that he is his own overseer, each individual thus exercising this surveillance over, and against, himself.[17]

While Dewey explicitly spoke of the rational and autonomous individual, an experimental and nonabsolute positioning in life, his mode of inquiry is very susceptible to the "modern gaze." A dialectical effect of this gaze, constituted by reason and shaped by institutions, however, has been to structure a "disciplinary regime"[18] whereby civilization or culture and its dominant, seemingly necessary, relations "lock" us up while dangling the key in front of us. For example, Dewey's progressivism regarded the *student* as a "whole child" who would become increasingly the *object* of schooling and the focus of a certain humanistic investment in her/his development. While the emphasis may be different in a number of respects, some more humane than others, hierarchy and control remain the central values to the debate because the material conditions of liberal democracy still require that an "inspecting gaze," *which is technologically possible and scientifically legitimated,* be constant.

This is not to suggest that there is anything reactionary in Dewey's agenda, but little about it suggests an educational praxis appropriate to the critical-ness of contemporary conditions. With intentions of liberating thought and unshackling movement by aligning itself to the dominant strains of the culture, liberal discourse and the methods of reform ignore the structural conditions of the problem/crisis. A major thesis of this book is that the shaping of schooling and education by the levers of economic organization and social control is a counter-productive basis for facilitating globally democratic societies. By misunderstanding the nature of existing functions in American society, their deep grounding in relations of domination, Dewey's proposed pedagogical instrumentalism is unlikely to transform the schooling process.

The limits to which Dewey's pedagogical progressivism would go were evident in his parting company from other progressive colleagues in the thirties who were arguing for a more radicalized schooling program. Though not overtly socialist, the reconstructionism of George Counts, Harold Rugg, John Childs, and Theodore Brameld challenged the formalism of Dewey's problem-solving methodology and his blindness to a world framed in terms of ideology and power. He agreed with them that educators should be aware of social injustice, but did not find this awareness to be central for an educational praxis. He argued that he did not

> see how the terms of a social problem are identical with the method of its solutions, certainly not with a solution by any experimental method. I [Dewey] do not see how they constitute the leading ideas that will give direction to the efforts of educators.[19]

He claimed that social "crises" exist only insofar as techniques have not been perfected, operations properly managed, consequences predicted, knowledges classified. He tended to explain the obvious breakdowns in American society as a collective misunderstanding, whereby the capacity, methods, and will of human beings to adapt to the rush of technology and new forms of social existence were incompletely assimilated. While Dewey was concerned to locate the concrete problems which confounded human beings, the general solution he offered was largely "epistemological"; i.e., he was "concerned to arrive at an hypothesis as to how this great change [modernity] came about so widely, so deeply, and so rapidly"; or, how we might better facilitate "men and women of good will" into the political process.[20] In *Liberalism and Social Action*, what I regard to be the problem-oriented perspective of liberal reform was succinctly put forth:

> Every problem that arises, personal or collective, simple or complex, is solved only be selecting material from the store of knowledge amassed in past experience and by ringing into play habits already formed. But the knowledge and the habits have to be modified to meet the new conditions that have arisen.[21]

In a more concretely pedagogical example, his early study of progressive practice, *Schools of Tomorrow* (1915), has heaped educational praise upon a teaching technique which had realized an instrumental aim—to understand the function of the Panama Canal. But he apparently found nothing remiss with a lesson that left major structural considerations like the commonsense acceptance of war, imperialism, and the paradoxes of pragmatic solutions, all of which were factors in the making of that canal, unquestioned.[22]

Well-known voices of the educational establishment today, echoing the need for schools to adjust to the demands of political economy, to merge "school and corporate interests explicitly," to fit curricula to "short range and long term business prospects," to acquire "cultural capital"[23] also seem to be holding out the reform promise—one which maintains more schooling will enable "our students to apply their knowledge, values, and experiences to the world they must create."[24] What continues to define this movement today (in either the liberal or conservative guise) is the nearly total lack of acknowledgment, let alone inquiry, towards the construction of *what* is to be reformed and the socialization process it would require. While the dominating discourse in reform today has been the so-called back-to-basics movements[25]—an aspect of the larger hegemonic control of the conflicts and inherent contradictions of the modern industrialized world—the liberal (in general) is far too accommodating in his analysis of social reality.

I am not unmindful of the many educators troubled by the plight of schools, the functions with which schools are currently burdened, and the critical edge that humanity itself is navigating, who find in Dewey a voice that speaks to contemporary issues of legitimation, limits, learning, and the reclamation of a hopeful future. Dewey, indeed, saw that the forces propelling modernity—plurality, science, technology, corporatism—required a greater participation of the populace and a more diverse input of ideas to consider in the organization of social policy. For those whom silence has been the less troublesome course for guiding their lives, for those who remain fearful and hesitant of pursuing alternatives to established praxis and mainstream order, Dewey today embodies a platform of progress, innovation, and practical thinking amenable to any condition of crisis.[26]

In this book, however, I attempt to deconstruct the premises of liberal reform while not losing sight of its progressive capacities. I suggest that the theory of liberal reform is plagued by its lack of ideological critique, its unifying dialectic, and an incomplete recognition of the issues effecting school and society. In putting forth the condition of "nuclearization," which I will describe in the next section, a pedagogical context is proposed which illustrates and investigates the politicized character of all social reality. Dewey's own suggested context—the democratic ideal—informed by a nineteenth-century faith in reason, science, progress, good will, and the more benign transportation of the white man's burden, cannot stand up to the intense thrashing it receives in a nuclearized world. Liberal democracy, science, and efficacy of schools to create social and economic equality are assumptions which can no longer stand by themselves.

Removing Dewey from the contemporary discourse on education and schooling, however, cannot be approached lightly. Henry Giroux, for example, one of the leading exponents of a critical praxis, has become more explicit in situating his own radicalism in the legacy of Dewey. I suspect that this is very much a maneuver for attracting the less-radicalized audience as well as countering the conservative hegemony by working from within the larger sphere and influence of liberalism. This tactic, or strategy, in the opinion of Stanley Aronowitz, while politically necessary, should not be construed as any attempt to "reconstruct" the position of Dewey.[27]

To pursue the power and control issues in socialization and individuation, which I regard to be fundamental to our situation of crisis, Dewey's philosophical premises must nonetheless be challenged.[28] A pedagogy (examples of which are abundant throughout *Democracy and Education* and *Schools of Tomorrow*) which prioritizes the functional rather than the concrete event, the surface rather than the depth, the empirical rather than the ideological, and the uncontroversial rather than the conflictual, I am arguing, will not engender a critical praxis. Rather, as Giroux writes, a radical perspective is enhanced by

> an extended analysis of class relations and historically conditioned inequalities in society . . . perceiv[ing] the self- and social empowerment of students as involving not just the politics of classroom culture but also political and social struggle outside of school sites.[29]

Like Michael Apple, I am concerned with an inquiry that begins "to grapple with ways of understanding how the kinds of cultural resources and symbols schools select and organize are dialectically related to the kinds of normative and conceptual consciousness required by a stratified society."[30]

The fault line which has been already assessed in Mann's time, one which subsequent reformers regularly reassure us may be bridged, is the gap flanked on either side by issues of socialization (the Platonic model) and individuation (the Rousseauean model). Where is the locus of the self-society relationship? My main criticism of reformism is that it wants to repair a system that may be better left behind.

Nuclearization

Crisis denotes the critical-ness of the human condition at the present time and the eventuality of a turning point. The nature of the *problematique,* an expansive phenomena which I will symbolize by the term *nuclearization,* is better understood not as a problem of the temporary incompatibility of the subject with the environment, but rather as a consequence of the structural conditions ordering the social construction of human be-ing. While the crisis is manifested symptomatically in individual behavior, the etiology of crisis is revealed in the dominant ideological structuring of social relations. In Bowles and Gintis, this structuring was the result of production relations and the mechanisms of control to define, condition, and determine the hegemony of American (and global) political economy and, in turn, the praxis of schooling. I am not in disagreement with their structure-superstructure analysis as much as I am with the incompleteness of traditional class arguments. Its origin in the foundations of our social order, however, and its clear intent to examine the inequity and injustice of social reality propose an explicit radical critique which I share. Certainly, it indicates an assessment that the historically dominant discourses and practices which have organized social reality do not speak to increasing numbers of people, are not concerned with nonviolence, nor with the expansion of democratic power through social justice avenues. My purpose in this introduction is to illuminate a further dimension of crisis.

The concept of crisis introduced here, of course, is not unique and its details need not be elaborated.[31] The launching of Sputnik in 1957 by the Soviet Union completely exposed the line of modernity which increasingly had been overwhelming American social consciousness: the technicalization of reason, militarization of the economy, and the forms of social subordination rendered by realpolitik and its pragmatic base. Historically, liberal reform in its many cultural manifestations attempts to solve problems *within* that continuum.

To some, however, the intrusion of atomic weapons into the world has "forced us to rethink the direction of our history."[32] The effects of "nuclearization," a collective symbolic *and* empirical term I use to characterize the (explicitly postwar) organization of human relations, are more easily discernible (and more troubling) today. The particular conditions delineating "crisis" today have been cogently stated by Karl-Otto Apel's essay wherein he locates the present crisis

> in the danger of a nuclear war of annihilation or in the perhaps greater danger of the destruction of the human eco- and biosphere...[and] of organizing the responsibility of humankind for the consequences (and side-effects) of their collective actions on a planetary scale....
> Here for the first time in world history, a situation is visible in which, in face of a common danger, men and women are called upon to assume a common moral responsibility.[33]

From Dewey's hermeneutic, obviously this specific aspect of crisis could not have been perceived. My argument claims that the philosophical principles inherent to reform discourse do not readily permit such structural elements of social reality (such as a war system) to be examined. As the components of this discourse, as constituted by Dewey, are unpacked, the limit which reform will not cross emphatically suggests a pedagogical alternative.

However, before I address these largely philosophical arguments, a more specific description of nuclearization may help the reader to situate further the phenomena of crisis.

In order to secure and maintain a more controlled economy an increasingly militarized society has been needed to defend domestic and global hegemony. The associations developed between "defense" and "security" in the postwar era have led to

> not just a permanent standing army, but a permanent mobilization of economic, social, and intellectual resources: higher peacetime military expenditures than ever before, a rapidly growing arms economy, massive investment in military R&D, and a large permanent military and security planning staff. National security doctrine, in sum, consecrates that tension-filled marriage between the economy, the military sector, and the State that is called the "military-industrial complex."[34]

Exacerbating the socialization process along the taken-for-granted structures of this historically continuous complex of domination (war), "nuclearization" has approached the critical point of no return. In addition to the obvious potential destructiveness of existing nuclear arsenals, consider the pervasiveness of its social repercussions: the expenditure of research and development upon nuclear weapon systems and "defense-related" technology; economic priorities assigned to the maintenance of nuclear security and military readiness; the incorporation of greater numbers of people in the development, manufacture, transportation, deployment, and safeguarding of both nuclear and so-called conventional weapons; the vertical and horizontal proliferation of nuclear and non-nuclear weapons among nations; the increasing internal security measures required to maintain military secrecy; the incidence and continuous threat of radioactive pollution in the storage, handling, transporting, and recycling of nuclear materials; the psychological, emotional, and cognitive effects felt from the preparation for nuclear war/security; the perpetuation of hostility, violence, economic exploitation, and peripheral warfare to maintain nuclear hegemony; the increasing need for protection from ourselves.[35]

The greater socialization/normalization process (attributable in no small measure to schooling institutions) into passivity, complacency, fatalism, and the aggrandizement of atomism have taken on more sinister consequences during this period. The prevailing sentiment of powerlessness, defined by a number of criteria, but lamented nearly unanimously, is not only a social but a pedagogical crisis as well. Stanley Aronowitz has described a "military model" of schooling practice central to this process which

> encourages subordination of a conceptually illiterate population whose skills extend to the technical plane. They are able to follow orders under the direction of managements that are responsive to the bureaucracies and capital, but unable to critically examine public and private life, to determine how and what should be produced and by whom, and to make the public choices that become policy.[36]

Two considerations emerge from this contextual "situation" which are vital to a transition from "problem" to "crisis" and, therefore, an agenda away from reform and toward a radical pedagogy. In the first place, the progressive liberal tradition tends to separate schoolwork from its politicized dimensions and to exclude from daily school practices the identification of the political with the personal. Representational democracy, scientific and technological elitism, quasi-positivistic methods, specialization of labor along economic functions, the "natural" stratification of social relations, and a certain disengagement which isolates the student/teacher from the politicized structures of consciousness are latent in Dewey's thought. While Dewey maintained in the dimming prenuclear light that

> the problem of democracy becomes the problem of that form of social organization, extending to all the areas and ways of living, in which the powers of individuals shall not be merely released from mechanical external constraint but shall be fed, sustained and directed,[37]

we are left to wonder why he also felt that the social pedagogy of his colleagues, Counts, Rugg, and Brameld,[38] would detrimentally inject an orientation "whose spirit and method are opposed to science."[39]

Secondly, given the highly visible and global events of "brutality and bestiality of the twentieth century,"[40] the four pillars of a Deweyan worldview—science, social democracy, nature, and experience—do not easily allow educators to explore the structural characteristics of domination, stratification, hierarchicalization and alienation of peoples historically preserved and maintained by racism, sexism, classism, and violence. As Mark Poster remarks (and Adorno before him), "No perspective on modern history could be adequate after Auschwitz if it portrays the past centuries as the march of reason."[41] Let me reiterate that Dewey is not being blamed for an undiscerning eye on the aftermath of the Second World War and the patterns which it revealed. But I think that it is important to see him as a denouement to the epoch of instrumental reason and the view that the march of history is an evolutionary testimony, if you will, of human progress.

Whether or not the impasse in consciousness—the proportions of which in the nuclear age are critical—can be dismantled, is the impetus for my inquiry. Americans have expected much from the schools, but this book does not project that the cessation of the cold-war mentality and its social forms is to be yet another goal. The barometer of the everyday world cannot be gauged solely by reading the discourse of nuclearization. But more modest questions can be asked; e.g., how do schools contribute to that mentality? how can schooling practices be transformed? what type of agenda wiil facilitate a plurality of educational concerns? A critically edged educational praxis which takes the possibilities of social change as originating in the formation of counter-hegemonic discourses begins to address these concerns. Central to this premise is a concept of ideology.

Ideology

Dewey's project—"to detect and state the ideas implied in a democratic society and to apply these ideas to the problems of the enterprise of education"[42]—is flawed, as I have suggested above, by an inattentiveness to the structural determinants of socially constructed reality and a depoliticalization of pedagogical praxis. While sharing Dewey's concern to reinvest in student-centered schooling, my argument claims that without an ideological critique of existing concrete conditions—social, political, philosophical, economic—prominently developed in a pedagogical agenda, the role of schooling in a democratization process will be too little too late.

The ideological basis of the West has always been reinforced, never challenged, in educational practice, writes William Bean Kennedy, and forms "a deep ongoing current in the stream of conscious choices and behavior patterns." By not having "penetrated deeply enough into the subcurrent of ideology,"[43] liberalism and educational reform fail to engender a praxis which initiates the structural transformation necessary in the age of nuclearization. Dewey's articulation of "democracy" and the "democratic" which frame his pedagogical vision, a conceptualization deeply rooted in "enlightened reason," is too dependent upon a "selective" pragmatic reading which either ignores or conceals the social contradictions in American society. One of the central paradoxes which I find in the Deweyan analysis is his pragmatic mode of "recovery" and the reclamation, as Dewey's writings often seemed to suggest, of some essential Jeffersonian democratic ideal. His concept of liberal democracy (the theme of *Liberalism and Social Action* was a defense of Western liberalism) did not intend to address the concrete and contradictory conditions of social existence. In general terms, it leaves relations of domination and structures of control that were incompletely settled in Jefferson's time— racism, sexism, authority, violence, poverty, and inequity— unexamined; insofar as it accents functional imperatives, continuity, and a naive reinforcement of growth/progress, social reality is distorted and/or camouflaged; it remains indentured to economic values and ignores or deproblematizes the limits of growth and the nature of problem/crisis; and, of course, it desensitizes the politicized quality of school work. For these reasons a secondary premise of this book claims that "democracy and education" was not fully conceived by Dewey. Historically recovering democracy from this tradition, I am arguing, cannot be a contemporary project because *democracy* has not yet been fully constructed. I am not unpersuaded by Ramon Sanchez's claim that

> the conditions for an honest, fair, and just ideology, and authentic democratic ideology, do not exist in the United States today; nor have they ever. Not only have we not had the social conditions, but we have not even had the correct theory for a democratic ideology of the whole society or for education.[44]

My primary concern, however, certainly connected to that claim but less historical in scope, finds the current renascence of the progressive assumptions to be constructed on similarly fallacious grounds. From his later writings, *The Public and Its Problems* (1927), *Individualism Old and New* (1929, 1930), *Liberalism and Social Action* (1935), as well as the earlier and more explicit pedagogical associations in *Schools of Tomorrow* (1915) and *Democracy and Education* (1916), Dewey spelled out the variety of ways he understood "democracy." The ameliorative or progressive quality of democracy which Dewey never tired of extolling (which will be presented in Part One) bypassed the relationship between educational theory and practice, the reproduction of power/knowledge, and the inequality of the social hierarchy. My critique of Dewey's pedagogical position, quite simply, does not see a transformational praxis emerging. His ideological assumptions will not permit it.

A concept of ideology will introduce and frame the subsequent distinctions I aim to draw between the socialization into "democracy" in the Deweyan sense and the pedagogical task of "radical democracy," or what I am elliptically referring to as "social justice." With some "ideology guides," we can glean the bindings shaping and defining Dewey's concept of democracy, and its rather nonthreatening modification to the hegemonic structure and critical condition of American society.

Ideology is a concept far too complex, too widely interpreted, to be presented here in nearly the richness that it deserves. Even a sampling of those who investigate the ideological constructedness of consciousness cannot begin to encompass the vastness of the concept.[45] Nor do I attempt to treat the specific ideology literature on liberal democracy.[46] Necessarily, there will be a certain eclectic quality to this section which (hopefully) can still convey a notion of ideology as well as my own ideological position.

On one hand, ideology refers to the production of meaning; on another, more existential level, it forms the ground, reference, justification, and value for those meanings and the particular responses/activities of one's life; in other words, how we interact. Thus, the materialized world, our institutions and instrumentalities, *and* our thinking, beliefs, and laws about them comprise a *terrain* of ideology. In these two senses, a concept of ideology refers to "a level of the social formation and not [merely] the sum total of the workings of individual consciousnesses."[47]

Human reality is always ideologically constructed. Our educational ideals, for example, and their associated practices, methods, rules, and languages are products of ideological construction which inform and shape the everyday world while simultaneously validating that construction. Ideology refers to a historically defined context where social reality is produced and ordered including the networks of relations created and maintained by power. Antonio Gramsci (1891–1937), the Italian thinker imprisoned during Mussolini's fascist reign, significantly revamped the notion of ideology. He offers a fuller explicaton of the relation between consciousness or subjectivity and structure (the socially produced), what Anthony Giddens refers to "as an intersection of presence and absence,"[48] contained in the everyday forms of social reality—language, commonsense, religion. In our cultural collective-ness we share a "spontaneous philosophy"—the basic orientation and understanding of the world acquired through language, customs, stories, myths, religious "answers," reinforced and conditioned by experiences and intuitions of our immediate surroundings and events, and the ritualized or institutionalized modes of our social lives. Gramsci's point is that habitual, ritualized ideas and practices—"commonsense"[49]—are never inevitable or just-the-way-things-are, but always a social, human construction. Ideologies are not to be viewed as possessions, texts, or creeds, but as ongoing social processes, always a dialectic of perception and deception, of acceptance and rejection, both present yet not felt, visible yet hidden, a quality philosopher Jean Grimshaw calls "second nature." Ideology may be defined, then, as the constituting medium of our activity, the historically contextualized, materially produced nexus of human be-ing where both consciousness and structure are formed, reconstituted, reproduced, understood, and resisted. In the following passage Raymond Williams, a contemporary thinker influenced by Gramsci, succinctly illuminates the pervasiveness (hegemony) of the terrain in our lives.

> [Hegemony] is a whole body of practices and expectations; our assignments of energy, our ordinary understanding of the nature of man and of his world. It is a set of meanings and values which as they are experienced as practices appear as reciprocally confirming. It thus constitutes a sense of reality for most people in the society.[50]

Consciousness does not come individually "but always through the intermediary of the ideological terrain," explains Chantal Mouffe.

> The self's acquisition of consciousness is in effect only possible through an ideological formation constituted not only of discursive elements, but also of non-discursive elements. . . . Subjectivity is always the product of social practice. This implies that ideology has a material existence and that far from consisting in an ensemble of spiritual realities, it is always materialised in practices.[51]

The "scene," what was "environment" in Dewey's inter-actionalism, is indeed part of consciousness, but it is always contestable, always political, never "natural" or taken for granted ontologically. This point is not entirely unattended by Dewey; e.g., when he sketches a "new individualism," it was to be framed by the "attention to the scene in which it must perforce exist and develop";[52] but his interactionalism is only remotely dialectical and certainly not ideologically grasped. Rather, Dewey argued that the relation between self and society is biological and psychological (a conjunction which forms the social). As we will investigate in Part Three, his concept of experience was inadequately conceived to include this material constructed-ness of social reality.

Ideology appears in the social areas where each of us is intertwined—school, religion, work, law, family, language[53]—and in the theories about the material world—literature, health, psychology, media, philosophy and theology, folklore, commonsense. One dimension of ideology, therefore, involves individuals in the defining and constituting of themselves. In Goran Therborn's terms, "The stakes of an ideological battle are either the reconstitution, desubjection-resubjection and requalification of already constituted subjects, or their reproduction in the face of a challenge."[54] However, historically, who has spoken, how much will be said, what may be spoken and at what times have been regulated by the few and accepted by the many. Therborn writes:

> The existing order of ideologically constituted subjectivity implies that, in a given situation, only persons of a certain age, sex, knowledge, social position and so on are allowed to speak (or will be listened to), about a set range of topics for a set length of time.[55]

As Dewey himself argued in *Individualism Old and New*, modern conditions necessitated new categories by which human beings could understand their world.

While the production of the terms of these self/society formations typically has been dominated by elites—intellectuals, clerics, monarchs, militarists, scientists, capitalists, or bureaucrats—for whom the institutionalization of ideas and behavior is more readily at their disposal and control, and accepted by the rest of us, ideology encompasses more than a set of beliefs produced and distributed by a class of political manipulators or religious protectors,[56] or our own "false consciousness" or mystification. Indeed, the duration or persistence of ideological positioning in any given location (individual or institution) may be the result of acquiescence, toleration, repression, and/or acceptance, but the more noteworthy fact is that it must be continuously sustained or preserved in order for it to be regenerated in human be-ing. One certainly recognizes that ideologies "differ, compete, and clash not only in what they say about the world we inhabit, but also in telling us who we are";[57] consequently, they may be resisted as well because the set of "lived meanings, practices, and social relations"[58] is not met nor agreed to by some elements of the society. A more useful concept of ideology, therefore, refers to the variety of forms or structures of and in everyday life (discursive and material) that have been or can be systematized or institutionalized in order to continue, confirm, legitimate, or replicate certain actions.

In order to understand Dewey's project clearly, then, it is vitally important to see that he too, in an explicitly ideological vein, was flushing out a progressive modification of the hegemonic order of American society. While Dewey and a progressive contingent were aware of problems in modern American society, democracy (defined in large as the rights of free inquiry) relied far too much upon transhistorical *ideas* of "democracy," as well as other empirical "results" such as intelligence and science to have transformational force. Dewey's agreement with Jefferson's conception of American democracy, for example, as the formation of a "natural aristocracy," wherein a leadership can be "raked from the rubbish,"[59] gives an important clue towards how Dewey's "new" democratic society would take shape.

Insofar as the schooling institution represents an ideological site, formally constructed in order to encourage, produce, and/or continue certain behaviors and certain notions of "human nature," a question posed by the conditions of nuclearization asks, how are existing sites functioning "as carriers of a modernizing and nihilistic mode of consciousness?"[60] The consequences for a pedagogy which claims to be democratically structured and radically inclined, of course, are significant. How might school practices and the assumptions about what it means to be educated, to be an American, to be human preserve existing social structures which exacerbate rather than transform those conditions? To assess this correlation completely is beyond the scope of this book.[61] More modestly, it is argued that the deficiency of the reform model lies in its failure to include an analysis of the ideological makeup of our lives including the organization, methods, and formation of how we constitute and legitimate our own analysis.

Towards Social Justice

Dewey's ideas are grounded in a historical context of American liberal democracy and the continuation of post-Enlightenment rationality. In my opinion the progressive orientation of Dewey's praxis draws from the presumed viability of that socio-political organization. The gaps in this tradition stemming from economic, social, and psychological aberrations—the alienation of the individual from systems of authority, the objectification, reification, technologicalization, and commercialization of needs and values by capitalism, the absence of absolute standards of truth and morality, and the deviance from the rational-scientific spirit—were assumed to be soluble by "more democracy."[62] In Part One, Dewey's concept of democracy will be further examined, but let it be initially acknowledged in its republican associations. He asked us:

> For what is the faith of democracy . . . except faith in the capacity of the intelligence of the common man to respond with common sense to the free play of facts and ideas which are secured by effective guarantees of free inquiry, free assembly, and free communication?[63]

A concept of (progressive) liberal democracy is the central value and organizational principle in Dewey's reform ideology. The strength and longevity of Dewey's social and pedagogical appeal undoubtedly lies in a common reading of democracy as an "evolutionary universal"[64] structuring American society wholly positively, naturally, and progressively. However, from an analysis more sensitive to the demands of power in the ordering of social reality, sociologist Todd Gitlin sees the dominant complex of ideology in American culture to be anything but democratic. In concrete ways (and via patterns already discernible to Marx in the nineteenth century), Western liberal democracy continues to be defended primarily by reasons which legitimate private control of production, the concomitant need for a militarized state to insure both privatization and control, in "the necessity of individualism, of status hierarchy, of consumption as the core measure of achievement; and overall, as in every society, the naturalness of the social order."[65] Democracy, as an ideological construction, encompasses a dialectic of human be-ing with aspects of both liberation and repression, necessity and freedom. From this perspective, Sanchez, writing in *Schooling American Society,* asks us to consider

> [when] comparing the means with the general goals of an ideology, one should never assume that something is honestly being done to preserve justice or eliminate injustice. One must observe suspiciously whether the laws and actual practices of the society's institutions are carrying out the goals of the ideology or are serving to perpetuate an unjust status quo.[66]

"He was a philosopher for an era," writes Charles Frankel, "when democracy was, in a neutral, descriptive sense, the hope of the world."[67] Whether that hope *in that form* should be sustained any longer, of course, marks the distinction between a praxis of reform or transformation. While liberal democracy remains an ideal, one often in abeyance with the middle class and co-opted by those whose continued struggle to see its fruits keep its paradoxes concealed, there are enough indicators which suggest a reconceptualization of the paradigm. For their part, schools can no longer be satisfied to sort, classify, categorize, prepare, and eliminate components for the economic organization of society—the socialization process of liberal democracy—but to become potentially liberating sites of an expanded public sphere where a radical democracy can be practiced. I am very much in agreement with Sanchez who effectively argues that "America needs a new ideology of democracy and a philosophy of education suited to a democracy."[68]

Insofar as Dewey remains the prototypical reformer of schooling, it is his ideal of democracy as the social basis for education that I wish to contrast with one of social justice.

While designating "social justice" as the basis for a new language of (radical) democracy and the backbone of an educational praxis, I will not fully conceptualize it in this work. Rather, I have to hint at it, to uncover it in admittedly partial and imperfect ways. Explicating a concept of social justice, then, involves (in historian Paul Buhle's phrase) cutting through a "web of forgetfulness."[69] It awaits a complete analysis.

Social justice, however, can be distinguished from the philosophical treatises of Locke, Mill, Rawls, Ackerman, and others.[70] That is, "social justice" in this book does not refer to a principle of justice considered *socially,* or how justice is *distributively* administered. In these senses, justice, as Marx noted, is largely a juridical concept, negotiable only by the State and confined to issues of equal opportunity and equal access. It has historically drawn upon premises of individualism and structural indifference. From this perspective, as Robert Lichtman explains, liberal theory

> combined a passion for democracy, equality and freedom with a system of devices designed to ensure that democracy would not displace the dominance of those whose authority lay in economic power, that equality would not manifest itself in the equalization of the material and social existence of all citizens and their equal access to self-determination, nor that freedom could be employed to freely overcome the exploitation of laborers within the system of liberal capitalism.[71]

Similarly, Kai Nielson, who has extensively critiqued the liberal notion of social justice, wonders whether justice and capitalism, equal liberty and capitalism, full and equal moral autonomy and capitalism are compatible at all.[72] It is important according to John Thompson, that

> when deliberating on the justice of a particular social arrangement we are concerned, not with adequacy of the evidence that can be adduced to support a claim to truth, but rather with the extent to which that social arrangement is capable of satisfying the legitimate needs and desires of the subjects affected by it.[73]

For example, it is certainly no subversive task to read from the annals of American history the continuing story of domestic and foreign imperialism. Nor were slavery, the exclusion of women from suffrage, the violence of twentieth-century war, economic stratification, and uncorrectable ecological destruction simply malfunctions in an otherwise well-thought-out, socio-political philosophy. Liberal democracy has and continues to require unequal and essentially exploitive hierarchies, and if those structures do change we will no longer be able to identify American society with the same ideological terms.

Social justice, then, originates in "a concrete sense of the historical moment,"[74] various moments from the conditions of everyday life which capture the paradoxical aspects of the personal and the political. It draws from those movements guided by the precept "that more things will be done and the work better accomplished when every person has a part to play in the things that have to be done."[75] In this respect it is a *transformative* (rather than a reformative) concept insofar as it addresses and prioritizes the structural basis defining social relations (e.g., egalitarian rather than hierarchial). It may be therefore characterized by a *resistance* to the dominant ordering of gender, race, class, and interpersonal positioning.

For the time being, three broad criteria can be introduced which shape my notion of "social justice" and from which an educational theory can begin: the pedagogical, the political, the philosophical. These will be presented as method and means whereby the relation of the personal and the structural is revealed and from which an understanding of social justice emerges. Power is inherent in these criteria; by which I mean the fundamental shaping and conditioning of our lives, what Foucault more harshly designates as the modes by which human beings are made subjects—philosophically, politically, and educationally—are ideological and structural. At those points where specific "arrangements" have been constructed, institutionalized, and disseminated, where reason has been constituted and practices shaped, struggles of power for social justice can also be discerned. As I stated above, the historical examination of social justice would carry us into other directions. For my purposes here these struggles must be broadly designated by issues of race/color, sex/gender, class, nature/ecology, and violence. In identifying these themes my intention is not to illuminate them in any philosophical or ethnographical way but to emphasize that the liberal tradition cannot transform those structures, nor that it especially wants to.

By the pedagogical I wish to refer to what is designed to take place, what does take place, and what can occur in the classroom—what informs the techniques, methods, organization, content, exercises, drills, guidance, and relations of the schooling process. It is an explicitly dialectical concept which includes the co-intentionality of desires of learner-teacher, their preconceived notions/values of authority and selfhood, as well as the norms, objectives, behavior, and their prescribed formation at designated sites. Pedagogy is a process of co-investigation in the tradition of Socrates' aporetic method[76] and his nonformal public teaching whereby the dynamics of the personal and experiential (as Dewey advocated) become linked to the creative agency shaping self/community/history.[77] Myles Horton, an American educator and founder of the Highlander Folk School in Tennessee in the early thirties,[78] locates the pedagogical stance in "the feeling that for people to be really free they must have the power to make decisions about their lives, so that they can acquire knowledge as tools to change society."[79] Similarly, Paulo Freire presumes (and I agree) that

> students [and teachers], as they are increasingly posed with problems relating to themselves in the world and with the world will feel increasingly challenged and obliged to respond to that challenge . . . because they apprehend the challenge as interrelated to other problems within a total context.[80]

Pedagogy is thus a confrontation (in an ethical sense); it is the engagement with freedom and knowledge, with texts and the concrete conditions facing people, but more radically, with power. Pedagogy is always explicitly infused with ideological posturing. With these considerations in mind, a distinction between schooling and education will further help us to grasp this notion of pedagogy.

> Schooling . . . takes place within institutions that are directly or indirectly linked to the State through public funding or state certification requirements. Institutions that operate within the sphere of schooling embody the legitimating ideologies of the dominant society . . . defin[ing] their relationship to the dominant society in functional and instrumental terms. . . . Education is much

more broadly defined, and...refers to forms of learning and action based on a commitment to the elimination of class, racial and gender oppression.[81]

Pedagogy is conceived by the further consideration of the political, or the activity directly and consciously concerned with initiating, changing, and preserving social reality. The "political," as I will use the term, refers to this influencing and shaping of social relations—the interactions of people and the structures conditioning them—and the environment—cultural and natural—by people in their everyday lives. This designation offers, then, to expand the political from its normal associations with government, politicians, and bureaucracy. I am mindful of its derivation from the Greek word *polis*, "a public space constituted and maintained by praxis."[82] Such a praxis, as it is understood pedagogically, alternates between the dialectical tensions lived as an individual-student and the structures within which one acts (school, family, peer group, community, nation, planet). The school is one place, argues Giroux, "where radical educators can battle for emancipatory interests." He goes on to say that "it is a sphere that must be seriously considered as a site for creating critical discourse around the forms a democratic society might take and the socio-economic forces that prevent such forms from emerging."[83]

This characteristic of struggle or confrontation in the political not only refers to a praxis or a certain engagement with our socialized lives, but tied with the pedagogical sense, implicitly includes the third criterion, the philosophical. The notion I am pursuing is taken up by Agnes Heller who describes philosophy as "nothing other than a means to give one's own life meaning or to reveal the meaning of one's life."[84] We are philosophical in seeking to bridge the gaps between being and becoming, between the is and the ought, between the personal and the political. That dialectic always exists, and when we attend to it, we need to determine not only the politics of the relation but a pedagogical stance toward it. Philosophy is, with the inclusion of this sense of praxis (pedagogical/political), the creator of the polis. To philosophize, therefore, one poses questions not to oneself but to the world. The philosopher further problematizes the world rather than only shedding light and/or unifying it. Philosophy becomes "radical" in Heller's terms because it doesn't give us "a norm to the world or a world to the norm...[but] wishes the world to become a home for human beings."[85]

The "recovery of philosophy," as characterized by the method of science (Dewey's project), is to be distinguished from radical philosophy in the same way that critical theory is distinguishable from scientific theory (see Part One). Rather than take the continuity between society and culture as a functional given, and its (re)production as evolutionary and empirically uncontestable—a philosophical stance in which science is indeed well suited to mediate—philosophy is to be understood as a deconstruction. Dewey spent his life *reconstructing*, a position which takes for granted that the foundation is sound. This orientation, in its concession to "solidarity rather than of despair,"[86] tends to mask the paradoxes of the lived world. "In a fit of utter utopianism disguised as pragmatism," writes Michael Harrington, "...liberalism reaffirms a faith in gradual, incremental change which, even more mystically than the Hegelian providence, will stop the ground from quaking under its feet."[87] A pedagogical stance which engages the always-politicized concrete conditions of social reality proposes that power/ knowledge, what I call the ideological, locates teacher-and-learner in potentially transformational contexts. Social justice is the inclusive term by which I identify these various themes.

Educational Praxis

The last consideration to pose in contrasting the reform sense of "problem" and the radical perception of "crisis" is the term *praxis.* In presenting a concept of praxis as having pedagogical-political-philosophical referents, I am distinguishing it from Dewey's analogous expression of "human activity." As a reconstructive and scientific designation, he not only depoliticized the pedagogical dimension of praxis but in returning its philosophical sense (liberal democracy) to an epistemological function he left the issue of power to a "scientific cadre." Whether or not the replacement/displacement of the clergy by the Enlightenment and liberal democracy has advanced democratic life is not the real question; rather the issue before us is still the micro-politics of control.[88] Dewey's grasp of agency, therefore, which was developed in his concept of experience, was conceived in typical functionalistic terms which did not pay particular attention to issues of institutional analysis, power, or the interstices of social change.

To move past these limitations—which Dewey himself believed he had circumvented with an interactive notion of experience—a contrasting theory of action less wedded to the subjectivity of the individual and nineteenth-century consciousness must be advanced. Giddens' theory of structuration, for example, seems to overcome the determinism of the French Marxist, Louis Althusser, as well as liberal social theorists like Talcott Parsons, by accounting for "how action is *structured* in everyday contexts and how the structured features of action are, by the very performance of an action, thereby *reproduced*,"[89] while not unmindful that "social actors are knowlegeable about the conditions of social reproduction in which their day-to-day activities are enmeshed."[90] Such an analysis is at the heart of the notion of transformational praxis.

I am arguing that there remains in liberalism and, therefore, in pedagogies derived from it, asymmetrical relations of power. I have (incompletely) identified these in the broadest way along the following socialized dichotomies: male/female; white/black; capital/labor; human/nature; violence/reconciliation. The theory of praxis I would like to offer takes shape from its dialectical movement, among the contradictions, the shadows, the forgotten, and the taken-for-granted, and for this, praxis has explicitly ideological objects. It refers to a sense of dialectic, Socratic rather than Hegelian, Nietzschean rather than Darwinian, antithetical rather than synthetic, which directs my formulations.[91] In Giroux's words:

> It is in the tension between the recognized oppression that underlies our daily lives and the critical understanding that demands a call to rectify it that the dialectic becomes more than a neutral social science category.[92]

In other words, while Dewey is in some key respects a dialectical thinker (in the Darwin/Engels scientific tradition), insofar as he acknowledged the Janus-faced pose of reality, he explained the "comedic" side where a critical dialectical praxis brings to its audience the "tragic."[93] Such a praxis investigates knowledges, including commonsense, the everyday world, and its (so-called) norms as "specific kind[s] of production with definite relations to the social and material world."[94] In a positive sense praxis is social justice.

In distinction to Dewey's presentation of "experience," which certainly is a praxeological concept, I will try to tie together the various elements already mentioned—ideology, deconstruction, social justice, and the philosophical-pedagogical-political synthesis—with the critique of the Deweyan pillars (to follow) and put forth a radical or critical notion of praxis. A final distinction, thus, will be made between the methods of reform and a "pedagogy for liberation."

The glaring absence in educational theory is this means for addressing its own legitimacy—what do we teach about our planet, how, and why? The preservation of unjust relations of power embedded in school practices, and the unintended consequences of the contemporary organization of social reality which disempowers students (and citizens) are explored in the remarks which follow, hopefully speaking to teacher, student, and citizen alike.

Part I
The Scientific and the Transformational

Theory in the traditional sense established by Descartes and everywhere practised in the pursuit of the specialized sciences organizes experience in the light of questions which arise out of life in present-day society. The resultant network of disciplines contains information in a form which makes it useful in any particular circumstances for the greatest possible number of purposes. The social genesis of problems, the real situations in which science is put to use, and the purposes which it is made to serve are all regarded by science as external to itself.
—Max Horkheimer, *Critical Theory*

Pedagogically, philosophically, and politically, ideology is the primary focus/object of any inquiry or critique which claims to be exploring the social construction of the lived world or human be-ing, e.g., education and schooling. Because education has a teleological or developmental orientation, the ideological matrix for an educational praxis has certain definable characteristics. I have identified the pillars of Dewey's social theory as democracy, science, nature, and experience. In Part One, two of these cornerstones will be examined.

Democracy

Dewey's idea of democracy is the ideological key to his entire philosophical/pedagogical/political *oeuvre* and, ironically, a source of paradox in liberal theory. In general terms democracy is a political tradition in which the establishment and securement of individual rights—involving the consultation and discussion of an informed public concerning those rights—effect an equitable distribution of such rights.[1] While Dewey maintained that an *idea* of democracy could not be embodied and secured only by a historic moment, he obviously identified a democratic process being carried forward by the industrializing nations (particularly America) and enlightened reason (particularly Jefferson). "Democracy [is] the crucial expression of modern life...not so much an addition to the scientific and industrial tendencies as it is the perception of their social or spiritual meaning."[2] Democracy is (epistemologically) the result of a changed conception of intelligence, an evolution of intelligence in interaction with "a change in intellectual conditions...the ordering of life in response to the needs of the moment in accordance with the ascertained truth of the moment."[3] Dewey saw in American democracy

> the conception of a social harmony of interests in which the achievement by each individual of his own freedom should contribute to a like perfecting of the powers of all, through a fraternally organized society, [and] is *the permanent contribution of the industrial movement to morals.*[4]

Along a similar ideological track, he stated in *The Public and Its Problems* that "it is even more important to realize that the conditions out of which the efforts at remedy grew and which it made possible for them to succeed were *primarily non-political in nature.*"[5] For Dewey democracy was largely a social idea and understood (in part) as the "improvement of the methods and conditions of debate, discussion and persuasion."[6] He maintained that American society has been the most significant manifestation of this evolution, but "because the conditions of life change,"[7] democracy is always a continuing experiment; there has never been complete democracy. He would have no part of an indoctrination into some metaphysical notion of democracy; there is never enough democracy.

> Since it is one that can have no end till experience itself comes to an end, the task of democracy is forever that of the creation of a freer and more humane experience in which all share and to which all contribute.[8]

Dewey regarded democracy as a highly cooperative, integrated form of social organization which had evolved in modern industrial times capturing both the autonomy and collectivity of individuals. In this sense he saw "democracy" as an "ideal" and wished to secure a perspective on its historical, philosophical meaning. He sought to develop a democratic ideology and referred often to the special values, purposes, and aims of a democratic society which

> must receive such distribution that they become part of the mind and the will of the members of society...to the democratic idea of making knowledge and under-

standing, in short the power of action, a part of the intrinsic intelligence and character of the individual.[9]

He stated that democracy is a social idea "wider and fuller . . . than can be exemplified in the state even at its best. To be realized it must affect all modes of human association, the family, the school, industry, religion."[10] He understood it as a generation of "a general will and social consciousness: desire and choice on the part of individuals"[11] involving a "community" towards the shared appreciation of goods and concomitant access to them.[12]

The expansion of rationalism along more explicitly scientific categories (the natural sciences) in the nineteenth century precipitated a social, political, and epistemological release from the clerical domination of private life.[13] The rights of participation in the organization of socio-political activities were claimed, thereby engendering a new notion of "freedom" which Dewey felt could unify the relation between the individual and society. According to Charles Frankel, Dewey's approach to the concept of democracy has an analogy to the Greeks and the evolution of those qualities imbued in the notion of *Paideia*.[14] Dewey (in more modern guise) sought to shape the social vision inherent to Plato's *Republic*

> to the themes and perspectives of a massive industrial democracy with Puritan traditions and a Hobbesian frontier experience in its recent past . . . [and] continuous with Jefferson's belief that America was a promise not simply to itself but to mankind.[15]

In this summarization of Dewey's notion of democracy we might consider *The Public and Its Problems* where he elaborated the social and political ideal (towards his notion of the Great Community) along the following principles: 1) the fluid or "experimental" nature of practice and policy to better accommodate the fluctuation in human desires; 2) the integration of shared knowledges to facilitate desired ends; 3) activity shaped by purposes of fraternity, liberty, and equality; 4) the associated activity of the public conditioned by moral purpose into the formation of "community"; 5) the recognition of the primacy of "meaning" in human affairs; 6) the awareness of personal power and responsibility in forming communities; 7) the predisposition of care in activities; 8) the governmental or political organization of the state designed to serve the needs of its constituents; 9) the participation of the public in the transformation of government policies.

We certainly can appreciate these functional characteristics and aims, and their political and historical significance for social justice. Liberal democracy, indeed, opened up new relationships of power, but my argument is that "democracy," *as the empirical ideal,* is too laden with associations to economic freedom and concomitant themes of growth, of evolution, of development, of progress, and the universal panacea assured by scientific method to deal satisfactorily with the burgeoning paradoxes of modernity. American life is concerned primarily with "freeing" the individual with the pseudo-promises of opportunity, and replacing the authority of the supernatural with the control affected by "the modern gaze." Democracy today is "inauthentic" to use Alan Wolfe's term. "Inauthentic democracy," he explains, "exists when the structure of choices present in an otherwise open political system either does not allow such fulfillment or actually works to negate it."[16] Liberal democracy is being construed today, as a result of the necessities of cold war rationality, as a

> social contract in which people receive the benefits of modernity, in return for not asking too many awkward questions about it.... If the quality of public life must be sacrificed a bit to keep the quantity of private life plentiful, it seems a small price to pay.[17]

But Dewey did not arbitrarily select "democracy" in a visionary or historic manner. Democracy was a pragmatic reality.

Pragmatism

When Dewey argued in *Democracy and Education* that "the conception of education as a social process and function has no definite meaning until we define the kind of society we have in mind,"[18] the inference is that not only a philosophical-historical *idea* of democracy existed, but an empirical approximation as well. For Dewey and contemporary neo-pragmatists, social planning begins by rejecting "objectivity," or the appeal to absolute or transcendent principles, that "truth" has some intrinsic nature, or that there are "real" essences.[19] Dewey, who Richard Rorty suggests found "truth" to be simply a complement to that which works,[20] nonetheless required that a past model,

a socio-historical account—"it has to be in *some* vocabulary"[21]—
be used to guide and direct. Having proposed a philosophical
basis for democracy Dewey's pragmatism further required that
democracy be empirically and historically identified from *some*
concrete source. I believe that a major paradox of liberalism may
be located in this curious circularity.

Both Dewey and Rorty refer us to what is historically
"available" as both source and end—liberalism as an ideological
designation expressing in part the "free play of intelligence," a
theory of life[22] and, empirically, what is called democracy in
America. Rorty has written that

> no other American writers have offered so radical a
> suggestion for making our future different from our past,
> as have James and Dewey.... They asked us to liberate
> our new civilization by giving up the notion of
> "grounding" our culture, our moral lives, our politics, our
> religious beliefs, upon "philosophical bases"...a
> permanent ahistorical matrix...and the "nonhuman
> nature of reality".... There is no epistemological
> difference between truth about what ought to be and
> truth about what is, nor any metaphysical difference
> between facts and values, nor any metaphysical
> differences between morality and science.[23]

Dewey's pragmatism and "metaphilosophical" relativism
rejected theorization which attempted "to ground some element
of our practices on something external to those practices."[24] By
following this line of reasoning, and everything I have read of
Dewey indicates he condemned the barren soil of metaphysics
as a basis of the "true," one source of the paradox of the liberal
model is exposed. In the broadest terms, Max Horkheimer
outlines the issue in his 1947 *Eclipse of Reason:*

> Man has gradually become less dependent upon absolute
> standards of conduct, universally binding ideals. He is
> held to be so completely free that he needs no standards
> except his own. Paradoxically, however, this increase of
> independence has led to a parallel increase of passivity.
> Shrewd as man's calculations have become as regards
> his means, his choice of ends, which was formerly
> correlated with belief in an objective truth, has become
> witless.[25]

Pragmatists, Rorty maintains, fill this void by stressing that our loyalty is to other human beings, not our hope of getting things right.[26] Democracy, then, or the designation used to describe certain identifiable practices originating in the "concrete details of the culture in which...[it] grew up and developed," is legitimate or valid, or true, only to the degree that its practices ("the successive stages of European thought")[27] are agreed to. The fear of parochialism and the "relativism" in the modern symptoms of irrationalism and nihilism, which premise Horkheimer's condemnation of pragmatism (and Dewey), may be dismissed by recognizing that the pragmatist's "inquiry into the nature of knowledge can...only be a socio-historical account of how various people have tried to reach agreement on what to believe."[28]

The aspect of the paradox (accepted as inevitable by both Dewey and Rorty) undermining liberal reform is its pragmatic requirement that a past model/discourse/history be acknowledged, ideologically secured, and from which guidance and direction may be drawn. Rorty states:

> The pragmatists' justification of toleration, free inquiry, and the quest for undistorted communication can only take the form of a comparison between societies which exemplify these habits and those who do not....Such justification is not by reference to a criterion, but by reference to various detailed practical advantages....
> We must, in practice, privilege our own group, even though *there can be no noncircular justification for doing so.*[29]

It would be "utopian to try to imagine the details of a social state such has never existed" Dewey told us in *Freedom and Culture.*[30] Yet, by his own admission democracy—"the best means so far found"[31]—does not exist. What does exist is a set of ideas, historically determined, philosophically rendered, and ideologically reproduced which by virtue of their ownership in the minds and hands of the few have exercised remarkable hegemonic control. Ideologically operative in Dewey's employment of democracy, as the remarks above suggest, is what Williams refers to as the

> *selective tradition:* that which, within the terms of an effective dominant culture, is always passed off as "*the* tradition," "*the* significant past". But always the selectivity

is the point; the way in which from a whole possible area of past and present, certain meanings and practices are chosen for emphasis, certain other meanings and practices are neglected and excluded. Even more crucially, some of these meanings are reinterpreted, diluted, or put into forms which support or at least do not contradict other elements within the effective dominant culture.[32]

The paradox existing in Dewey, liberalism, the resurgence of neo-pragmatism and the progressive spirit of reform, then, is barely concealed: what historically is being selected, why, and how is it being legitimated and reproduced? In order to appeal to or defend one's own cultural language of "solidarity" and the "self-image our society should have of itself,"[33] the ideological terrain of our social construction must be grounded by various references, standards, practices, and beliefs hegemonically selected, ordered, and disseminated. Pragmatism, as a philosophy of *present* experience, assigns ontological status to the "natural" and the "social" or "functional." By describing the "present" as the evolutionary empiric, its analysis and/or diagnosis is dependent upon continuity with a "selected" past. Pragmatism cannot, however, deal with the fundamental questions of structure and determination other than to relativize them (to be discussed in Part Two.)[34] Consequently, as a recent essay by Cornel West argues, Rorty's neo-pragmatism and by extension what I take to be Dewey's position as well, only satisfy "a self-conscious post-philosophical ideological project to promote the basic practices of bourgeois capitalist societies while discouraging philosophical defenses of them."[35]

Where have these "ideals," this terrain, predominantly come from? What was the historical context which defined them and continues to shape them? And which are the philosophical premises used to articulate them? Dewey stated that "We cannot set up, out of our heads, something we regard as an ideal society. We must base our conception upon societies which actually exist."[36] He acknowledged that "the chief source of social welfare and the ultimate spring of social progress"[37] was in the bourgeois movement of the eighteenth century. Democracy, characterized in the social sense as "the liberation of a greater diversity of personal capacities [was] caused by the development of modes of manufacture and commerce, travel, migration, and intercommunication which flowed from the command of science over natural energy."[38] Indeed, if "freedom is something to be achieved and the state has the responsibility for creating institutions under which individuals can effectively realize the potentialities that are theirs,"[39] then the contemporary problem was to *continue* the notion of freedom (and democracy) he believed inherent in the *socially* enlightened projects of Jefferson, Rousseau, Mill, Spencer, and T.H. Green with the *economic* structures requisite to modern bourgeois industrial organization. In Dewey's view, "as economic relations became dominantly controlling forces in setting the pattern of human relations, the necessity of liberty for individuals which they proclaimed will require social control of economic forces."[40]

The designation for this ordering is liberal democracy. C.B. Macpherson states that liberal democracy has typically promised "to reconcile the claims of the free market economy with the claims of the whole mass of individuals to some kind of equality. It...is strictly a capitalist phenomenon."[41] In Macpherson's terms:

> With a liberal state guaranteeing a free market, everyone's natural desire to maximize his own utility, or at least not to starve, would bring everyone into productive relation which would maximize the aggregate utility of the society.[42]

Dewey was not entirely blind to the problems of this association though due to his ideological position he regarded the worker-capitalist division (for example) to be socially natural, not economically determined, and functionally necessary even if the relations were hierarchical. In *Individualism Old and New* (to which we will turn in greater detail below), Dewey theorized that

> it would be in accord with the spirit of American life if the movement [between capital and labor] were undertaken by voluntary agreement and endeavor rather than by governmental coercion....A coordinating and directive council in which captains of industry and finance would meet with representatives of labor and public officials to plan the regulation of industrial activity.[43]

Now, in a utopia, such a partnership makes perfect sense. In a society that has been stratified along class, race, and gender relations, Dewey's position is extraordinarily naive.[44] He assumed that the moral progressiveness of rationality and the goodwill of the state to control technology and the marketplace would ultimately promote the "new" individual. In this respect, following Mill, Dewey had sought to "turn away from the market"; but he also was left with Mill's problem:

> helpless, unable to reconcile his notion of values with the political economy which he still believed in. The world's work had to go on, and he could see no way in which it could be carried on except by competitive private enterprise.[45]

Dewey clearly spoke from the pulpit of liberal pragmatism: "For in the long run democracy will stand or fall with the possibility of maintaining the faith and justifying it by works."[46] Thus far, democracy "has worked to keep factional disputes within bounds."[47] What is urgently needed, Dewey pleaded in 1939, was "a faith based on ideas that are now intellectually credible and are consonant with present economic conditions, which will inspire and direct action with something of the ardor once attached to things religious."[48] Liberalism was that faith; it has been "associated with generosity of outlook as well as with liberty of belief and action."[49] He felt that a socially evolving intelligence towards scientific, industrial and technological values and structures would provide not only the securities of life, but individual movement and invention.

This political and philosophical framework, I am arguing, has historically been utilized by reformers—liberal and conservative—not only with the zeal of secular faith, but to monitor and control political participation. Women and people of color, for example, remain in peripheral roles, analogous to the limited democratic reality of ancient Greece and the unresolved racist/sexist/classist presuppositions of "revolutionary" America. The opportunities to enter the system and fully embrace the ideal had been narrowly defined, and where entry presently occurs, the concomitant prerequisition prevails to conform or adapt to its socially and economically stratifying rules. Equal opportunity, insofar as it has come to define democracy in America, continues to be a principle of ("natural") aristocracy, a concessionary adjustment to an essentially unfree society.[50] Equal opportunity is based on the somewhat fallacious premise that social equality exists, as well as on the premise that opportunities for all exist. Pragmatism attempts to unify the dialectic of liberal democracy. Picking pieces of Locke, Bentham, Mill, and Green as if they constituted some evolutionary continuum, Dewey was not defining American life so much as the ideals of a philosophic tradition concerned with humanizing *but not changing* the structures of power. Social justice, as I will suggest below, posits that democracy begins only after reasonably egalitarian conditions and structures have been prioritized, after the absence of discrimination toward women and minority populations, the gross disparities of economic distribution are rebalanced, and the welfare of the planet to sustain life is insured.

Less astute than Marx, Dewey did not analyze the *politicized* conditions, the ideological and structured conditions, in which "enlightenment" can flourish. He remained wedded to a functionalist view which, "on the one hand assumes a unitary social domain, and on the other leaves unproblematized the content and take-up of those attitudes."[51] In one telling passage Dewey offered the complete scenario of the limited democracy and *aristoi* empowerment behind the pragmatic liberal vision:

> There are *few individuals* who have the *native capacity* that was *required* to *invent* the stationary steam-engine, locomotive, dynamo or telephone. But there are no one so mean that they cannot *intelligently* utilize these *embodiments of intelligence* once they are a *part of* the organized means of associated living.[52]

Hidden in this instrumentalism which is derived from an economically framed vision of "genuine industrial freedom"[53] is the same disempowering tendency which marked Lenin's vanguard cadre, the same organization of social life into the shepherds and the (knowledgeable) sheep, precisely the same typology of Plato's "republic." Yes, a degree of social unity is captured by these views, but the freedom or capacity of the individual to make critical inquiries into the system itself is denied. The ideal, glimpsed from real existing conditions, typically has been the product of limited ideological perspectives. If the real has been structured with racist and sexist assumptions then an ideal will necessarily incorporate aspects of these characteristics.

Ultimately, pragmatism and its ethnocentric presuppositions must be derived from the ideological baggage they inherit from their sources. When it is further assumed, as Rorty states, that "there is nothing wrong with liberal democracy,"[54] what *is* wrong becomes desensitized, depoliticized, rendering its nonideological reforms lukewarm. In order to defend the concepts of liberal democracy, of rationality, of scientific method—what Rorty refers to as toleration, free inquiry, and the quest for undistorted communication[55]—a language is used and a history selected that has been primarily constructed by economic and chauvinist values and exclusive of women, people of color, and other social justice concerns. In citing Winston Churchill's defense of democracy—democracy as it has been lived—as the worst form of government imaginable, except for all the others,[56] neo-pragmatist Rorty also seems to be trying to reinvigorate a Deweyan liberalism by similarly preaching an old-time faith.[57]

Individualism

A third paradox and, perhaps, the most glaring because it reaches the heart of an American worldview, is the notion of the individual, or subject. Dewey's interactionalism sought to integrate a self (subject) with the needs of modern capitalism/production (object) thereby highlighting the inter-dependent, cooperative bonds of self and society. From the standpoint of Dewey's *Individualism Old and New*, the reproduction of the "possessive individual" (Macpherson's term) was an unfortunate consequence of the latent laissez-faire tendencies of liberal democracy. The original dialectic historically had separated individuals from authority, the state, and metaphysics, releasing them from their social ties, work, authority, moral standards, as well as economic constraints.[58] Democracy, as the socio-political-economic ideal, was the attempt to reconnect those individuals collectively under certain common concerns.

Our views of the world—how we should or can conduct our affairs—are manifest in our actions and materialized in forms of social organization and structure. The intellectual, emotional, psychological, and behavioral relationships we have within the prevalent ideological terrain in our lives significantly condition the responses we will make. The paradox here is exemplified by Dewey's lambasting the aberration of laissez-faire individualism in *Individualism Old and New* while still concluding that a new individuality depends upon fulfilling the preconditions of the corporate and industrial world. If that dominant terrain, as I have suggested, has been constructed along certain unequal and/or unjust power relations (which in the postwar period has culminated in the militarization/nuclearization of the planet), then it is little wonder that pedagogical practices which left those relations in place would not succeed. Dewey, of course, bemoaned many of the results of the modernization process, as do contemporary "liberal" conservatives today; yet, one reads little if anything which suggests a transformational praxis of the social relations which bind people. While the release of the individual from external restraint obviously has been spectacular and unprecedented (quantitatively) in America, the "creativity" of these expressions also has been magnetic enough to convince many people that it must never be sacrificed or compromised. Consequently, the focus of reform has remained wedded to a *psychological* account of crisis, inevitably blaming the bad attitudes, misconceptions, and faulty reasoning (dualism) of individuals. Underlying this approach and below the discourse of Dewey's interactionalism is the assumption that our social relations are the result of mutual exchange.[59] This tension, I believe, is where the radical perspective begins.

My position proposes that (contra Dewey) the social origins of the individual be further problematized. I have already stated that Dewey's project of recovery is not possible because what there is to recover may not satisfactorily service present transformational needs; hence, to construct an "individual" from what is the contemporary social ordering or what can be imagined, seems to maintain the circularity. A pedagogy of (Deweyan) democracy is less likely to encourage critical inquiry into the constructed-ness of self and society. If in fact Dewey regarded a progressive pedagogy to be

> founded on a number of new principles: society as the ultimate bedrock of the values expressed in notions of the social good; the utilitarian understanding of the maximization of the happiness of the greatest number; the health of the social body; national prosperity and the sacralization of the state . . . [then] such a foundation is both a condition and a product of the new forms of production and administration and of the new processes of subjection/subjectification.[60]

Hence, Dewey's efforts to collapse dualisms (self-society) are undermined by functionalistic designations of the respective poles. In fact, to posit some notion of the "authentic subject," which claims agency in history, we are susceptible to yet another of the "games of truth" of which Foucault has spoken.[61] In arguing that various apparatuses,[62] institutions, and "truths" mediate social relations, I am further stating that any notion of the individual (of self) is an ideological construction intimately affixed by those social constructions. Couze Venn writes:

> Any discourse which aims to speak of the subject must at the same time speak of the social, and it must do so *not* in terms of a complementarity but on the basis of the fabrication of subjects in and for signifying material practices.[63]

On this point, Foucault's "animus against the subject," and the hermeneutic circle of inquiries "which take 'man' as their object, also have 'man' as their subject" thus producing, what Poster explains as

> a certain blindness which allows the human sciences to avoid reflecting upon their effects on practice. Foucault thinks that, by taking a point of view other than that of the subject, one can decipher the mechanisms through which the human sciences come to dominate, not liberate, the subject.[64]

From these brief considerations, let us contrast the four "individualisms" Dewey referred to in *Individualism Old and New* with Foucault's argument in "What is Enlightenment?".[65] Here as David Hiley explains, Foucault allows a *distance* between a "modern" praxis and the grip of modernity itself. Rather than regard the present as "heroic," in the sense of an evolutionary culmination, Hiley maintains that Foucault did foresee the "achievement of maturity," or freedom, or liberation, and what I am proposing is the context for social justice, only when the tables were turned on the "blackmailers" of the Enlightenment. Foucault sees "an attitude toward ourselves and the present which is an historical analysis of the limits that are imposed on us and a transgression that opens the possibility of going beyond the limits."[66] We will keep this analysis in mind while examining what sort of "individual" Dewey saw emerging from the productions of schooling.

The "old individualism" of revolutionary America possessed certain positive qualities for Dewey which had become distorted and misdirected over the century and a half since Jefferson. The qualities of individualism Dewey appreciated in the emergence of the American state as manifested in the small farmer and businessman, craftsmanship, and the activities of leisure life have been consumed by "our materialism, our devotion to money making and to having a good time."[67] Nevertheless, he was not advocating romanticism, some return to a less complicated individual/social existence. It was useless to bemoan the departure of the good old days.[68] Rather, with "an enormous command of instrumentalities, with possession of a secure technology," his explanation in *Individualism Old and New* was that we have not developed "the means at our disposal . . . to form an equitable and stable society."[69] He regretted the loss of the "spiritual factor of our tradition" and the present orientation towards "the practices of a pecuniary culture."[70] The corporate mentality ("for better or worse, we are living in a corporate age," Dewey told us) had negatively generated "impersonal and socially undirected economic forces"[71] and removed individuals from the traditional bonds and grassroots participation Dewey recalled from an earlier age. He lamented

> that the loyalties which once held individuals, which gave
> them support, direction, and unity of outlook on life, have
> well-nigh disappeared. In consequence, individuals are
> confused and bewildered.[72]

From these excerpts, three "individualisms" can be detected: 1) the pre-industrial individual constructed in an agrarian and petty-bourgeois context with an "ideal of equality of opportunity and of freedom for all"[73] now usurped by 2) the "present" ordering of the individual by "corporate mechanisms"[74] leaving 3) the *lost individual,* "confused and bewildered."[75] The fourth, of course, was Dewey's conceptualization of "a new individualism," a position covering the remainder of the text. Here again we recognize the pragmatic thrust of his analysis in which the "present" is always the most facilitative means for addressing the future, and "problem-solving" replaces critical theory. As mentioned above, the problem for Dewey was that the advance of industrialism and the corporate way of life have not been sufficiently accompanied by a scientific planning of consequences around social development.[76] The prescientific and preindustrial individual was not to be resurrected but reconstructed to meet "the realities of the social estate."[77] "A new individualism," he advised, "can be achieved only through the controlled use of all the resources of the science and technology that have mastered the physical forces of nature,"[78] thereby equipping the youth "to be masters of their own economic and social careers."[79] The failure of an educational system to prepare its youth for membership in modern, scientific, industrial life was being hampered by an "old individualism" not yet cognizant of its unity with the rest of society, as well as the bastardization of the frontier individualism. Dewey's (new) individualism, a sort of secular rebirth, characteristic in all of his writing, thus required the formation of "a new psychology and moral type."[80] He argued that

> recovery of individuals capable of stable and effective self-control can be had only as there is first a humbler exercise of will to observe existing social realities and to direct them according to their own potentialities.[81]

My contention in this section is that Dewey's "new individual" remained a product of economic forces in the terms of a base-superstructure analysis, without ever coming to grips with the issues of growth, expansionism, imperialism, class, gender, and partial or incomplete democratic practices concomitant with it. Furthermore, my argument rejects Dewey's attempt to create a "subject"—no matter how ideally—from the ideologically construed "harmonious society" envisioned by the liberal discourse. The "problem," as Joel Kovel explains,

> does not lie in the workings of the economic system, but in the fact that the system is economic in the first place. And the solution is not to grease the wheels of an archaic machine, but to see to it that the machine itself is replaced by something more suitable to the well-being of life on earth.[82]

Subjectivity, or the ideological premises for the construction of the individual in a society, was settled pragmatically by Dewey and liberalism, i.e., according to the mandates of the prevailing power structures. Freedom and the development of the "new individual" could be gained "only by participating in the common intelligence and sharing in the common purpose as it works for the common good."[83] This alignment of means and end, of possibility and consequence, of self and society seems to be more deeply rooted in the Hegelian separation of consciousness from material structures ("forces" in Dewey's usage) than Dewey was aware.[84] However, by regarding how the ideological refers to the discursively, bodily, and emotionally interpellated (to use another of Althusser's terms)[85] social formations by which individuals define themselves as subjects, we get at the deeper foundations from which consciousness and meaning are constructed. "Subjectivities," then, exist prior to the individual and define what is "American," "student," "teacher," "citizen," "democracy," "social justice," "learning," "gender," "race," "excellence," "knowledge," and "power." As Mouffe's account explains, if social agents

> are not the constitutive principle of their acts, but supports of the structures, their subjective principles of identity constitute an additional structural element resulting from specific historical practices.[86]

"The problem consists," as Mouffe continues, "in determining the *objective* relation between these subjective principles or ideological elements."[87]

My argument is that "democracy," as an ideological totality in which schools should be ordered, is philosophically unable to accomplish its own ideals let alone the more far-reaching investigation into nonviolence and social justice. To continue the ordering of values defined by liberal democracy is to be impotent before the crises facing the world's peoples. While Dewey did not regard "democracy" to be a product of a particular class (capitalists), I tend to agree with Macpherson ("liberal-democracy is strictly a capitalist phenomenon"), and it is within that political and economic ordering that its contradictions and/or failed promises may be located. The transformation of liberal democracy is the transformation towards social justice, not the abolishment of an open society. Whereas he held that the "realities of the social estate" which define, construct, and reproduce individuals could not be changed, a radical position does challenge those structures. Information, scientific rationalism, and the traditional assumptions of school practices regarding the "normative" and functional organization of society ignore this analysis. The contradictions of that attempt during the development of the American school has been illuminated by a number of works during the past fifteen years.[88] Social justice and nonviolence, as it will be sketched, imply the transformation of priorities from the pragmatics of realpolitik to the human.

Democracy and Education

In developing the pedagogical dimensions of this democratic project in *Democracy and Education,* Dewey asked, "Why is it, in spite of the fact that teaching by pouring in, learning by a passive absorption, are universally condemned, that they are still so intrenched in practice?"[89] Twenty years later he asked a similar question:

> What are our schools doing to cultivate not merely passive toleration that will put up with people of different racial birth or different colored skin, but what are our schools doing positively and aggressively and constructively to cultivate understanding and goodwill which are essential to democratic society?[90]

In the fabled "Chicago Experiment" (1894–1904) to which Dewey's early educational writings *The School and Society* (1900) and *The Child and the Curriculum* (1902) refer, he identified the progressive agenda: "Let us then ask after the main aspects of the social movement; and afterward turn to the school to find what witness it gives of effort to put itself in line."[91]

It is not that reform hasn't addressed huge tears in the social fabric nor expended repairs, but that in accepting functional categories and pragmatic solutions for the problems of social reality, it fails to challenge the economic basis for organizing human life and the ideologically related structures which promote individualistic, isolated tactics. The paradox in liberalism has been well-camouflaged in Dewey's theorizing because it *does* express a social organization concerned to bridge the gaps historically dividing self and society. As we have seen: "At whatever level, state, factory, party, family, the *existing* social order is the implicit framework in whose official but unspoken terms people's actions are understood and assessed as criminal, disruptive, disloyal, naughty or whatever."[92] Of course, the ideology of reform finds *something* problematic with the existing social order, but *within* the parameters or logic of the paradigm itself. Consequently, in order to begin his (pragmatic) pedagogy Dewey had to accept America as a continuously evolving democracy in which the socialization process was an ongoing

> communication of ideals, hopes, expectations, standards, opinions, from those members of society who are passing

out of the group life to those who are coming into it. . . transform[ing] uninitiated and seemingly alien beings into robust trustees of its own resources and ideal.[93]

Rather than accuse Dewey of formalism[94] I would emphasize that it is his pragmatism which is problematic. If "a part of wisdom [is] to utilize the products of past history so far as they are of help for the future" and schooling; or, if schooling is "the training of our original impulsive activities" and consists "in *selecting* from the diffused responses which are evoked at a given time those which are especially adapted to the *utilization* of the stimulus,"[95] then an ideological critique is appropriate rather than pragmatic adaptations. Dewey's concept and image of "social environment" were not only very selective, dependent upon a naive, apolitical, and idealized reading of American history, but pedagogically impotent to engage teacher-student in critical practices. To have investigated the structures of liberalism and how they are ideologically maintained would have opened a door Dewey probably was not ready to walk through. In this light, we can understand Clarence Karier's objection that the Dewey School experiment only

> emphasized social unity, cooperative living, and the rational, orderly, progressive development of technology from the spinning wheel to the modern, industrial, corporate society. The violent, bloody history of Indians, blacks, and immigrants, as well as the labor conflicts of the previous decades, were peculiarly missing in the school's history of the progressive evolution of American technology.[96]

Dewey himself stated "that this [industrial] revolution should not affect education in some other than a formal and superficial fashion is inconceivable."[97] In *The Child and the Curriculum* we are introduced to the holistic evolutionism that marked "the cumulative outcome of the efforts, the strivings, and the successes of the human race generation after generation"[98] guaged by scientific, technological, and political events. Dewey was setting forth in his early educational work a pragmatic basis for schooling which would address the experiential adaptability called for in the modern industrial state.

The "social environment forms the mental and emotional disposition of behavior in individuals by engaging them in activities that arouse and strengthen certain impulses, that have certain purposes and entail certain consequences."[99] "The very existence of the social medium in which an individual lives, moves, and has his being is the standing effective agency of directing his activity."[100] "The inclination to learn from life itself and to make the conditions of life such that all will learn in the process of living is the finest product of schooling."[101] "The statement of aim is a matter of emphasis at a given time."[102] "In directing the activites of the young, society determines its own future in determining that of the young," and "the latter's nature will largely turn upon the direction children's activies were given at an earlier period."[103] Education, ideally, is a growth process that should "make individuals better fitted to cope with later requirements."[104] "It is the business of the school environment to eliminate, so far as possible, the unworthy features of the existing environment from influence upon mental habitudes" and "provide something like a homogeneous and balanced environment for the young."[105] Social environment is defined by Dewey to be "constituted by the presence and action of the habits of thinking and feeling of civilized men."[106] "The continuity of any experience, through renewing of the social group, is a literal fact. Education, in its broadest sense, is the means of this social continuity of life."[107]

In general, then, Dewey assumed a typically functional social ontology that prioritized the empirical facticity of the self-society relation. Learning as doing, the legacy of Deweyan progressivism, therefore, was to be linked to "social conditions" and their production of "the appliances which are requisite if new ideas are to be adequately elaborated."[108] Dewey, can be seen (again) to be exalting the "Great Community" in phrases like "the formation of the proper social life," the "maintenance of proper social order," the "securing of the right social growth," and the teacher as "the prophet of the true God and the usherer in of the true kingdom of God."[109] In Sanchez's view this meant putting "the schools in step with a modern, industrial democracy... [where] children would develop the critical intelligence to help push the wheels of progress in a society 'which is worthy, lovely, and harmonious'."[110] Politically and educationally, the nature of reform "was to make the system work efficiently and effectively"[111] and, if necessary (as Dewey argued in *Liberalism and Social Action*), increase the role of the state.

As I have been arguing, Dewey initially defined democracy functionally and abstractly: common interest, interaction, cooperative discussion with others, "of conjoint communicated experience."[112] Democracy is a "particular social ideal"[113] which demands a social return from everyone, while providing the opportunities for the development of individual capacities,[114] and reflects a "society in which all share in useful service and all enjoy a worthy leisure."[115] "Socialization depends upon the habits and aims of the group."[116] The greater realization of universal education was drawn from the potentiality of the new, bourgeois-developed need to produce a growing industrialized society. From this rationale, society, or "whatever binds people together in cooperative human pursuits and results,"[117] along with the values instrumental to its preservation have been already defined. These relations, as we have seen, which bind people together, were construed in social and functional terms, not as a result of a struggle for ideological turf.[118]

Due to the gains of experimental science, he believed that American democracy had transformed both the Platonic and Rousseauean formulations of self and society. Schools could begin to develop the imagination and sympathetic insight into "the social and scientific values"[119] of the workplace which the evolving Western consciousness had produced. However, according to Sanchez, *The School and Society* and *Democracy and Education* unequivocally proposed "an educational solution for alienation in industrial society."[120] "The stick of mindless labor," writes Sanchez, "poor working and living conditions, and skimpy salary would be ameliorated by the carrot of understanding that each individual worker was part of a great industrial, corporate society which would in time bring a cornucopia of goods."[121] Karier, too, critiques the reformist position and ties it to the argument (cited above) against the pragmatic view. Dewey, he says,

> never seriously challenged the power sources within American society; his nonviolent socialist views threatened few in power. In fact much of his philosophy of nonviolent, reasoned, and orderly change (albeit toward a kind of welfare-state socialism) was adopted by those who directed and managed the corporate industrial state.[122]

Dewey's answer, thus, never problematized "democracy." It was never a question of "do I fight?," "do I flee?," but "how do I accommodate?" By assuming a pragmatic stance, he was philosophically wedded to that which already existed (American democracy); by his naturalism and functionalism (more of these in Part Two) he took for granted the relation of self-society and its internal hierarchies; and by his non-confrontational and somewhat formalistic curricular agenda he implicitly admonished us to bend our will to the "common good."

In hindsight, Dewey can be situated at the cusp of a recognizable shifting of a cultural paradigm, but one which has been only incompletely transformed.[123] As I have noted, Dewey's many reservations, as expressed in his later works, revealed his own dissatisfaction with the results inherited from the "old individuals." His acknowledgement of social democracy—intervention of the state into the economy—was an attempt to deal with the frustration characterizing the thirties. Of course, it is important to locate Dewey's effort to salvage liberalism at that time in its violent confrontation with fascism and totalitarianism, the twin specters challenging democracy and, therefore, to contextualize his pedagogical vision. In a series of lectures collected under the title of *Liberalism and Social Action*, he warned that the danger of abandoning liberalism in crises is to relinquish "things of enduring and priceless value."[124] And, I suppose, that some may feel that the shock of World War I, the impact of the Russian Revolution, the "era of excess" (1920s), the nature of the American depression, yet another war, more drastically distinguished by fascism, nuclear weapons, and the advancing anti-democratic positions required of the cold-war relationships in the world, which were producing tools of reactionism rather than of transformation, were simply "problems" which liberalism would certainly handle.[125] Subsequent "rifts," which I have symbolized by the phenomena of nuclearization, e.g., issues emergent in and after the war in Vietnam, of continued imperialism increasingly less disguised by the rhetoric of democracy, of the decay of urban centers, increasing stratification of class/race/gender discrimination, psycho-social dysfunctioning, and the felt-pervasiveness of environmental pollution, continue to expose the underside of the liberal paradigm.

Not because I disagree with the idea of democratic schooling, but for the reasons I have been arguing, the reconstruction of Dewey's pragmatism or progressivism seems misguided. The idea of democracy, *as a political concept,* is historically drawn from, even imbedded in, the ideologically hegemonic practices of economic individualism and statist leadership, a paradox that

Dewey was aware of, to be sure, but without either a historical or ideological analysis, clearly unable to transform. The idea of democracy, *as a social concept,* emerges from and remains determined by nineteenth-century notions of freedom, of representation, of participation, liberty, necessity, technology, science, biology, and the purity of enlightenment via rational discourse, ideas which Dewey assumed would continue to embrace the masses. Obviously, there have been concrete social gains issuing forth from the dominant discourse. That is not the point; rather, it involves reconstituting the "democratic as oppositional," as counterhegemonic. Finally, the idea of democracy, *as a pedagogical concept,* not only incompletely realizes or reproduces democratic, participatory politics and socially responsible citizenry, it fails to achieve, on the basis described in the previous two points, the desired empowerment of students and teachers and the emancipation from social contradictions.

Before we turn to the more historically situated and dialectically concrete perspective from which a social justice pedagogy begins, the next two sections pose the contrast in methods of reform and transformation, and the scope of scientific analysis and ideological critique.

Scientific

The ideological construction of Dewey's liberalism and pedagogy has been aided considerably by the "tools" of science. The difference in orientation between "scientific method" and "critical theory"—what sort of project is made—should further clarify the issue of ideology, the nature of reform and the boundaries of "progressive" pedagogy, as well as my own methodological approach.

If, as I have suggested, the social and epistemological position of liberalism lies in its adherence to the persuasive power of reason to condition and prescribe change (growth), then Dewey seemed to be continuing the *reform* perspective of the Enlightenment, a secularized religious morality which replaced the clerical voice with the bourgeois, revelation with reason, and principle with empirical evidence. In largely acquiescing to the bourgeois interpellation of self (either in its theistic or naturalistic guises), framed in Dewey's mind through the liberation of scientific intelligence, the discourse of American democracy has been unable to promulgate a social vision other than through the categories of the "possessive individual." My point in this section is not that Dewey was an ideological lackey of capitalism, but that he virtually ignored the structural relations between the "problems of men" and modern political economy, and in the undialectical thrust of his instrumentalism "overlooked" the contestable nature of "science." In identifying "scientific" with "democratic"[126] Dewey made a similar mistake to the one Plato had made, only where Plato's was metaphysical, Dewey's carried the punch of science. Both presumed an epistemological basis (idealism) for their social theory. Ordering the world in that way, the scientific or metaphysical approach, argues Brian Fay, is bound to become "instrumental" whereby "social theories increase power by providing appropriate knowledge in terms of which one can manipulate the causal mechanisms that characterize a certain social order so that a desired end state is produced."[127] This critique was central to the critical theorists, and Marcuse, in particular, spelled out the implications of a scientific ordering in *One-Dimensional Man* (1964):

> The principles of modern science were *a priori* structures in such a way that they could serve as conceptual instruments for a universe of self-propelling, productive control. . . . The scientific method which led to the ever-more-effective domination of nature thus came to provide the pure concepts as well as the instrumentalities for the ever-more-effective domination of man by man *through* the domination of nature. Theoretical reason, remaining pure and neutral, entered into the service of practical reason. . . . Today, domination perpetuates and extends itself not only through technology but *as* technology . . . and provides the great rationalization of the unfreedom of man and demonstrates the "technical" impossibility of being autonomous, of determining one's own life.[128]

Now, we need not follow Marcuse to the end of his argument—the subordination/alienation of humanity to its technological apparatuses—but it is equally as frustrating to regard the theory and practice of science neutrally, as the force of modern enlightenment, and the organizational principle for the modern world. Brian Easlea points out that even in early capitalism, scientists "recognized that their own interests lay in serving the interests of the emerging bourgeoisie and thus in allowing their exploitable new science to be exploited in the interests of private profit." He cites the early example of Galileo's "prompt and lucrative sale of the telescope as a war instrument to the Venetian Senate."[129] In Galileo's words, "Great and remarkable things are mine but I can only serve (or rather, be put to work by) princes, for it is they who carry on wars, build and defend fortresses."[130] There is no question that scientific inquiry, method, and end prioritize the new, the developing, the buds of growth, the potential, the improved (the very modus operandi of contemporary capitalism and its need to create necessary obsolescence) which is materialized (at one important locus) in technology. Technology is used by the society, of course, but is increasingly invented, produced, owned, and controlled by the managerial and corporate aspects of the society. Increasingly, the subordination of the many to the few—a technological minority rather than either an intellectual or a clerical/fedeistic leadership—has contributed to the spiritual vacancy that is the legacy of the nuclear age.

Dewey clearly had advocated the "systematic utilization of scientific method as the pattern and ideal of intelligent exploration and exploitation of the potentialities inherent in experience."[131] He stated in *Schools of Tomorrow* that "the real question is one of reorganization of all education to meet the changed conditions of life—scientific, social, political— accompanying the revolution in industry."[132] "It is sound educational principle," he later stated in *Experience and Education* (1938), "that students should be introduced to scientific subject-matter and be initiated into its facts and laws through acquaintance with everyday social applications." The methods of science illuminate how "a better social order can be brought into existence."[133] His emphasis upon scientific method as pedagogical principle, I am arguing, was turned towards reinvesting preindustrial values/functions to use in the technologically constructed, industrial/capitalist political economy. This troubling tendency of Dewey's to put all his eggs into the basket of science has been noted before. Karier has written:

> Although theoretical science may be open-ended, technology concerned with serving particular social institutions may not be so dedicated to truth or an open community of discourse. On the contrary, a social institution dedicated to survival may find it expedient to sacrifice truth. The new liberalism of Dewey and others

> failed at this critical juncture. Perhaps in some ideal
> world where all men were governed by "rational self-
> direction," Dewey's idea of science might be applicable.
> In the world of twentieth-century power politics, however,
> most scientists and technologists became hired men of
> the industrial militarized state.[134]

Karier's point is simply that technology has been always wedded
to a ruling elite, appropriated because it can buy it. By positing
science and its methods as ideologically pure, sacrosanct, moral,
and progressive, Dewey failed to consider that "neither
democracy nor individual freedom had any inherent connection
with science and technology."[135] The deeper one is invested in
the power of the paradigm, the less likely will there be the
inclination to question it.

Science typically seeks the manipulation of the external
world to cope effectively with Nature/environment; it is
objectifying insofar as it stands apart from that which it
examines; its epistemological and concrete value is empirically
fixed by what is given. Having determined the naturalness and
functional necessity of the self-society relationship, scientific
method (and pedagogical practice) take it for granted that the
relationship as it exists empirically and ethnographically can be
made to work. Aronowitz brilliantly debunks this by showing the
ways in which scientific practice by virtue of its own concepts
and methods "promotes a universe in which domination of
nature is linked to the domination of humans, or the *way* in
which science is a form of power."[136] As an unintended
consequence of a reform approach this marriage of science and
liberal democracy preserves the same structural conditions (at
more subtle levels) that have always repressed the great majority
of human beings.

Scientific method, to the extent that it continues an
intellectually transcendent means to induce, assess, and control
social reality, is, therefore, a cart before the horse. It cannot be
applied objectively, it does not supercede false consciousness,
nor is it benign. Its usurpation by the dominant discourse has
rationalized the interests of military-industrialist production, the
maintenance of a hierarchical society, the legitimation of
inauthentic democracy, and the displacement of alternatives/
resistance to deconstruct the debilitating structures. A critical
method, or what Brian Fay has termed *the educative approach,*
questions the legitimacy of the options themselves; i.e., it begins

with a critical stance towards one's reality and engages in the contradictions which the option-makers have hidden. While not abandoning the empirical means of science, critical theory takes aim at hidden coercions, at the concrete contradictions consequent to any world picture, at an entirely different sort of emancipation.

Ideological Critique or Educative Method

Alternatives have always existed to dominant ideological paradigms. Particularly in a politically free society, peace activists, the voices of Black, Hispanic, and women dissenters have been concerned not only with the struggle of inclusion, the usurpation of democracy by its liberal and reactionary wings, the subtlety of its power, but also (positively) to create the "free spaces" where the atomistic democracy of individualism and class divisions are minimized and greater social justice maximized. The received images of authority, responsibility, freedom, autonomy, duty, community, and purpose, transmitted and reinforced (and rejected)[137] in no small measure through formal schooling, are bloated with prenuclear associations and conceptions of democratic plurality that are (and always were) inadequate for many.

Part One of this book strives to reorient an analysis of education and schooling away from a diagnosis of individual failings and weaknesses and towards unsatisfactory structures and institutions. My argument throughout takes issue with Dewey's correlation of experimental inquiry or scientific method and democratic life. These two discourses constituted the ideological and front-facing pillars of his social philosophy. He accepted those ideas pragmatically and rationally as uncontestable, satisfactorily realizable, justly structured, and amenable to educational activity. As we have seen, Dewey maintained that a scientific method could best investigate the dichotomies of existence (subjective-objective, or human-physical) and render obsolete the false dualisms obstructing their unification, thereby revealing the natural compatibility between the seeming polarities (the unification of the dialectic). He fully explicated the logical pattern of this inquiry in his *Logic: The Theory of Inquiry* (1938).[138] The following passage from *The Public and Its Problems* typifies the social thrust of this logic:

> We have also held that a considerable part of the remediable evils of present life are due to the state of

imbalance of scientific method with respect to its application to physical facts on one side and to specifically human facts on the other side; and that the most direct and effective way out of these evils is steady and systematic effort to develop that effective intelligence named scientific method in the case of human transactions.[139]

The assumption of science is that it transcends ideology, it is objectively pure, and "in the right hands," socially progressive.[140] It regards the relations between "physical facts" to be fundamentally ontological (must there not be some empirical relation between the individual and the group?) which have been intellectually misconstrued (ironically by metaphysicians). Its own ideological basis is subsumed by this slight of hand. While an experientially based pedagogy informs Dewey's agenda—*Schools of Tomorrow* and *Democracy and Education* give multiple references to an experiential pedagogy—the structure or determined quality of social existence is largely taken for granted. These seemingly natural, historically evolved, and socio-biological givens—family, community, work, social hierarchy, order, democracy, knowledge—while continually susceptible to further evolution, constitute the forms in an otherwise dynamic world. The fluidity of scientific experimentation transcends structure. Science replaces history as the synthesizing element of progress. This is not to say that scientific discovery and method have not facilitiated many developments in the human condition. Rather, I would like us to consider that scientific method, as a basis for an educational praxis, circumvents the structure of domination, the reality of oppression, and the paradoxical consequences of its own rhetoric. Dewey is defined as a "liberal" because he seeks to reduce the tensions and ignore the dialectics (the contradictions), rather than identify social reality along ideological orderings of power.[141]

What I am calling "ideological critique" never assumes that the dialectic between "dependency" and "independence," for example, or the aims of schooling and the functional values declared by the state, to be necessarily in place. Furthermore, it rejects the positivistic strain among those "pleading for science"[142] for categories purporting to "transcend" the ideological quality of social constructed-ness. As such, ideological critique and the praxis it generates can replace the long-valued "scientific method" which simply "can't handle any of the more interesting cases of ideological delusion."[143] Apple articulates this aim, as well, in the following passage. As educators, he argues, we need to

> examine critically not just "how a student acquires more knowledge" (the dominant question in our efficiency-minded field) but "why and how particular aspects of the collective culture are presented in school as objective, factual knowledge." How concretely may official knowledge represent ideological configurations of the dominant interests in a society? [What in fact are those interests?] How do schools legitimate these limited and partial standards of knowing as unquestioned truths?[144]

In seeking different aims ideological critique establishes a different method. While science is concerned with ignorance, ideology seeks emancipation.[145] Following Fay's distinctions,[146] the positivistic assumptions inherent to science are to be challenged, to be replaced with a "critical" model of education theory. A new concept of "critical social scientist" (or educator), explains Fay, refers to one

> who seeks to disclose how the historical process was such that the social order which he is examining was incapable of satisfying some of the wants and needs which it engendered, and in so doing he will have accounted for the structural conflict and accompanying social discontent which he perceives.[147]

Briefly, ideological critique in its application at the formal pedagogical level may be understood as a hermeneutic which addresses:

1) ways to uncover and examine schooling, its basic day-to-day regularities, and its relation to economic production, political control, and culture. The necessity of interpretive categories for examining social phenomena, which is to say, situating or historicizing both agents and their circumstances within the nexus of meanings by which they live their lives, is vital. Apple, who specifically addresses his remarks to schooling, describes this "relational" viewpoint:

> . . . any subject matter under investigation must be seen in relation to its historical roots—how it

> evolved, from what conditions it arose, etc.—and its latent contradictions and tendencies in the future. . . [and] anything being examined is defined not only by its obvious characteristics, but by its less overt ties to other factors.[148]

2) the means by which social relationships central to school practices can be recognized, assessed and transformed (e.g., sexism, racism, authority, control, power, knowledge, individuality, responsibility). The existence and impact of "structure" within "systems of social relationships which determine the actions of individuals and the unanticipated, though not accidental consequences of these actions"[149] more clearly demands an inquiry on the determined quality of our everyday lives. Structure refers to the "binding" properties in space and time of social systems "which make it possible for discernibly similar social practices to exist across varying spans of time and space and which lend them 'systemic' form"[150] (to be developed further in Part Three). From a context of schooling, the architectural and physical properties/design of a building, the ad hoc "rules" habituating teaching methods, or the commonsense and/or unconscious beliefs ordering personal interaction such as our "habits" of competitiveness, gender, etc. have this structural quality.

3) the organizational procedures for selecting curriculum and educational objectives with consideration of how knowledge and what constitute knowledges are to be selected. Herein lies the distinctiveness for a theory of education which purports to "revolutionize" school practices. As well as a curricular issue, (what I am calling) a transformational praxis examines the concrete conditions of school and community, of self and the larger political spheres. My argument claims that the terrain of "social justice," as it commences in the concerns of the vanquished and the vanished, better grasps the dialectics of self and society.

The liberal-reform agenda offers today the same 150-year-old bromide it has always offered: an intercession between necessary structural transformation of school and society and the mechanized, authoritarian military models of stability and order.[151] In Part Two the difference between Dewey's *social* scientific method and a *historical* critical one is further developed. In identifying the "social" with the "natural"[152] Dewey sought to include the specifically human within the larger categories of natural science and thereby eliminate the dichotomy between the natural and the social sciences. Whereas "social" is largely a functional concept for Dewey illustrating those aspects of human activity which extend an evolutionary or continuous development, "historical" is to be understood ideologically, i.e., the social relations in human history are organized by concerns of power. By replacing the anthropological fact that human beings and human societies have survived by adapting to their environment, a historical perspective initially secures, in Apple's pedagogical terms, "an understanding of how the kinds of symbols schools organize and select are dialectically related to how particular types of students are organized and selected, and ultimately stratified economically and socially."[153]

While Dewey referred to the various relations and needs observable in human existence, e.g., community, mutual benefit, security, and economic collectivity, his conflation of the natural (scientific), fortified in its conceptualization by evolutionary theory,[154] with the social (ideological) left him ill-equipped to confront the reified pockets of power. In the next section I will suggest that a concept of social justice, insofar as it includes a dimension of critique, initiates a praxis *outside* the dominant discourses of democracy and science.

Social Justice

While acknowledging Dewey as an innovator in classroom practices, I find unsatisfactory his tendency and that of the liberal/progressive tradition in general to take the structural conditions of a human-constructed world and the impact of those forms in the mediation of consciousness for granted. As argued above, his undialectical faith in scientific method, his satisfaction with the social ends of the Enlightenment, his staid middle-class consciousness, and the absence of materialist and/or class analysis qualifies Dewey, in T.H. Wilson's phraseology, as one of the carriers of the "American ideology." Before we examine the forms of this "ideology" in Part Two, Wilson's remarks may hold this marker for the moment: "The idea that knowledge is inherently neutral, that there is a unitary scientific method, or that science provides the pre-eminent explanatory model...

constitutes the epistemic foundation of the American ideology."
Its advocates, Wilson continues, argue that change "is built into
the development process in 'open' societies in a way which does
not sacrifice continuity to either a noncirculating elite or to
revolutionary disorder." At the heart of the American ideology
is an "uncritical criticism...a commitment to the Western
project with second thoughts threatening, but never quite
becoming, first thoughts."[155]

The context of the nuclear age should be radically changing
our social commitments towards a qualitatively different ground
of egalitarianism, social responsibility, and politicized participation. To distinguish social justice from democracy as the
philosophical and social context for an educational praxis is to
walk the line between their respective historical intentions and
origins and their everyday expression. As stated above, "democracy" promises "the legal entitlement of 'citizens' to participate
in the determination of the policies to be executed by the state
in its capacity as sovereign legal subject and, in addition, to the
legal conditions of existence of such participation."[156] Reform
offers us this "democracy" as a right and in return expects us
to mind our own business.

An aspect of the social justice concept, on the other hand,
while not dismissing the egalitarian gains in the history of the
United States, requires that we not only rethink the blatant
contradictions of that history,[157] the sources and conditions for
liberal democracy, but also to what ends is it leading us. Already,
by the middle of the nineteenth century, Marx had recognized
that the relation between political emancipation and human
emancipation had been not fully examined.[158] Today, from such
a premise, writes Nielsen, the fundamental organizational
assumption of American society must again be re-examined.

> If we are committed to a society where human beings are
> treated with equal concern and respect, where their lives
> are taken to count, and taken to count equally, and where
> they are to have equal liberties, it is a very real problem
> whether justice and capitalism, equal liberty and
> capitalism, full and equal moral autonomy and
> capitalism are compatible.[159]

And to the extent that Dewey acknowledged this incompatibility,
for example, in his *Liberalism and Social Action, Individualism
Old and New,* and his writings in *The Social Frontier* (1934–1936),

his reluctance and adverseness to see an educational praxis that could more explicitly confront these dichotomies illustrated that he would take his cues from a functional and pragmatic acquaintance with the world.

Reform proposals for improving and democratizing the schools during the past decade of "what's to be done about the schools?" have not wavered from a praxis of validating the functional relationships necessary to liberal democracy. Following in Dewey's progressive footsteps, the fundamental concern of the Education for Democracy Project[160] with the "poverty" of traditional schools reuses the same conception, methodology, and platitudes which Dewey had extracted from the dominant discourse (even less acceptable now because the project is apparently ignorant of the many sociological studies of everyday school practice which have exposed numerous paradoxes). The educational claim of Education for Democracy is that a "fullness of knowledge, an objective and balanced picture of world realities,"[161] or a glut of "right" information provides the ground for intuitive "right" decisions. Following a neo-liberal line, it states that our political heritage is "the vison of a common life in liberty, justice, and equality, as expressd in the Declaration of Independence and the Constitution two centuries ago."[162] It makes no bones that "democracy is the worthiest form of human government ever conceived" but, like Dewey, aware that "very much still needs doing to achieve justice and civility."[163] Values like human dignity and freedom, equal rights, social and economic justice, and the rule of law, civility, truth, toleration of others, cooperation, civic responsibility, self-respect and self-restraint "must be taught and learned and practiced."[164]

The problem of the schools, as this position sees it, a problem increasingly materialized throughout the public domain, is that young people are not being sufficiently introduced to their national history. The position advocates that students need more ideas, more historical information that promotes the ideal of democracy as a particularly American project. As their pamphlet implores, unless students have a clear grasp of the alternatives to freedom, they will not be in a position to defend it. These ideas, then, (not at all dissimilar to Dewey's), embodied in American history and American heroes, are to be conveyed in American schools. The Education for Democracy proposal asks: Can not these ideas be taught through an expanded curricula of history (in particular)? Will not the presentation of ideals in turn foster citizens who see and accept their places in the American hierarchy? Can't we then "leave it to our students to apply their knowledge, values, and experiences to the world they must create"?[165] Is there not a fundamental, even "natural" link between the rational and the real?

"Education for democracy" presumes that the existing power structures operative and necessary for the maintenance of economic growth are satisfactory; it educates students so that they will be able to enter into the continuing reproduction of that system,[166] what R.D. Laing referred to as "flying in formation." Can "democracy" as the philosophical, political, and pedagogical idea of American history be any more viable for latter-day progressives than it was? Apparently. Because, like Dewey, the Education for Democracy Project believes that the problem of schooling has been a lack of will or the subversion by "some educators . . . [of] a certain lack of confidence in our own liberal, democratic values."[167] The logic of this position fails to examine the daily contradictions of democracy in student experience of the world; it fails to create an environment in which praxis is established as a pedagogical practice; it continues to maintain the division of power, the leadership of the few, and the hierarchy of knowledges that have historically preserved inequality, possessive individualism, and the disempowerment of students (and eventual citizens).

Without grasping "the Second World War and its aftermath" (a concern for the Education for Democracy people), for example, how can students understand the process of nuclearization? the Three Mile Islands? Without "knowledge of our own struggle for civil rights," how can students understand the continuing history of racism in this country? the Howard Beaches and Fulton Counties? Without studying how the United States is economically committed to intervene, colonize, and exploit the "Third World," how will the democratic citizen "know what is worth defending"?[168] The historical emphasis is vital, but without critically approaching history, educational reform lacks the cutting edge to induce transformation.

Progressivism, the spirit of reform, unfortunately, is etherealized in decidedly ethnocentric and pragmatic forms that cannot be reconciled with the global structure of social reality today (contra Rorty). Not discounting the authentic humanitarian concerns fueling the liberalism of Dewey's time, progressivism still masked the shifting to other countries of the grosser forms of exploitation. Dewey's example of a "progressive" technique (taken from *Schools of Tomorrow*) reflects to what extent liberal reform would pose a serious inquiry into the hegemonic terrain. Lacking the whole picture, the "whys" of social reality could not be investigated. In that example, the function of the Panama Canal could not be grasped by the students, so the teacher "changed her method entirely and starting from the beginning, asked the class to pretend that Japan and the United States were at war, and that they were the Government at Washington and had to run the army."[169] It seems that war, American interventionism, military metaphors and teaching methods, while in this case functionally useful, had only the objective of the lesson— the location and function of the Panama Canal—as an educational goal. Gonzalez is harsh in his condemnation of Dewey's appreciation of this exercise and maintains that Dewey

> expressed an imperialist nationalism coincid[ing] with his scientific approach towards society . . . . The United States takeover of Panama, the forced treaty granting exclusive jurisdiction over the Canal Zone, and military value of the Canal to the United States' imperialist ambitions were facts not unknown to Dewey . . . . The teaching of the practicality of imperialism was, for Dewey, not the issue. The issue was whether one successfully connected the individual in a conscious and scientific manner to the existing social order.[170]

What sort of inquiry in the sphere of schooling could begin a transformative praxis? I believe that we need to consider some *postmodern* conception of social life. In proposing (what I admit is a still incomplete notion) a concept of social justice as a way to think about a postmodern world, the philosophical-political-pedagogical thrust is a further radicalization of democracy, explicitly through nonviolent channels, and drawing upon the "daily struggles at grass roots level, among those whose fight was located in the fine meshes of the web of power."[171] Various elements of the world's people have remained unimpressed and untouched by the liberal discourse. Sexism (or patriarchy), racism (or the minority as pariah), underdevelopment, violence, and ecocide remain grossly uninfluenced by laws, logic, and rational analysis (enlightenment). The project of a social justice pedagogy for American schools *selectively* counterposes an inquiry in which a "dialectic of the concrete" is encouraged to surface.

A social justice education, or the inquiry into the structures of social relations, is much more than the formal attempt to address ad hoc "crisis" situations. That is the work of reform both conservative and liberal. To locate the roots of social justice we would need to investigate an irregular and discontinuous discourse largely peripheral to the mainstream. Though I can't trace these roots in their historical detail here, the philosophical basis of social justice is the structure of social relations.[172] But during the last fifty years in this country, the work of the social reconstructionists during the Great Depression, free speech, antiwar, and civil rights activists/educators and, more recently, the antinuclear and antipollution concerns poke at the festering wounds of liberal democracy. Today, as I have contended, the crisis is the culmination of militarism, regimentation, disempowerment, and the prospect of global annihilation, phenomena which because of their pervasiveness seem to have alerted more people to the danger of nonparticipation. In these numbers there are movements, sometimes diverse, which can find solidarity, crossing ideological lines hitherto rigid.

Hegemony, as noted above, refers to a family of related concepts involving the relationships of ideas, structures, and institutions (and their relativity to each other), the "truth" of which lies in the extent to which it is accepted. It is to be identified with the "totality of a community's attitudes, beliefs, values and purposes embodied in social relations, customs, laws, institutions and political constitutions, but also expressed in a more intellectual way in art, religion, science and philosophy."[173] The performance and continuity of the ideological strains in a social configuration must be constantly reinforced and, as such, are located at those sites where they can be both produced and reproduced. They "explain" to us our everyday world. They claim to fulfill (though not necessarily) the promises or ends they advocate; they are, however, dependent upon the consensus of individuals who accept them—intellectually or habitually.

Transforming the existing hegemonic structures perpetuated by the phenomenon of nuclearization, then, as both Gramsci and Dewey might have claimed, is a process which could be assisted by schooling. However, as the sociology of education has illustrated in the past two decades,[174] the function of schools has been that of an "accomplice" in reproducing oppression or, less harshly, silencing opposition. Educators at every level of instruction, knowingly and/or unconsciously are crucial actors in struggles of ideology. Schools, in their existing form as compulsory institutions attending to the reproduction and transference of knowledge, are a vital factor in the maintenance of any ideological agenda: actively, through discursive, symbolic, behavioral, and structural forms; and passively, in the forms of resistance taken by teachers and students. It is at this point of dialectical tension between (the potential for) education and (the domination of) control where schools become liberating sites. Educators, in this sense, presume a position of social responsibility in which social justice becomes the raison d'etre of teaching. The origin of social justice, I believe, lies in its counter-hegemonic basis, fundamental to which is the notion of educator as intellectual and "agitator" (which in this sense commences with the Socratic gadfly).

In proposing preliminary considerations for a concept of social justice, however, it is important (methodologically) to avoid both an overly general set of concerns which are invisible to particulars or a specificity which undermines a claim of universality. Social justice does identify and designate a sentiment and/or concerns involving human relations (characteristic of Dewey's ideal of "democracy"), but it does not claim or attempt to describe an ideal (or historically available) state of affairs via pragmatic concession. Interestingly enough, it is the pervasiveness of fragmentation, which I have symbolized by the social fallout of nuclearization, that is actually drawing together what had been antagonistic perspectives, perspectives which are not simply generated by their claims to be included in the American Dream. We can see this in a new role of the churches, the alliances of secular and religious positions, the working class with ecological movements, human rights issues for Blacks/ Hispanics with the confronting Gays, and the middle classes joining disarmament campaigns and protesting environmental pollution. Rudolf Bahro (optimistically) cites the poet Holderin who beautifully captures the dialectic here: "God is near and hard to grasp. But where there is danger the force of salvation grows too."[175]

A second source of social justice is rooted in its "global" orientation, which can be defined initially as a recognition of the relationship between one's own situation and that of other people.[176] "Global" is expressed within the context of relations delineated by particular collectives (family, community, institution, state, nation) and includes what I have referred to as political. It further refers us to the relational structures holding together international capitalism and nuclearization, for example. From this consideration, a social justice concept includes the premise that persons are to be defined and understood in their relation to other persons (locally and globally), not as autonomous and antagonistic agents who have a right to compete for a limited list of goods and services, or functional cogs in an economy. The language of rights, which in our society is "largely concerned with this tension between what is owed to the common good and what the individual can insist on as his right even in the face of the public domain,"[177] is reconceptualized.[178] The educational objective, as Robert Aspeslagh states, is "to strengthen the ability of people to act on their own responsibility with others in relation to people outside their own social group as well as with those in other parts of the world,"[179] i.e., to see the world dialectically. The unity which Dewey saw and felt as overarching the American enterprise of democracy, can no longer sustain the increasing contradictions of its premises. Hence, social justice emerges from a dialectical grasp of the macro-structures of social reality.

In more concrete usage, a third aspect of social justice specifically refers to the investigation, illumination, and eventual transformation of existing structures of violence, heretofore identified along issues of race and gender, distribution of wealth, conflict resolution, and ecology. In a point which I will argue further in Part Three, social justice *is* a praxis which initiates and reinforces egalitarianism, responsibility, and solidarity.[180] Such a concept of praxis is vital to an integrated approach of education-research-action focusing on social justice. It initiates structural alternatives to violence (to include the disempowerment of students) and acts as an organizational value and principle for pedagogic content and form. It requires that engagement or dialogue be conducted at the various levels of interchange—student/teacher, student/administrator, teacher/administrator, administrator/parent, parent/student, parent/teacher—correspondence we defined originally as political.

Fourthly, a concept of social justice also requires that significantly "radical" positions be considered—practices, policies, models, and values which go beyond the logjam of modern thinking. The recent expansion of the concept of peace and peace education/research has made considerable gains in this direction.[181] Necessary for a full articulation of social justice is a radical philosophy, or a formulation for recognizing possibilities and putting "forward recommendations for help and relief everywhere and in every situation."[182] As Foucault has written:

> There can be no possible exercise of power without a certain economy of discourses of truth which operates through and on the basis of the association. We are subjected to the production of truth through power and we cannot exercise power except through the production of truth.[183]

A discourse in which social justice is fundamental, as it produces truth, poses possibilities (dialectical) and practices that *expose* the strength and weakness of its claims. A significant premise of a social justice concept is derived from a perspective of the "situation of humanity," i.e., the negativity of human being in the contemporary world. The dialectic of the Enlightenment is the further inquiry into the voices of those for whom enlightenment was but another link in the chain of oppression. The praxis is a process which initiates an inquiry from a rejected world through a real world to a preferred world. It originates from whom Paulo Freire calls the "silenced," expanded here to consider the etiology of silence as well.

It has become increasingly apparent to me that significant numbers of people share some concern about the present and the forecast of crisis. Their starting points emphasize different concerns. But it is only at those points at which the situation is *felt* that real changes and the possibility of systemic transformation will be actualized. Part of the social justice concept, as I believe Dewey must have understood his concept of democracy, is in its "universal" appeal to the conditions of the lived world. However, in posing a concept of social justice as a postmodern source by which the contemporary ideological ground for the organization of schooling can be developed, I think that it must be further distinguished from "democracy."[184] In the following Chapter, I further challenge the moral terrain, which Dewey claimed infuses his notion of democracy, with a critique of the paradoxical conclusions and the opacity of his perspective of philosophical naturalism. As an ontological base from which the inquiry into the material and socialized conditions of human be-ing can begin, it is only capable of piecemeal solutions.

Part II
The Natural and the Historical

This modernity based on rationality and the Enlightenment, on science and technology, nationalism and imperialism, on humanity's dominion over itself and the world, and the consequent loss of nature and God, now faces a *crisis*....In the midst of our farewell to modernity we are already *in transition to something new*....Postmodern means an immanent critique of modernity, means an enlightenment on the Enlightenment.
　　　　　　　—Hans Küng, *Theology for the Third Millennium*

To acknowledge the ideological components of American society and the hegemonic organization of its reproduction and socialization processes is no longer a foreign discourse. From a considerable diversity of points of view, the locations where social relations are materialized have been identified and assessed. Sociology of education, since 1970 particularly, has illuminated the relationship of schools to economic considerations.[1] Feminist theory has revealed the forms of patriarchal domination that have subordinated women and the feminine.[2] One does not have to be a scholar or a person of color to see the preservation of oppression by race.[3] Social ecology increasingly gives evidence that the capitalist mode of production/organization premises "an ideology of growth"[4] that exacerbates problems rather than reduces them. At the international level, the presuppositions of the development decades (1950–1980) initiated by the Western bloc of the United Nations have been increasingly rejected.[5] It is not my intention to restate or reaffirm these positions, but framing them as a historical-sociological backdrop, to critique the "metaphysics" of Dewey. The task of this book has been to identify the foundation upon which Dewey's educational philosophy rests and to argue that many of the "problems," the social injustices, and the critical condition of liberal democracy concomitant with the organization of modernity, are *hidden* by that philosophical/social discourse. In Part Two the "third pillar" of Dewey's philosophy of education—Nature—is examined. We have touched upon two already—democracy and science—and in the following sections I extend my argument which claims that

71

the progressive elements of reform pedagogies are diluted rather than strengthened by Dewey's philosophical premises.

Nature and the Natural

As a philosopher Dewey established a starting point, a source which could logically ground what he subsequently had to say. This source seems to me to be Nature, the biological and organic world, and the patterns of existence (objects of knowledge) which Darwin and nineteenth-century scientific inquiry had discerned and legitimated as the only possible basis for any metaphysic. In *Experience and Nature* (1929), which more than one commentator has referred to as Dewey's "principal work on metaphysics,"[6] Dewey alluded to the capability of the naturalistic method to reveal "the nature of things."[7] This source similarly had guided Rousseau's educational premise of the natural qualities of human beings. Dewey, however, sought to correct Rousseau's separation of "Nature" from "existing social organization"[8] and thereby unify a longstanding philosophical dualism which romanticism had obscured. In *The Quest for Certainty* (1929) he prophesied that "the perplexities and difficulties" of modern "experimental knowing" will vanish when "we see that knowing is not the act of an outside spectator but of a participator inside the natural and social scene, [and] the true object of knowledge resides in the consequences of directed action."[9] Such a relationship shapes a praxis and, while possessing "no claim to be final," is the context and guide for the inquiry into self and society.[10] By collapsing the social/cultural world with the natural world, the world which science was equipped to disclose, Dewey was on sound philosophical ground to proceed with a functionalistic analysis, a neo-evolutionist social theory, a theory of history as progress, and an educational agenda which could *never* challenge the machinations of liberal democracy.

Dewey recognized the value of the "natural" foundation for his educational theory and democratic practice.

> "Nature" is indeed a vague and metaphorical term, but one thing that "Nature" may be said to utter is that there are conditions of educational efficiency, and that till we have learned what these conditions are and have learned to make our practices accord with them, the noblest and most ideal of our aims are doomed to suffer.[11]

The goal of education, therefore, was to develop the natural being in accordance with the order which scientific rationality had revealed. As he stated in *Schools of Tomorrow,* "education which finds out what children really are may be able to shape itself. . . so that the best can be kept and the bad eliminated."[12] Nature was the key to understanding human experience. Dewey's intellectual development in this respect was consistent with the progressive thinkers of his time. I call this philosophical framework "naturalism," or in Dewey's terms, "naturalistic empiricism." In general terms, Arthur Danto explains, naturalism

> is a species of philosophical monism according to which whatever exists or happens is *natural* in the sense of being susceptible to explanation through methods which, although paradigmatically exemplified in the natural sciences, are continuous from domain to domain of objects and events.[13]

Furthermore, as John E. Smith claims, the principal point for Dewey was that "there is a vital and practical relation existing between the generic traits of the universe on the one hand and the issues of life and death faced by those who live in it on the other."[14]

In the last section of Part Two I sketch an alternative to this organic and naturalistic metaphor, history, or genealogy, which in conjunction with the critical method alluded to in Part One, proposes to the educator a mode of analysis for organizing educational practice which illuminates social reality more concretely. As we will see, it was Dewey's unwavering identification with "organicism" which I believe philosophically inhibited his pedagogical transformation (as opposed to reform). It is the reluctance to examine the ideological knots between *political* emancipation and *human* emancipation and the distinctions between natural and social/political relations which still renders "progressive" reform insufficient.

Initially, my argument claims that Dewey's ideologically neutral concept of the "natural" must be *deconstructed*; i.e., as was the case with "democracy," it must be further problematized, and the historical constituency of certain fundamental, taken-for-granted, commonsense assumptions about it reexamined. Julian Henriques explains that "deconstruction involves prising apart the meanings and assumptions fused together in the ways we understand ourselves in order to see them as historically specific products, rather than timeless and incontrovertible given facts."[15] It challenges a pattern in much of modern thinking (including Marxism) and further exemplifies the considerable paradox (which Aronowitz so thoroughly captured) embedded in Western epistemology, viz., Dewey's replacement of a theology of heaven with one of science.

This biological metaphysic, which Dewey termed "empirical naturalism," had its genesis in the premises of natural law, itself an impressive building stone of liberal democracy. Jürgen Habermas points out that the incorporation of the natural law premise, for example, in the formation of the U.S. Constitution assumed that "through the interests of liberated private persons these principles [of constitutional government] will assert themselves with the same natural force as the laws of nature and the instincts of animals."[16] The order of Nature, given a clarity by Darwin and his successors never available to the history of naturalism and natural law, became the metaphysical key to the understanding of human be-ing. Human existence, albeit more sophisticated, complex, evolved, is analogous to the rest of the living world. Dewey regarded social reality to be (empirically) represented in "the structure and workings of human nature."[17] As Morton White has shown,[18] Dewey learned to think of the world as organic through and through. Much earlier than the following passage from *Human Nature and Conduct* (1922) reveals, Dewey had been guided by "the influence of Darwinism."[19]

> Human nature exists and operates in an environment.
> And it is not "in" that environment as coins are in a box,
> but as a plant is in the sunlight and soil. It is of them,
> continuous with their energies, dependent upon their
> support, capable of increase only as it utilizes them, and
> as it gradually rebuilds from their crude indifference an
> environment genially civilized.[20]

In the conditions of life and the necessity of interacting with an environment, a human was analogous to "a problem forming animal, in conflict with himself over the constitution of the problems and with himself and the rest of nature in their solution."[21] Dewey believed that he had mediated (theoretically) a major philosophical dualism which had divided how humans grasped reality. But in that mediation, Dewey glossed over the "real problem," which is

> to discover the various precise ways in which what actually exists, in nature as well as society, affects the ways we conceive of and label it; and how the latter, in turn, reacts upon what exists, particularly upon what we take to be "natural" structures.[22]

It is useful to contextualize Dewey's reasoning in the initial efforts to develop a science of society/education which could account for the continuity and change of society, an orderly process of socialization, and the appropriate management of social lives. By linking the cultural with the biological, the scientific and the natural, Dewey implicitly was establishing the ideological parameters of his social theory. In the following, rather long, passage, a contemporary of Dewey and a fellow pragmatist in the American tradition, George Herbert Mead, to whom Dewey acknowledged a great debt, stated this connection:

> The animal, even the plant, has to seek out what is essential to its life. It has to avoid that which is dangerous for it in its life. . . . The getting of food, the avoiding of enemies, the carrying-on of the process of reproduction, take on the form of an adventure. Intelligence consists in the stimulation of those elements which are of importance to the form itself, the selection of both positive and negative elements, getting what is desirable, avoiding what is dangerous. . . . What the animal needs is food [and] freedom from its enemies. If it responds to the right stimuli, it reaches that food, that safety. The animal has no other test . . . [of] whether it has made such a proper selection except [in] the result. . . . You can test your stimulus only by the result of your conduct which is in answer to it. . . . That takes the research method over into life. The animal, for example, faces a problem. It has to adjust itself to a new situation. The way in which it is going brings danger or offers some unexpected possibility of getting food. It acts upon this and thus gets a new object; and if its response to that object is successful, it may be said to be the *true* object for that stimulus. It is *true* in the sense that it brings about a result which the conduct of the animal calls for. If we look upon the conduct of the animal as a continual meeting and solving

> of problems, we can find in this intelligence, even in its
> lowest expression, an instance of what we call "scientific
> method"...developed by man into techniques
> of...science. The animal is doing the same things the
> scientist is doing. It is facing a problem, selecting some
> element in the situation which may enable it to carry its
> act through to completion. There is inhibition.... It tends
> to go in one direction, then another direction; it tends to
> seek this thing and avoid that. These different tendencies
> are in conflict; and until they can be reconstructed, the
> action cannot go on. The only test the animal can bring
> to such a reconstruction of its habits is the ongoing of
> its activity.[23]

Here we see not only Mead's and Dewey's naturalism, but the
metaphysical basis for science, democracy, and experience
which would render previous philosophical dichotomies
obsolete.[24] Dewey's position was grounded by his analogy of
society and the biological organism, and he saw the "problems
of men" to be temporary disturbances of the organism. If we take
Dewey's apparent regard for democratic practices to be central
to the activities of schooling—that an "organic" relation exists
not only between school and society but also between the
individual and society and between the individual and the
school—then it is vital to any assessment of the efficacy of Dewey
and progressivism to locate the terms of those relations. While
I am aware that Dewey *conceptually* had distinguished himself
from "the tendency to take natural law for a norm of action,"[25]
his acknowleged debt to Hume with which he opened *Human
Nature and Conduct* is also a clue that his empiricism would
generate the same ideological problems that his pragmatism did.

　　We might focus this analysis towards the critique of liberal
reformism by initially recalling my claim that Dewey's work has
as its principle end the unification of society. The self-society
union—biologically evident—was to be further advanced on the
anthropological view that the "psychology of instincts and
habits"[26] could be successfully controlled toward a worthy,
lovely, and harmonious society.[27] For example, in "My Pedagogic
Creed" (1897) Dewey maintained that "the child's own instincts
and powers furnish the material and give the starting point for
all education."[28] In the following passage Gonzalez takes issue
with a possible repercussion of this premise.

Dewey contended that "instincts and tendencies" were meaningless unless translated "into their social equiva- lents".... Instincts found their correlate in the existing structure of society, in industrialization, and in its massive development as well as in the distribution of property in poverty and wealth, in the power of the few and the powerless of the many.[29]

Dewey, of course, was hardly reticent about the terms of that relation; as stated in *The School and Society,* he wished to see "the impulses which lie at the basis of the industrial system" aligned with those selfsame "instincts of construction and production" in the child.[30] The essential components of any social philosophy—self and society—obviously have some relationship, but in this section the claim is that in order to accomplish this, Dewey's ontological *foundation* would not permit certain crucial aspects of the relation to be exposed. The dialectical unity he sought is my bone of contention, and with several brief points my initial objections can be posed.

In the first place, Dewey seemed to see social reality—natural and/or human—as uniform or whole, a "given," if you will, which presented to the observer its functional and emphatically unideological categories. From this perspective, as Gonzalez puts it, the totality would always take precedence.

People randomly came together and separated themselves out for purposes of production, but they nevertheless constituted a social body, a cluster of individuals, not of classes, and this cluster or community constituted a social organism. All societies were social entities, capitalist as well as primitive societies. The social had to be predominant over the individual, region, class, ethnicity, or occupation.[31]

However, as I illustrated in Part One, Dewey's grasp of the "nature of our social scene" was heavily influenced by the pretensions of science, technology, and industry, and the possibility of a democratic ideal. In moving to "a condition of dominant corporateness," the influence/power of business to determine "present industrial and economic activities...more and more defined the opportunities, the choices and the actions of individuals."[32] Because his ontology would not include the ideological dimension in the construction of social reality, the political economy of America appeared natural and evolutionary.

Secondly, it is clear that Dewey's naturalism depended upon integrating the cultural with Nature by which both would fall under the domain of science. To locate human be-ing within Nature afforded Dewey a seemingly neutral, objective, i.e., natural basis for understanding and determining future human activity. His naturalistic theory of logic stated,

> on the one side, that there is no breach of continuity between the operations of inquiry and biological operations and physical operations. "Continuity," on the other side, means that rational operations *grow out* of organic activities, without being identical with that from which they emerge.[33]

Dewey required of his social philosophy that it address movement, variation, transformation, and change in human be-ing, the very characteristics which the natural world afforded for contemporary, scientific observation. His "naturalistic metaphysics,"[34] as George Santayana (in another vein) called his scheme of things, took Nature as the source and context of Reality, an empirically based theory in which human be-ing (of course) was central. In an early essay, "Psychology as Philosophic Method,"[35] Dewey provided the basis for his metaphysic by stating that human nature is the proper, indeed, the only object of philosophy, and psychology is the science which explains our nature. Early in his career Dewey had forged the link between the environment and the human which would accompany him throughout every piece of his writing. Psychological experience, not ideology, not power, not historical materialism, was the methodological key to understanding human be-ing. The psychological was disclosed by scientific method because it too is part of Nature, the domain of science.

Finally, an important issue that surfaces is the one of the "leviathan," *homo lupus,* or the survival of the strong. While Dewey distinguished his *social* position from both the Hobbesian and Spencerian conclusions, he did not altogether abandon their scientific naturalism. A theory of human nature which originates in natural instincts, in impulses, is essentially subjectivistic, although in a way that denies overtly ideological representation. It is also dependent upon the form of socialization and collectivization of the State apparatus. When he wrote in *Experience and Nature* that individuals are "free to direct change to new objective consequences,"[36] he seemed to be aware that human beings do indeed make their own history, but unconcerned that those "consequences" may be anything but objective, anything other than neutral. Here the essence of the paradox is boldly before us. The ideological make-up of "self," "society," "science," "technology" had been completely ignored in Dewey's unification of Nature and culture. Whatever problems humanity faced—and Dewey, of course, was not unaware of the problems in social organization from the residual of laissez-faire capitalism—each was part of the natural scheme of things. He left interpretation and production of the "natural" to the same historically select elements which have always defined reality. He found this arrangement perfectly natural, as the following remark in *Experience and Nature* suggests.

> Since modern natural science has been concerned with discovery of conditions of production, to be employed as means for consequences, the development of interest in attitudes of individual subjects—the psychological interest—is but an extension of its regular business.[37]

I would claim that social manipulation, as Foucault's analysis points to, is the most blatant consequence of this hegemonic method. By fortifying his social views with a metaphysic of naturalism, Dewey sought to humanize the natural and naturalize the human and thereby unify the domain of scientific inquiry to rationalize human activity. Dewey's entire pedagogical effort, unfortunately, smacks of the sort of creeping idealism which the materialist critique of Marx found unsatisfactory in Hegel. In so doing he seems to have covertly smuggled in his own "quest for certainty."

The Functional

From another point of analysis, Dewey was advancing a theory of social change. His concept of Nature accounted for and explained the metaphysical basis for the development (and importance) of social reality. Three empirical conditions were implicit in this metaphysic: 1) the interdependency of parts to the formation of the whole, 2) the mutual (if sometimes antagonistic) compatibility of the parts, and 3) the continuous readjusting of their relationships. The infrastructure of this theory of change and order, which attempted to account for the relational components within the natural world and apply their identifiable structures to human behavior, may be called "functionalism."[38]

In his own way Dewey had spelled out his functionalistic markings in an early essay, "The Reflex Arc Concept in Psychology" (1896). He argued against traditional empiricism and for the interdependency and mutuality of the parts to the whole in the behavioral situation. Organism and environment were two aspects of one interacting process. To his credit, Dewey was attempting to reinvigorate the classical Greek account of the essential unity or balance within the universe while disassociating himself from the positivist and determinist wings simultaneously flapping in the scientific breezes.[39]

Nevertheless, my argument in this section maintains that a functionalist social theory, while allowing for both dynamic and static processes within social systems, insufficiently accounts for historical concreteness and structural conditions (affecting school practices, for example). History, it will be argued, is to be understood as explicating events rather than roles, disparity rather than continuity, and the ideological terrain that conditions both.[40] Dewey (satisfactorily) offered in his evolutionist schema a nascent functionalist model, but one which purposely sidetracked the dialectics of historical concreteness. This functionalist orientation, even if Dewey cannot be classified as a hardcore functionalist in his educational theory[41], is very much the difference between reform and critical pedagogical stances. The talk of reviving Dewey and the progressive school movement as a counter to the dominance of the back-to-basics approach may appear viable, but as the philosophical assumptions and ideological basis for him/them are deconstructed, the reservations about such a tack will become clear.

Rather than diverge the critique of Dewey along the formal analysis of functionalism, however, a general assessment of this approach gathered from Dewey's works must suffice. Incomplete as such a critique may be, I think that it will provide a sufficient lens with which to locate Dewey's psychology of development, his theory of social change, progressivism, and a further clarification of a critical (historical) educational praxis.

Hardly a unique view, my reading of Dewey is that he was concerned to highlight the normative basis for social stability and equilibrium during a time of rapid and disorienting shifts on the social landscape. He believed he had recovered it with his concepts of the democratic and the scientific. According to Alvin Gouldner's thesis, however, he did not seem to have deviated much from the socio-political model of the Greek notion of democracy. He glossed over the ideological problems of Aristotle's "political animal" in the polis and his own liberal "democratic public." He did avoid the essentialist pronouncements of the earlier era but retained the organic functionalism (what Gouldner calls "the system") that both Plato and Aristotle saw originating from the state's priority and its organizational development over the individual.[42] In *Democracy and Education* he stated, in general, if somewhat chilling form (in the aftermath of Nazism), the socialization process:

> Setting up conditions which stimulate certain visible and tangible ways of acting is the first step. Making the individual a sharer or partner in the associated activity so that he feels its success as his success, its failure as his failure, is the completing step. As soon as he is possessed by the emotional attitude of the group, he will be alert to recognize the special ends at which it aims and the means employed to secure success.[43]

Giddens also finds the normative assumptions of the functionalist models deficient in their unideological and depoliticized framework. When Dewey stated in *Democracy and Education* that education is a social function, that "a society transforms uninitiated and seemingly alien beings into robust trustees of its own resources and ideals," that "the particular medium in which an individual exists leads him to see and feel one thing rather than another," that one "not merely acts in a way agreeing with the actions of others, but, in so acting, the same ideas and emotions are aroused in him that animate the others,"[44] he is setting up "a relation which calls for explanation, rather than explaining it."[45]

> It sets up a research problem, and understood as asking a question rather than as answering one, it is entirely legitimate. But the use of the term "function" can be misleading because it suggests . . . some sort of need that is a property of the social system, somehow generating forces producing an appropriate (functional) response. We might suppose that we have resolved a research problem when all that has been done is actually to establish a problem that demands research.[46]

My point all along has been that Dewey's understated nominalism, for example, in *Individualism Old and New,* exacerbated (not resolved) the dichotomy between agency and the system of structures. If there is a relation or interaction, then "society" must be regarded as more than an "artificial substitute" for "the cooperative consensus of multitudes of cells, each living in exchange with others."[47] Individuals indeed have come together to form what are commonly called "societies," but this organization, in Dewey's view, was generated by individuals' rational (historically progressing) assessment of the division of labor which would produce the greatest harmony. Social reorganization, if necessary, arises from the need to increase the smooth functioning of the social organism which must be kept viable. Dewey's "new individualism" was the attempt to reconcile the demands of industrial capitalism (modernity) with a democratic autonomy.[48] As Dewey admitted:

The world in which most of us live is a world in which everyone has a calling and occupation. . . . Some are managers and others are subordinates. But the great thing for one as for the other is that each shall have had the education which enables him to see within his daily work all there is in it of large and human significance.[49]

But "underneath the organismic image's rhetoric of inter-dependence there is the spiny substance of hierarchy."[50]

Dewey cannot be justly accused of mouthing the rhetoric of the capitalist state (though he is on less sure ground when labeled a "positivist" or a "theologian of science"), but by no means did he grapple with the structural characteristics and limitations of the liberal democratic society. The progressive vein of American life in which Dewey lived and wrote stressed the values of persistence, stability, compatibility, orderly growth, "common denominators"[51] that would more effectively realize the liberal democratic model twentieth-century (corporate) America was seeking; and his own white, middle-class, nineteenth-century American frame of reference was unconsciously assumed as norm. Along with his "progressive spirit" (see below) which aligned him to science, technology, and industry, this functionalist infrastructure would dictate the problems of reform.[52]

In functionalist terms his progressive outlook towards science and industry helped to account for the differentiation and reintegration—the dynamics—of reform (internally as psychology; externally as sociology). This flexibility of both the individual and the societal organism is explained by the evolutionary principle of adaptation. By this term Dewey refers to the subject's mediation in existing conditions in order that "they will be accommodated to [his] wants and purposes."[53] He believed that the "growing" organism regularly and naturally absorbed new values, more inclusive belief systems, greater participation which bridged the gulf with a previous orientation. The dualistic thinking, or the subject's mooring to the past, prevented new forms of autonomy and social organization to occur.

As I have argued, this scheme is grounded by Dewey's integrating the cultural with the natural. By employing a highly "naturalized" account of human beings he avoided the inevitable paradoxes presented by *concrete* historical conditions and the deterministic implications. But the "naturalness" of human being fails to anticipate the increasing "artificialness" of the modern Western world for resuscitating brain-dead structures and bloodless sociopolitical conditions. In the following passage taken from *The Public and Its Problems* the nominalistic tone indicates that an analysis of structure is a bark up the wrong tree.

> Individual human beings may lose their identity in a mob or in a political convention or in a joint-stock corporation or at the polls. But this does not mean that some mysterious collective agency is making decisions, but that some few persons who know what they are about are taking advantage of massed force to conduct the mob their way, boss a political machine, and manage the affairs of corporate business. When the public or state is involved in making social arrangements like passing laws, enforcing a contract, conferring a franchise, it still acts through concrete persons.[54]

Apparently, in a functionally smooth "modern" society a managerial elite rules the masses, white men oppress Blacks, men generally dominate women, science replaces tradition, corporations determine economic hierarchy, profit replaces ethics, and international relations are sustained imperialistically. Racism, sexism, and structural violence do not exist, only individual racists, sexists, and laissez-faire social Darwinists. Schools do not blindly reproduce the roles required of an industrial society that must be strictly managed, but individual teachers, who have developed specific habits, continue to filter out, track, and encourage hierarchical social divisions. The crisis in American schooling is attributable to "bad" principals, "lazy" teachers, "uncultured" students, and "short-sighted" communities.

There is a normative order characteristic of modern societies that can be functionally identified according to what Parsons referred to as "evolutionary universals."[55] Dewey's historical awareness, which resided for the most part in the background, recognized in the evolution of the Western political economy the roles and attitudes essential to a modern industrial state. In this model the capacity of a social system both to generate change and absorb the change it produces through rational or scientific understanding has been explained (empirically) by the "universal" administrative bureaucracy.

The problem of equilibrium, or in social terms, unification, is accounted for in the functionalist model by the a priori assumption that the conditions by which a given society maintains itself are to a large degree necessary; i.e., social organization reveals underlying "laws" by whch institutions and social relationships are ideally ordered and harmonized. To the extent that Dewey extrapolated upon "natural law" theories of the eighteenth century, he still could claim that a "natural" social order in a technologically advanced, highly industrialized America required a greater competency, a surer sense of participation, and a higher self-control in order that the complexity of the systems be maintained.[56] The tendency here is that the analysis becomes both ahistorical, insofar as the concern is on the realization of social roles rather than events, and depoliticized, to the extent that it does not regard contradictions to the infrastructure. It is not a matter of who will lead the society, philosopher or tycoon—that matter had long been decided—but how well we can adapt to the roles which corporate America has devised. Our paths, as in Plato's *Republic* and Aristotle's *Politics,* have already been established.

The pragmatic spirit ideally reflects the enthusiasm of American progressivism to capture the mechanisms of social control which are neither dogmatic nor totalitarian. As Aristotle found slavery to be natural to the functioning of the polis, a contemporary functionalist will also be reluctant to investigate the roles in industrial capitalism other than by their operative capacity in the system. Dewey accepted the recursive capacity of the society/state to structure its needs. The democracy which he recovered had grown from and developed along the needs for economic liberty without particularly coming to grips with the highly racist, sexist, and discriminatory structures necessary to facilitate it. It was a naturally developed democracy in an analogous way to the "form of government...in which every man, whoever he is, can act for the best and live happily."[57]

Little in such an outlook addresses power issues, nor the unintended but longstanding consequences from the institution-alization of structures, of exploitive and manipulative elements in the social sphere. The formation of a "public" (school) can only be naive or utopian, desensitized by its accountability to categories (roles) rather than concrete events. The aim of a "progressive" school was not simply to train young people "for any trade or profession, but to train them to be capable, happy members of society."[58] The issue which escaped Dewey's wide net of analysis was not who will be "happy," who can be a citizen, who can have a voice in political policy, who can acquire economic control, *but who in fact does.* By addressing problems as intellectual muddleheadedness, Dewey could not liberate theory from practice, create possibilities for emancipation (democracy), nor identify the durability of conditions to determine consciousness.

We are now in a better position to see Dewey's notion of democracy as a series of evolutionary changes, a succession of humanity's progressive realization of higher moral forms. In referring to the necessity to pass through "a machine age"[59] he utilized one of his strongest functional concepts to describe this "natural" occurrence, viz., growth. The open-endedness of this concept enabled Dewey to think "dialectically" (in the traditional sense of that term), or in his own terms, interactionally, while eliminating the transcendental synthesis characteristic of a Hegelian dialectician. Theoretically, growth allows for more growth. It had dialectical connotations (in the sense which both Engels' *Dialectics of Nature* and the more recent Richard Levins and Richard Lewontin book, *The Dialectical Biologist* have)[60]—albeit biological rather than historical—which grasped the interactional process of the subject to adapt to and/or change its environment. The metaphors of nature which abound in Dewey's work consistently captured this give-and-take relation-ship. However, to posit an analogy between a) an organism's activity which seeks alternative routes or habitats when confronted with a permanent obstruction, say a river or mountain range, and b) activity confronting the materialized world of human be-ing, seems to me not to consider fully the incredibly richer and deeper levels of that historicized and sedimented world. With the advances in methodology (science) and technology already dramatically changing the world and the perceptions of it, Dewey was confident (right up to his death in 1952) of the progressive quality of social evolution.

To even the most optimistic eye, *what* is growing, whether it be what Dewey maintained was democracy, some other cultivated flower, or a species not easily describable, has *overgrown* its niche. Dewey's functionalism was primarily a scientific reorientation to intellectual problem-solving. The oft-mentioned problem of dualism was one of erroneous thought, not those of concrete dilemmas in human be-ing. This vast difference, when applied to methodologies in school practices, will be further uncovered when Dewey's notion of experience, which is derived from this naturalism, is contrasted with a notion of praxis (Part Three). Hopefully, by now, the reader has been attuned to the possibility that a social theory and educational practice organized in such a discourse may have serious limitations, limitations which ultimately are regressive and mystifying. If "traditional" education, which has been premised on the acceptance of ideas, eternal and/or cultural verities, and hierarchic knowledge, is to be transformed, then Dewey's evolutionism and its alternative metaphysic is a vital advancement towards that goal. The ontological status of the "given" must be relocated on terra firma, reassigned and reinterpreted. Nonetheless, while the parameters of the natural world are dynamic, open to redefinition and new disclosure, the functional position which regards the individual and society in a holistic network is not without its problems too.

If we have considered the position sketched in Part One, viz., that all value formulations are tied to a prior ideological context, i.e., praxis is inescapably ideological, then we will more easily recognize that Dewey's functionalism had to be linked to a context, which will be examined in another section as American progressivism—industrial growth, scientific method, technological innovation, and liberal democracy. Before we look at that external framework, we will address the new individualism which would legitimate this social integration.

Development

The naturalistic metaphysic (and epistemology) were implemented by Dewey in order to counteract several of the assumptions of traditional educational premises. As noted, the individual perceives and acts while also being acted upon by the environment. With his interactionalism Dewey sought to reveal the transformative capacity of individuals—praxis—and a more democratic pedagogical agenda. Secondly, a more practical, more immediate, more personal educational experience is created by deriving the learning process from individual impulses. By also defining these impulses with particular reference to the liberal democratic worldview, I am arguing, Dewey bypassed a critical analysis of society and a more transformative promotion of democratic schooling.

My contention is that the implicit ideological determinants shaping the relationship of self-society were largely from the occupational categories of the industrializing, scientifically ordered and manufactured world, from historically embedded social relations, and from power/knowledge. I do not disagree with Dewey that the school years should begin to prepare one to enter the adult world. My objection stems from the "relative" autonomy which a functionalist reading assigns to this world and its historical "development." The "forces" or external conditions to which he referred throughout his works loom menacingly outside his purview. It seems to me that Dewey has taken Plato's "ideas," given them empirical credibility while reassuring Rousseau's Emile not to be afraid.

As Dewey saw it, his entire social and educational edifice could be legitimated with psychology. The mind was an instrument to mediate experience, not as the door to consciousness itself. The parameters of the scientific paradigm had greatly modified the epistemological discussion by establishing an empirical basis and limiting consciousness to the conversion of "the relations of cause and effect that are found in nature into relations of means and consequence."[61] As a new foundation for a pedagogical praxis, psychology could be perfectly integrated into a functionalist infrastructure. His use of "instincts," "interests," "impulses," and "habits" discloses an especially clear entry into the contradictory schema of the liberal model and the strategy of reform.

In *The School and Society,* for example, Dewey indicated that the ideas of heredity and evolution are empirically revealed in the "instincts" which have perpetuated the species. "Instinct," or "impulse" is the "primary fact" for human activity and an important concept in his social psychology.[62] Impulses originate in the biological functions necessary to survival, as reflected in William James' taxonomy of human instincts (including imitation, rivalry, pugnacity, acquisitiveness, greediness, and sociability).[63] The empirical or biological source is here again evident: to understand human be-ing we begin with humanity's common animal nature. As Dewey explained in *Experience and Education*, the development from an impulse to an end-view involved the "foresight of consequences" and the "operation of intelligence."[64] By rationally and scientifically isolating and identifying these, their continued prominence in the future socialization of humanity could be enhanced. Pedagogical development could be clarified as well. "In its practical aspect," he wrote, "this laboratory problem takes the form of the construction of a course of study which harmonizes with the natural history of the growth of the child in capacity and experience."[65] He had referred to the "active control of the environment through control of the organs of action"[66] whereby "habits" could be developed which would enhance the educative experience. He had previously identified psychology as the instrument which would provide additional insight into the relation of instinct and habit, individual structure and the environment.[67]

"Habit" is another vital term in the Deweyan scheme. Organisms become adept in their environment by developing habits of survival, ways which will maintain and enhance their existence. "In the first place," he stated in *Democracy and Education*, "a habit is a form of executive skill, of efficiency in doing. A habit means an ability to use natural conditions as means to ends."[68] In *Human Nature and Conduct* he explained that the

> essence of habit is an acquired predisposition to *ways* or modes of response. . . . Habit means special sensitiveness or accessibility to certain classes of stimuli, standing predilections and aversions, rather than bare recurrence of specific acts. It means will.[69]

In *Experience and Education*, he expanded the basic characteristic of habit as the modification of previous and subsequent experience.[70] One acquires the habit of piano playing (for example), of brushing one's teeth, of reading, of reflecting upon certain issues, of behaving in certain situations, of interacting with various aspects of one's environment by appealing to "convenience," standards, gradations of performance, and (simply) results. In a "unity of experience" a *meaning* is gained in these interactions, what Dewey referred to as an "end-in-view."[71] Individuals recognize the function or purpose, if you will, of their interaction. Individual and social functions are intellectually grasped as their relation to the object/goal or whole is psychologically developed. Insofar as Dewey understood the unity of experience in social terms, where the object of knowledge *and* the subject are accessible to scientific inquiry, his pedagogical task was to advance the basis of the functional relationship.[72] In terms of an educational program,

> this means to make each one of our schools an embryonic community life, active with types of occupations that reflect the life of the larger society . . . . When the school introduces and trains each child of society into membership within such a little community, saturating him with the spirit of service, and providing him with the instruments of effective self-direction, we shall have the deepest and best guaranty of a larger society which is worthy, lovely, and harmonious.[73]

"Habits are like functions," he stated in *Human Nature and Conduct,* "in requiring the cooperation of organism and environment,"[74] Dewey had been influenced by William James who had linked the plasticity inherent to the young child and her instinctual or impulsive nature with the notion of habit in order to establish the psychological infrastructure of the developmental approach.[75] Yet, Dewey could not be entirely satisfied wth James' subjectivist conclusions and reformulated a psychology of experience that would at least to some extent include the structural (in closer proximity to Mead's social psychology).[76] Intelligence, the subject's means for experiencing an environment, was also the product to be gained in an interaction with that environment, ultimately changing both subject and object. Dewey offered a corrective to the deterministic and behavioral views that had surfaced in the rush of scientific hubris during the late nineteenth century by assigning to the subject a liberating freedom of will that was empirically in interaction with its world. Not only had Dewey sought to circumvent the empiricist (sensationalism) position, but in his transactionalism he wished to avoid the idealist tendencies of James and the determinist inclinations of Marxism and structuralism. In so identifying experience as fundamental activity initiated by subjects, he located the *object* of inquiry within the subject.

At this point, I would argue that instincts and habits are hardly explained by their biological/psychological expressions but are distinctive responses to the particular (and historical) conditions of *materialized* reality. Zygmunt Bauman conveys more closely this notion of "materialized," and which structuralism defines as:

> the set of generative rules, historically selected by the human species, governing simultaneously the mental and practical activity of the human individual viewed as an epistemic being, and the range of possibilities in which this activity can operate... appear[ing] to the individual as transcendental law-like necessity...[but in] its inexhaustible organizing capacity it is experienced by the same individual as his creative freedom.[77]

Indeed, within the social and historical reality of hierarchies of power (sexism, racism, class, domination) which Dewey's analysis avoided, particular instincts are developed into habits for ideological reasons which preserve those hierarchies. As one example, Simone de Beauvoir points out:

> Throughout history [women] have always been subordinated to men, and hence their dependency is not the result of a historical event or a social change... however, the nature of things is no more immutably given, once for all, than is historical reality.[78]

A major source of the paradox in liberal reform is traceable to its disregard of a critical, politicized analysis of historical (concrete) reality.[79] Dewey only superficially, in my opinion, considered that the materialized world—structures, institutions, systems—intervenes, conditions, even determines consciousness; the materialized world is the creator of consciousness by putting forth what functions it requires of its membership. By explaining differences and hierarchies as "natural," Dewey's reform pedagogy would set specific parameters for challenging social reality.

Presently, the functional order of our postnuclear modern world—a highly technological, computerized, rationalized, and bureaucratized system of structures which produces not only products, food, and leisure, but also consciousness—tolerates and supports the pervasive condition of nuclearization. The nature of this paradox—along with the concrete manifestations resulting from the social violence fostered by racist, sexist, and economic divisions of American society constructed by domination—remains outside most of reformist pedagogical theory. While Dewey's intention was not to sustain, let alone foster such conditions, this progressive spirit left him rather tongue-tied with respect to those aspects of the modern American enterprise which seemed to be defying democratic progressivism.

In fairness, Dewey's humanism, generally characteristic of progressivism and liberalism, had sought to modify the coercive, positivistic, and overly disciplinarian wing of the scientific paradigm. In *Experience and Education* he described this conflict in terms of "traditional vs. progressive" education. He objected to the behavioral and possibly totalitarian practices which force the individual into the "Great Community"; he would rather see that individuals understand their function within the whole. Rationality, in the social sense, the means for fitting in with the social world, should be attained not through the often authoritarian methods of traditional educational practices, but through the development of the natural inclinations of the individual. To the extent that these inclinations can be controlled by the individual, i.e., the identification of freedom as the power to frame purposes,[80] one becomes liberated from external forces.

If in the reform agenda, the business of education was to develop "the correlation of instinctual structures with their expression as social, political, and economic structures,"[81] from a pedagogical perspective, which impulses can be coaxed into activity? What ends are to be envisioned? How can the experiencing subject better perceive her world and a relation to it? What traits better enable subjects to facilitate their experience in/of the world?

In an essay by Valerie Walkerdine her position states:

All that is required then is for the child to be provided with the conditions for spontaneous activity. It is observation, monitoring and above all normalizing of the sequence and effects of development which become the central pedagogic device. In these practices, early childhood was a crucial site for intervention in order to produce, in a medicalized sense, prevention of problems associated with adolescence and adulthood. These involved making sure that the individual developed away from passion, emotionality and aggression, towards love (*caritas*), rationality and sanity. The production of the democratic citizen was naturalized.[82]

Walkerdine's argument (with which I am in agreement) contends that the conditions of developmental psychology are constituted by the regulatory and classificatory practices central to science.[83] The improvement of scientific methods to locate, define, and categorize the given-ness of the world could be implemented as psychological (and educational) mechanisms to determine the normalization and regulation of the child (and, of course, the continuation of dominant practices). Through sociological observation, behavior can be selected, catalogued, and evaluated; norms and values determined; and patterns of development formulated, standardized, and promoted. The linchpin of developmental psychology—the developing child—thus becomes a relationship premised on 1) a knowledge of certain capacities (instincts) of the child, 2) the established organization of society (structures), and 3) a methodology for validating and propagating its findings. The child-subject also must be constituted as an *object* to whom and upon whom psychological (behavioral) observation, measurement, and evaluation is directed. We are back to Foucault's "gaze."

Developmental psychology, of course, can be situated progressively as an antithetical position to an earlier view of the child as a miniature adult. The evolutionary pattern of the natural world does provide a model by which the fundamental and unique characteristics of the individual may be nurtured and shaped. The issue at stake with Dewey is whether the developmentalism undergirding his educational theory inhibits rather than liberates; that is, to what extent are developmental models contradictory and linked to the preservation of dominant modes of social organization? From this consideration, "science envisaged as a tool of liberation [by Dewey] was by its naturalization the very basis of the production of normalization."[84]

The curious logical circle that the revealed religions had so vigorously (and dogmatically) used for centuries was being reinvested by the scientific community. If we are to understand human be-ing, we must first have the proper tools to reveal it; these tools are scientific (not metaphysical). With the book of science we can prove the natural properties of things; by indicating these natures we legitimate and validate the tools themselves. Science is the new theology. The functional totality of developing and the developed and the production of the normal (adjusted) subject are accounted for in this all-answering functionalist model. What Walkerdine's analysis contests is that the genuine concern for individual freedom and the promises of scientific revelations are thwarted ("impossible" in her words) by the very mechanisms of this process.

> It is perhaps the supreme irony that the concern for individual freedom and the hope of a naturalized rationality that could save mankind should have provided the conditions for the production of a set of apparatuses which aid in the production of the normalized child. It is the empirical apparatuses...of development...utilized in education. It is precisely this, and its insertion into a framework of biologized capacities, which ensures that the child is produced as an object of the scientific and pedagogical gaze by means of the very mechanisms which were intended to produce its liberation.[85]

The developmental idea, as a crucial aspect of the entire functional model we are examining, is legitimated on four important counts which continue to mystify educational reformers. There is 1) the patina of liberalism, the discourse of freedom, creativity, individuality, antidogmatism, openness, the child-as-center, and the teacher-as-hip appearances, not altogether undesirable, but significantly weakened when 2) their location within the hegemonic discourses of classification, regulation, and normalization is recognized (bureaucracy, science, militarism). Development in its relational location with 3) economic ordering and needs and the specifically capitalist divisions in America tends to 4) deproblematize the ideological constituency of reason and its concretely historic expressions.[86] While Dewey seemed to assign "freedom" to the individual to intervene in the developmental process, he retained the "psychologicalization" of experience[87] and the individualization of problems as the basis of interacting with and changing the world.

The direction of developmental processes, rather than lying within each individual unit, can be understood as a social construction; i.e., the totality of development requires that it be a dialectical construction of the individual and the social system; development requires production. "There is no objective 'meeting' of human needs in the case of men," writes Wilson, "for unlike animals men mediate and generate their needs through consciousness."[88] While this relation was crucial for Dewey as well, certain questions remain: developing toward what? what are we "growing up" to be? are the assumptions and conditions behind the progressivism of Dewey's work viable today? are developmental possibilities in the ecologically and militarily nuclearized era more promising to the realization of freedom and democracy? where are the historical origins of progressivism, its ideals of enlightenment, of democracy, of freedom, of justice, located? what about social conditions already existing which discriminate, which pollute, which demean and desensitize? where is his pedagogic creed when the issue is discriminatory schooling/hiring/housing or the perpetuation of war and violence? what about a unity of experience that daily contradicts sociability, cooperation, nonviolence, dialogue? Dewey's pedagogy must be examined historically, not simply as a set of timeless constructs/structures biologically latent within each individual and neutrally determined by science.

An acritical usurpation of Dewey's progressive ideas today is the liberal's fundamentalism. To ask, "Can progressivism be revived?" is only slightly less reactionary than the outbursts of the moral majority. The liberation produced by scientific method and its conclusions advanced the belief in social progress, advanced the hope that a smoother, more efficient, more harmonious functioning of society was but a statistic away. It is difficult to conceive of this framework, Walkerdine concludes, "as being the basis of any kind of pedagogy which could potentially 'liberate' children."[89]

Dewey's insights into the formation of better schooling practices cannot be severed from their context and the parameters of their possibility which existed in a pre-nuclear, pre-Auschwitz, pre-Manson era. He tried to open a door (of progressivism) which the weight of human history would not permit. The back-to-basics movement, the entire reactionary period of American history since Vietnam, propelled in the eighties without compunction by the most reactionary administration in history, sees all too clearly what is behind that door.[90] Fortunately, I think that there are elements within educational praxis which are building to challenge and extend Dewey's project. Indeed, to suggest that the door may need to be dismantled altogether no longer elicits the immediate reactions of the red-baiters, jingoists, and National Guard.

Dewey's concept of experience is located within this developmental discourse. I will offer a contrasting notion in Part Three with the concept of praxis, which as an epistemological activism takes as its initial dialectical interaction the historical and the concrete. The next section attempts to locate the basis for Dewey's curious grasp of the historical.

Progressivism

The natural universe is constituted as a relational whole by science, its parts in dynamic growth, an interaction of organism and environment. For Dewey, the universe became intelligible to the extent that scientific inquiry[91] assigns meaning to the various functions operative, i.e., to the nature of the relations within. The "climate of opinion," where reformers were basking in the late nineteenth and early twentieth centuries, spurred the next premise of the Deweyan metaphysic we will look at— progress. More overtly and ideologically, the evolutionary pattern which so marvelously accounted for stability and change in Nature could also provide some framework or design for human society. The society-as-organism view was viable for Dewey because a functional analysis of mutual exchange, orderly arrangement, communication, and reciprocity had been gleaned from the natural world. There are rules—natural, organic, cosmic—which, as discoverable empirical regularities within the natural world, reveal modes of development and social efficiency which could explain the continuity of human behavior.

With an evolutionary model and his social-scientific approach to understanding life, Dewey also had the foundational premise for a progressive pedagogy. It is not to those practices which we turn, but to the concept of progress as a further extension of the "natural" in the overall scheme of liberal reform.[92]

Historian Paul Violas places Dewey in the continuum of a modern and progressive spirit in America to meliorate the transition from an agrarian to an industrial society.[93] According to Violas, for American sociologists Charles Cooley (1864–1929) and Edward Ross (1866–1951), the vision of a good society was that of a rationally organized, corporate state. Existential autonomy of the individual was considered dysfunctional. Their [Cooley and Ross] good society was grounded in the belief that man received his self, identity, and humanity from the social group. They assessed their era as one of rapid change requiring ever-increasing functional specialization and the articulation of such specialization in a rationalized social system.[94]

The organic viewpoint, as Dewey clearly saw, could intellectually ground a teleological empiricism and allow him to describe "society" as a "natural" organization of individuals

> held together because they are working along common lines, in a common spirit, and with reference to common aims. The common needs and aims demand a growing interchange of thought and growing unity of sympathetic feeling[95] . . . [and] a common understanding.[96]

As individuals we come together and begin to institutionalize our social sphere. "Society" is just that collective term, a conceptualization given definition by its parts.

In this light, the ineffectiveness of those ideas to establish systemic social and pedagogical change, paradoxically, might be partly attributable to Dewey's attempt to align or reform the social functions of "human nature" with the requirements of a modern industrial state being created by the technological advances of scientific thinking. His functional analysis and reconciliatory pragmatism reinforced this view. Dewey was convinced that "the changed behaviors, perceptions, and insights of individual human beings" wrought by pedagogical changes would not merely "make citizens, or workers, or fathers, or mothers," as Lawrence Cremin explains, "but ultimately to make human beings who will live life to the fullest—that is, who will continuously add to the meaning of their experience and to their ability to direct subsequent experience."[97]

In *Individualism Old and New,* for example, Dewey argued that the rugged individualism that had been symbolic of America's origins had become distorted and misdirected as the result of the Machine.[98] Dewey's time, the century from 1850–1950, had become increasingly distanced from its social origins, transfixed by the rapid movements of technology and industrialization. The values which nourished and sustained the idea of the individual in a largely agrarian society were undergoing transmutations which when situated in the structures of capitalism were inhibiting social liberation. Simultaneously, the bonds of custom and tradition were also losing their hold on individuals. In this conjunction of old and new, Dewey sought in the past the threads of continuity with the present: initiative, personal ability, responsibility, free association, intercommunication, the honing of natural instincts, and a religious or aesthetic sensibility.[99] This theme of continuity is paramount in the functionalist-evolutionist perspective. Dewey's emphasis on how "societies survive and cohere in the face of external pressure and internal strain, not how they change," [100] was another paradoxical source of his "progressive," at times, teleological, faith in liberal democracy.

Individuation, as an ideological construction, was already showing signs of a sort of homogenizing process which was collectivizing persons rather than freeing them. The historical liberation of the individual, which Dewey found to be progressing in America, nevertheless, was being thwarted by a misguided understanding of the dominant corporateness towards which the modern world was evolving.[101] The occupations and activities which had nurtured the formation of the individual in an earlier era—the small farmer and businessman, artisanship, leisure life, amusements, sports—had "decayed," "broken down," become "bankrupt." The result was the "tragedy of the 'lost individual'."[102] Individuals were lost in the new complex of associations of the industrial world; there was no balance, no harmony, a not-yet-understood shadow over modern life.

Dewey's progressivism spoke to what he termed the serious and fundamental defect of our civilization: our materialism, our devotion to money making and to having a good time.[103] The individual was being consumed by the corporization of American life,[104] those "associations highly or loosely organized more and more defining the opportunities, the choices and the actions of individuals."[105] This "collectivistic scheme of interdependence"[106] was generating "impersonal and socially undirected economic forces"[107] which removed the individual from participating in the organization of society while at the same time creating the illusion of freedom. While he was quite harsh with the turns of economic management producing the bastardized individual, he formulated a response, as I have been arguing, in terms of "adjustments" in the thinking/acting of individuals. The chief obstacle to the formation of a new individuality, he constantly reiterated, was "traditional ideas."[108] The categories and parameters of reform, for Dewey, were already functionally given: modern, technological, industrialized, and democratic society provided the reasons and the tools to make the necessary adjustments. Progressivism foresaw indefinite prosperity, equalization of wealth and income, and the expansion of equal opportunity and humanitarian concern, as well as democratic participation. In not altogether different characterizations, the progressive spirit could be seen as "American Tory radicals . . . who as conservatives helped to democratize the society as part of the struggle against the vulgar nouveau riche businessman"; or, from a more liberal perspective,

> progressivism was a mild and judicious movement, whose goal was not a sharp change in the social structure, but rather the formation of a responsible elite, which was to take charge of the popular impulse toward change.[109]

Dewey's own stated solution—accepting the corporate and industrial world in which we live—then gives a clear picture of the *real* basis of progressive reform. By fulfilling the preconditions of the modern world "for interaction with it, we, who are also parts of the moving present, create ourselves as we create an unknown future."[110]

Dewey had to talk around the concrete facts of corporatism and the historical atrocities and social policies which it perpetuated behind the camouflage of economic opportunity and universal suffrage. Part of his mainstream appeal, of course, was that the discourse of reform spoke to everyone—everything gets better, just wait. There is a concession to the present, that pragmatic mode of thinking/acting which begins by accepting present external conditions as the most facilitative means to address the future. The past—and I am referring to its psychoanalytic connotations as well—is largely ignored; consequently, we don't read of culprits but saviors, not of historical events but functions, not the personal but the formal. In fact, the present is largely but a touchstone for the reconstruction of tomorrow.

The progressive aim was to harmonize the individual with the social changes being wrought by the new methods of production, with their relocation into urban areas, with the greater intermingling of races, creeds, lifestyles, etc., with scientific innovations, and the ideal of the democratic promise itself. As Dewey stressed in *Schools of Tomorrow,* students require the "proper material" in ways that "represent relations and conditions that actually exist outside the classroom."[111] Of course, as a functional prescription it is admirable that the socialization process of schooling be grounded in the concrete conditions of living. When the relations and conditions of socialization are exploitive, unstable, uncaring, possessive, anti-intellectual, destructive, and wasteful, when they are dependent upon historical, deeply sedimented structures of racism, sexism, class inequality, and violence, unfortunately our schools will be similarly constituted. As long as society is guided by "the revolution in industry"[112] educational praxis will follow suit. The revisionist contention is that progressivism in education was not distinct from nor in opposition to the capitalist organization of society, its division of labor, and its maintenance of the power/knowledge hierarchy. Moreover, by accepting the socio-politico-economic conditions apparently indigenous to that organization, for example, the fostering of social/global relations of dependency and the sort of endless growth idea which it shared with technocracy, "progressive" pedagogy alone would never and could never pose viable educational transformation.

My argument for rejecting Dewey's educational praxis ultimately stems from the *philosophical* refusal to critique the structure of liberal democracy's existing social relations. Dewey maintained that democracy in America would survive, the individual liberated, if each of us clearly saw our functional imperatives within a carefully circumscribed area. The *political* and *pedagogical* implications are no less of a concern. The greater socialization of labor in the economic sphere brought by increasing monopolization of capital production requires (at one level of reproduction) that schools produce fewer monopolizers and more to be monopolized, less of the Socratic-philosopher types and more of those who find their integration with the scientific-cultural-corporate leadership to be their best bet. We see this *fait accompli,* of course, in the theme of arch-conservative Allan Bloom's *Closing of the American Mind* as well as neo-liberal E.D. Hirsch's *Cultural Literacy.* Secondly, there is an increasing despair and/or rejection in regarding the schools as sites where social justice, both as an organizational and a curricular project, can be practiced. Dewey's "progressive" assumptions/practices, which ignominiously declined after the

Second World War, carried no oppositional clout, nor were they particularly appealing to the cold war crowd.[113] A third limitation should also be obvious, viz., the absence of a politics of education, either in curricular forms or sociological analysis. A critical assessment of the corporate state and the more longstanding construction of social relations would expose causes rather than effects of the hegemonic domination.[114] Power, in its many historical forms, becomes the center of inquiry.

Alan Wolfe in a particularly insightful article clearly addresses the repercussions of these deficiencies the nature of which had long ago been exposed by Marx. "Public life in the United States," he says, "can be understood as a mechanism for the translation of authentic urges into inauthentic responses."[115] Economic and political power in the U.S. has limited the structure of choices around the objectives of economic growth and military security. Modern liberal democracy is inauthentic, he explains, because it

> can only survive if the assumptions of modernity itself are selected out of the political process. . . . The social contract of modern liberal democracy, then, is one in which the state agrees to provide growth and security on the condition that the citizens accept the state's objectives as their objectives.[116]

The State stabilizes social organization, specifically to protect the private, singular, exclusive, possessive, unique, relative, disconnected notion of freedom while, ideally, at the same time collectivizing human beings into the necessary functionaries of its political economy. Hence, "progressive" pedagogies modify the harshness of the latter by encouraging the development of an individual, a free-thinking, sensitive but opportunistic, worldly agent who accommodates/manipulates the social environment. In Gonzalez' view:

> In placing an organic society as the goal, a break with the previous ideological underpinnings and role of the laissez-faire state was mandated. Anarchistic social relations governed by the marketplace gave way to the constant intervention of the state in the social process that was required to steer society away from class conflict. One particularly important group participating in the formulation of state interventionist policy were the academics, especially the social scientists. To the extent

that the Progressive movement attempted to resolve the contradiction between classes, it was forced to foster state intervention to dominate and guide social relations.[117]

The great phobia of indoctrination, the aftermath of the Enlightenment's liberation and construction of the subject, unfortunately, even in the production of more "individuals," leaves the bulk of students isolated, fragmented, with no discernible possibility to unify their experience along socially responsible avenues. Progressivism can offer no more (and no less) than a program of reform which facilitates the making of a unified, hierarchical society (functionally stratified); it strengthens (by leaving in place) the existing social and economic structures; it is and was a strategy of repair. The liberal tradition and its democratic objective can only be partially realized by the "progressive" praxis of current reformers. Dewey's philosophical ground simply would not engender a transformational critique.

The production of choice by the interests of political economy, transmitted through the primary systems and institutions of American life, less and less concerned with democratic practice, as Wolfe claims, has historically prompted reforms in public schooling in this country.[118] The intervention of the government, as a guarantor of one's right to education, has been compromised by its increasing role in the nuclear era to maintain hegemony and *remove from inquiry* the dominating objectives of this era: economic growth and militarism. Along with the discourse of the "new individualism," a component of which posited that the circumstances of poverty were "not social in nature but simply an effect of differing levels of industriousness,"[119] these structural dimensions of social reality conditioning our lives are posed (if at all) as functionally necessary by mainstream educational reformers (see Part One). For every "individual" developed in the Deweyan sense, it seems so many more never mature.[120]

Progress, then, functioned, as Feinberg explains in his chapter "The Image of Progress," as a conceptual device to displace the concrete disharmony, the exploitive and alienating conditions of modernity "into a larger, more purposeful context, thereby maintaining faith in the basic soundness of the larger institutions from which reform would issue."[121] Dewey, as I have tried to show, offered with his naturalist metaphysics and pragmatic recovering of "ideal aims and values...deep and indestructible in the needs and demands of humankind"[122] a rational consolidation with the powers that be. If democracy bogs down, he steadfastly maintained, there need not be cause for alarm "provided there is effected a union of human possibilities and ideals with the spirit and methods of science on one side and with the workings of the economic system on the other."[123] Reinforced in the reform position is the view that the problem is not structure (which are natural and therefore neutral), just bad or muddleheaded people. History, to which we will now turn, functioned in this scheme "as something 'found' not made."[124]

History

In this last section the argument claims that Dewey was not a student of history, that his thinking, if it may be called dialectical at all, remained idealistic, and that his pedagogical praxis, as a model for educational change today, insofar as a historical (not evolutionary) perspective is absent, must have strong provisos. He did not examine the deeper sedimentations of social life, the conditioning and determining structures which prevent and contradict the progressive ideal, nor the necessity of transformation rather than reform. In describing the functional "consciousness," Gouldner implicates an analysis which abstracts itself from the concrete:

> Functional sociology with its ahistorical character and its emphasis upon the *ongoing* consequences of existent social arrangements, reflects the loss of historical imagination that corresponds to the mature entrenchment of the middle class, which no longer fears the past and neither imagines nor desires a future radically different from the present.[125]

As I will argue, a dialectical praxis challenges the assumption of progress by fostering "critical consciousness," or the "awareness that there is an essential difference between the given-ness of the natural world and contingency of the social."[126]

Human history, insofar as it could be functionalized along categories of continuity, convergence, and cumulation, revealed itself as an evolutionary progression. Thus, in "the process of becoming" the scientific method is concerned with the discovery of a common and continuous process, and that can only be determined empirically.[127] Dewey was seemingly willing to exchange history for evolution, as evidenced by scientific rationality, control, and technological innovation. He explicitly identified history with evolutionism, with the experimental method, and ultimately with morality. The three pillars of Dewey's thought which I have examined—democracy, science, nature—all presuppose continuity and a pseudo-historical account of events. The relation of means/end in an organic or evolutionary theory emphasizes the utopian and ideal aspects without the necessary exposition of the concrete obstacles to any unification. The assumption that history or culture, is an evolutionary progression analogous to the biological/cosmic development of the universe is less and less probable today.[128]

This view of history as adaptation was evident in the work of fellow progressivist Jane Addams (1860–1935). More concrete in her historical selection, her efforts at Hull House in Chicago during the Progressive Era expressed the orientation of liberal concern "to make social intercourse express the growing sense of the economic unity of society."[129] For example, she devised an exhibit of spinning wheels chronologically arranged so that "even the most casual observer [could] see that there is no break in orderly evolution if we look at history from the industrial standpoint; that industry develops similarly and *peacefully* year by year among the workers of each nation."[130] Even in Addams' more explicit social history, what is naive in such a rendering, drawing upon Rebecca Comay's critique of Rorty, "is the willingness to embrace an abstract version of democracy and community at the expense of more substantive and concrete requirements."[131]

In identifying evolution and progress as history, Dewey had linked morality, the "ethnocentrism" of liberal democracy, and the individuation process as the standards and the terrain of reform. I am not claiming that Dewey should have foreseen the limits of such an approach or more clearly recognized the structural contours of liberal democracy which were being openly debated. He was certainly cognizant of the historical shifts that marked the transition from agrarian, decentralized, merchant functions to the heavily urbanized and industrialized society emerging in the West, obviously a concerned educator struggling with the issues of his time—problems of a prenuclear era and a social organization which could exclude Blacks, women, and the non-WASP contingent from the public sphere. But, as stated above, history had to establish a perspective.

A curious paradox exists, however, which the following passage from Walter Feinberg taps. On one hand, the liberal formed a historical interpretation

> from which conflicting events and social forces could be judged while at the same time supporting the development of technology and the secondary institutions formed around it.... He claimed that questions about the overall direction and pattern of the past did not have empirical significance and were not worthy of serious study,... that liberal history and philosophy stood as a reaction to large ideas with religious overtones.[132]

Yet, history was not a random recovery of the past. Not "everything" was worth the effort. History, indeed, provided a certain perspective, a point at which "the relations, the evolution, and the development of all aspects of life, of useful production, of art, of knowledge, of spiritual ideals, out of the matrix of the typical dominant interests of mankind—their occupations" [were disclosed].[133] Inquiry is historical, Dewey maintained, when it analyzes a phenomenon from the conditions which led to its coming-into-being. In Dewey's words:

> History is conducted on the principle that it is a means of affording the child insight into social life. It is treated...as a way of realizing what enters into the make-up of society and of how society has grown to be what it is...thus...great emphasis is laid upon the typical relations of humanity to nature, as summed up in the development of food, shelter, habitation, clothing and industrial occupations. *This affords insight into the fundamental procedures and instruments which have controlled the development of civilization.*[134]

As Feinberg puts it, Dewey believed

> that the recent past had revealed to man the method for favorably manipulating the natural environment towards progressive ends.... The historian...does not simply capture the past as it once happened. He reconstructs it by selecting out events, assigning degrees of importance to evidence, and postulating a direction to change. And he does so guided by problems that are foremost in the present.[135]

What is recollected is, of course, necessarily a selection; it is a judgment. We are always selecting those events, according to Dewey, which bring out

> the consecutive qualitatively continuous history. . . . Strains of change have to be selected and material sequentially ordered according to the directions of change defining the strain which is selected.[136]

In his *Logic,* Dewey referred to "events" as always involving judgment.

> The origin and development of the Appalachian Mountain Range is an event, and so is the loosening and rolling of a particular pebble on a particular ledge on a particular foot-hill. There may be a situation in which the latter sort of episode is much more important in judgment than is the history of long duration.[137]

By regarding history as progression, Dewey implied that change and growth were moving in evolutionarily desirable directions; he assumed, furthermore, humanity's ability to control those changes.[138] By "overlaying" or reading continuity on events, not only is a psychology of the subject and its natural development assumed, but he further extended continuity historiographically to social collectivity. We have seen that Dewey had largely accepted the dominant discourses. Merle Curti maintained these were formed from "upper middle class" values: faith in democracy; acceptance of capitalism; approval of the doctrine of rugged individualism; faith in the future; faith in human nature; belief in piecemeal reform; faith in the school; utilitarian interests; expression of (what I have referred to as) the "American ideology."[139] Continuity requires either an a priori or a pragmatic set of categories by which events can be synthetically rendered. Liberal democracy, for Dewey, was "the *means* by which conclusive and complete judgment about an entire course of sequential events, a history, extending from the past through the present into the future, is groundedly instituted."[140]

Dewey, of course, was not a historian per se, but he was concerned, as this book argues, to promulgate a so-called "American ideology" in its most favorable light. In Wilson's terms, Dewey believed:

> What is the knowledgeable society but a functional order in which substantially rational individuals participate,

exercising that intelligent insight into things and events whose rational auspices are to be discovered in the "success" their efforts exhibit, derived from proper "socialization" and correctly contemplated effects.[141]

Progressivism, as a particular Euro-American perspective, saw reform, for example, in the shift from the blatant exploitation of working people and people of color in America to the exploitation of foreign peoples and markets. Dewey also assigned urgency to the social problems "developing out of the forces of industrial production and distribution."[142] Inherited instincts, developed into habits, as we have seen, structured and determined appropriate behavior (ideally). The materialized world and the environment, though central to Dewey's notion of experience, were nonetheless secondary to "the child's own instincts and powers" in their impact to shape human activity.[143] As Gonzalez explains:

> Dewey contended that "instincts and tendencies" were meaningless unless translated "into their social equivalents" and carried "back into a social past and [we] see them as the inheritance of previous race activities." Instincts found their correlate in the existing structure of society, in industrialization, and in its massive development as well as in the distribution of property, in poverty and wealth, in the power of the few and the powerlessness of the many.[144]

Consequently, we get a historical picture like Dewey's fellow progressive (and historian) Charles Beard (1874–1948) had recommended. In *The History of the American People,* he explained the rationale of selection:

> The space given to the North American Indian has been materially reduced. They are interesting and picturesque, but they made no impression upon the civilization of the United States. In a history designed to explain the present rather than to gratify curiosity and entertain, Indian habits of life and Indian wars must have a very minor position.[145]

Here we see from where history was to gain its power. Native Americans and the chronology and interpretation of their exploitation by "progress" is made insignificant, it sheds no light on the "problems of men." Praising the "progressive" methodology used to inform young students of the Panama Canal (in his *Schools of Tomorrow*), we have seen that "the teaching of the practicality of imperialism was, for Dewey not the issue. The issue was whether one successfully connected the individual in a conscious and scientific manner to the existing social order."[146] The implicit justification of the U.S. takeover of Panama, its exclusive rights of control, and the strategic usefulness as a military site which the takeover of another country could provide is the essence of realpolitik.

Yet, his activist (experiential) extraction of continuous principles was not simply "ethnocentric" but contained elements which were classist, parochial, and jingoistic. Like Plato, Dewey was willing to accept a society of unequals. However, Dewey argued that the inevitability of inequality and nonparticipatory democracy was validated by genetic or psychological or social conditions, not metaphysical ones. He maintained that the hierarchicalization of society was a natural and therefore objective basis for the organization of society:

> The business of education [was] to discover what each person is good for, and to train him to mastery of that mode of excellence, because such development would also secure the fulfillment of social needs in the most harmonious way.[147]

Education was to be the preparation of unequals for equality because Dewey and reform accepted "the order of things."[148] In both *The School and Society* and *Schools of Tomorrow* the necessity of vocational schooling for certain classes, further defined along gender lines, was emphasized.[149] What sort of occupations did Dewey find in American society which would be appropriate training models for Blacks, or for that matter, women? Here again I think that the lack of professional and intellectual concern in American schools already marked by blatant and legal racist/sexist/classist structures, "reformed" by vocationalism, but abandoned when immigrant, ethnic, and working-class populations became too high, leaves the progressive ideology with questionable credentials for its application today.[150]

Dewey's evolutionism was both liberating and concealing. For those whom the culmination of social life as a historical evolution—the empirical record of the human endeavour—is the premise of analysis, the "events" selected will be the features and fundamental qualities which fostered the growth. As Smith states: "The aim of all neo-evolutionist models is to discover and systematise the processes which serve both to maintain and to change social systems,"[151] i.e., the presupposition of certain patterns or laws of nature to which human be-ing necessarily conforms if it is to survive. The need to locate human be-ing—society as an organism—within those processes or patterns precipitates a pedagogical perspective which is heavily ontogenetic, a psychology of development that excludes the structural environment in its diachronic effects, and a depoliticizing of the categories which ultimately are used.

> Instead, the environment is treated as a quarry from which the relevant stimulus or catalyst (that is, relevant from the point of view of that aspect of the system changes which is thought to require explanation), is carried off, torn out of its context and injected into the system, like some stone thrown into a pool to see how many circles it will form. In this way, the environment is broken up into a series of disparate stimuli, which as they impinge upon the system, turn into so many "accidents[152]."

My conclusion is that Dewey's naturalism could not then, nor cannot now collapse concrete contradictions in the *materialized world* but rather can attend only to the *dualisms of thought.* Therein springs the fountain of paradox. To this mode of inquiry historical events constitute appearances, a certain epiphenomenal quality;[153] it is the hidden (progressive) current of evolutionism which has carried forth the species manifesting itself in various histories, epochs, cultures.

In the final part of this book, I will attempt to reconnect these initial criticisms with the pedagogical theme of praxis. An alternative notion of "historical" will be emphasized, one focused around power configurations rather than functions, one that conjoins the personal with the political, towards the structures or frameworks in which individuals are located, a politics of culture, if you will. These, as such, have a chronicle to be read, a history of change, yes, but not necessarily growth or progress. Foucault, perhaps the most widely acclaimed of the so-called historians of *discontinuity,* argues against the evolutionary view and the "seamless web" theory of socio-cultural movement. His objection is against those who see continuous history [as] the indispensible correlative of the founding function of the subject: the guarantee that everything that has eluded him may be restored to him; the certainty that time will disperse nothing without restoring it in a reconstituted unity; the promise that one day the subject—in the form of historical consciousness—will once again be able to appropriate, to bring back under his sway, all those things that are kept at a distance by difference, and find in them what might be called his abode.[154]

Dewey sought to explain everything in general but addressed little in particular. In stressing the complementary and unifying qualities and relations of the growing, progressing organism to which it owes its continued status, he sociologized history, as Habermas explains, where "cultural traditions are no longer taken at face value, but are studied in terms of their latent functions."[155] I am not denying that Dewey's interactionalism attempted to deal with the problem of structure and agency; his concept of experience, to which we now turn, was a major pedagogical innovation. My argument is that it is inadequate as an epistemological premise for theory and schooling today and that it speaks for reform when a transformation is needed.[156]

Part III
The Personal and the Political

While saints are engaged in introspection, burly sinners run the world.
—Dewey, *Reconstruction in Philosophy*

Philosophically, the notion of praxis has a long history.[1] In general, praxis conveys the dialectical nexus between the "theorizing," or thinking dimension of human beings and the "practicing," or doing. It refers, more specifically, to a certain kind of human activity manifested in "the realm of culture and history,"[2] an engaging or intervening in the multiple forms of social reality which have moral, social, and political implications for us. In the sense relevant here, I take praxis to signify "activity by means of which people transform their nature and social environment in order to improve their living conditions."[3] I would further wish to situate such activity in its relation to the pedagogical design and import of Dewey's "democracy" and to the notion of "social justice" which I am positing. Even in its basic sense—the relation of thought and action—I believe that praxis is *the* pivotal concept in any theory of education. The paradox of reform, then, ultimately lies with the particular expression of the conditions for and forms of school "activity."

Several preliminary remarks should be made. Without agreeing with the (possible) implications of Marx's concept of ideology,[4] his emphasis upon the relationship of the ideological and the materialized as the context of praxis is worth recalling. In *The German Ideology* the authors say:

> we do not set out from what men say, imagine, conceive, nor from men as narrated, thought of, imagined, conceived, in order to arrive at men in the flesh. We set out from real, active men, and on the basis of their real life-process we demonstrate the development of the ideological reflexes and echoes of this life process . . . . Life is not determined by consciousness, but consciousness by life.[5]

Praxis, then, (at least in a Marxian sense) refers to activity directed towards the materialized and ideologically infused, to

111

embedded concrete social relations and practices, to the *politicized* (in the sense posed in the introduction) construction of social reality in toto. It is these referents which I find lacking in Dewey's notion of experience, a concept which I believe cannot engender nor even address the situation of crisis and critical consciousness. Dewey was convinced that as the "progressive" reform impulse became infused into schooling the stratification[6] visible in American society eventually would diminish. But without an educational praxis that begins with these concerns and the critique of the power relations involved, reform in education, which is illuminated by the many permutations clinging to Dewey's concept of experience, necessarily will be piecemeal.

Secondly, I have understood Foucault in a rather Marxian way and Marx in a way considerably illuminated by my reading of Foucault. I have also planted (in admittedly rocky soil) in this book a notion of ideology which neither would completely support (though neither would entirely disagree). Both, however, seem to me to have recognized the "terrain" of human be-ing in its discursive and material forms. For example, when Foucault writes that "discourse is not the majestically unfolding manifestation of a thinking, knowing, speaking subject, but, on the contrary, an arena in which the dispersion of the subject and his discontinuity with himself may be determined,"[7] he implies these contingent, socially constructed, and, ultimately, politicized forms of human be-ing wherein individuals are always engaged dialectically with those forms.

Not unmindful of Foucault, but in an analysis which better captures the dialectical tension of praxis (located in the relation between agent and structure), Anthony Giddens has developed what he calls a "theory of structuration" which posits the "duality of structure," or a picture of an intentional agent within "the unfolding of the routines which constitute day-to-day life."[8] In making the linkage with praxis, he argues that locating agents in the "duration" of structures (and institutions), which are their daily lives, allows us to better understand both; e.g., a-teacher-in-a-school. While he does not explicitly expound a pedagogical agenda, I think the implications are clearly present.

> The basic domain of study of the social sciences, according to the theory of structuration, is neither the experience of the individual actor, nor the existence of any form of societal totality, but social practices ordered

across space and time. Human social activites . . . are not brought into being by social actors but continually recreated by them via the very means whereby they express themselves *as* actors.[9]

The relation between individual and society has been a primary theme of this book. In Parts One and Two the Deweyan social theory and its reliance upon a naturalistic metaphysics was critiqued along with the inadequacies resulting from a unideological, and unpolitical analysis. There I try to show that reform cannot investigate certain "crisis" situations because of its epistemological structure. Dewey's well-conceived theory of social reform, I am arguing, was and continues to be undermined by its absence of "contradiction," which, in Bertell Ollman's terms,

> is a way of referring to the fact that not all . . . developments are compatible. In order to progress further in the direction made necessary by its own links of mutual dependence, a component may require that the probable course of change of another component be altered.[10]

Contradictions are created by the fact that human be-ing is an ideological construction, that it is a product of human activity. Human beings engage in a world that is not of their making and seldom (in the initial confrontations) to their liking; social reality is, in powerful and binding ways, structured. To see human be-ing as contradictory, that is, as constructed and imperfect, rather than natural (biological and functional) is to shift the level of inquiry from the organic to the ideological. Giddens' work brings this contradictory aspect of human be-ing to the forefront by illuminating how the "recursive character" of activity not only draws upon the "rules and resources" (structures) of social life, but in so doing also reconstitutes or reproduces them. In his theory of structuration,

> there is no circumstance in which the conditions of action can become wholly opaque to agents, since action is constituted via the accountability of practices; actors are always knowledgeable about the structural framework within which their conduct is carried on, because they draw upon that framework in producing their action at the same time as they reconstitute it through that action.[11]

People do things unnaturally (dye their hair), illogically (smoke cigarettes), irrationally (believe in ghosts). But people do not grow like mushrooms out of the earth in accordance with some essential organic design. Nor, let me stress, can an effective analysis of what may help us to understand human be-ing be gained from such a starting point. Contradiction is an element of praxis because it refers to the many situations where human beings "differentiate," their "status" changes, they re-identify themselves. It is recognizable, for example, in the struggle of the infant to differentiate from the parent, or the slave to transform its relation of (natural) servitude, or a student to rebel against the positioning of the teacher.[12] Conflict, or the multiple ways in which humans act, resist, and struggle, is essential to human be-ing simply for the reason that human be-ing is *not* "natural." Consequently, the "pragmatic turn" directing Dewey's concept of thought and action—experience—and its insertion into the discourse of liberal reform leads into a social and pedagogical cul-de-sac.

Thirdly, the relation of praxis to the "polis," or to a more contemporary notion of "public sphere,"[13] which includes public schools, is significant for my use of "praxis" below. In regard to creating public spheres within institutional and formal pedagogical contexts, Giroux states an organizational approach that clearly points towards an educational praxis focused in social justice issues, and which I find missing in Dewey's democratic experience.

> Education has a direct link to the creation of alternative public spheres, and it represents both an ideal and a strategy in the service of struggling for social and economic democracy. As the embodiment of an ideal, it refers to forms of learning and action based on a commitment to the elimination of forms of class, racial, and gender oppression.[14]

Indeed, intimately connected with the notion of educational praxis is the material transformation of the schools towards increasing social justice concerns. To envision the schools as sites where the intellectual underpinnings of social reality are invested, where discourse and practice can be challenged when appropriate and creatively enhanced, as well as the basic development of literacy and critical thinking, seem to be nothing more than granting to a theory of education its latent potentiality. Such a movement cannot be separated from the politicized awakening of publics themselves to re-conceptualize the role of schools. In linking the school with a concept of public sphere as a referent for social transformation, Giroux maintains, opportunities expand for the

> critique and restructuring of social experiences based on new forms of communicative interaction and the reappropriation of cultural modes of communication. . . . As part of an alternative public sphere, it organizes and uses, where possible, the technology of science and the mass media to promote dialogue and democratic forms of communication.[15]

In Part Three I am contending that Dewey's concept of experience (the fourth pillar), while claiming to develop individual empowerment, also does not (nor intends to) address the relationship of the individual to the structures of the materialized world. The translucency which his commonsense reading of the world gained him, what I have referred to as "natural," and what is the basis of the concept of "experience," simultaneously blinded him to unintended consequences. Dewey's most advanced concept, experience, only intended to capture education in the terms of science, ethnocentric enrichment, developmental functionalism, and vocational familiarity. It does not address reappropriation, restructuring, nor liberation.

Experience

Briefly, let us examine several of the components upon which Dewey's notion of experience rests in order that the later distinctions with a more radical praxis can be understood. It is my contention that "experience" was for Dewey, expressed in somewhat hyperbolic fashion, the basis for "a criticism of criticisms."[16] It philosophically serviced (among its other uses) his concern with social reform, "especially as it is expressed in the education process."[17] Significantly, Dewey attacked the absolutist and transcendentalist views which dichotomized thought and experience, value and fact, while illuminating the significance of experience in the formation of reality. He insisted that human beings do not simply react to an environment—this position is uncontroversial for Dewey and for me—but are continuously and actively engaging it. Experience is a thinking and an acting, cognitive and sensational, naturally and logically linked to "the experimental," and the basis for a "scientific praxis."[18] Pedagogically, he sought to legitimate experience by advancing its centralness in the everyday lives of human beings. Generally, these characteristics pertain as well to a modern concept of praxis.

As we have seen, Dewey found continuity in nature by regarding events, values, patterns, etc. from a consideration of their functions within the larger constellation of collective associations, the "facts" of evolutionary survival, and his own selected ideals. He regarded humanity and the world as natural, as an organic process of life and death, of movement, of growth, an evolutionary spiral towards freedom.[19] Opposition, conflict, contradiction, or to use the term in his lexicon, *problems,* are not ontological to human be-ing, but the result of aberrations in thought, muddleheadedness. Reality is not dialectical or contradictory; it is our thinking that creates conflict.

My objection with this orientation is the ease with which it has been taken over by the scientific hubris inherent in positivism. Karl Popper, defender of the open society, claimed that conflict is a matter of attitude:

> it is only our critical attitude which produces the anti-thesis. . . . The only "force" which promotes the dialectic development is *our reluctance* to accept, and to put up with, the contradiction between the thesis and the antithesis.[20]

With such a position, things *are* what they appear to be; they have an identity, an evolving core which defines them. Things can be grasped in their essence, their essential unity understood, and their function determined, not in some metaphysical fashion, but empirically. The identity of human be-ing is an objective realization, insofar as it is assumed natural, and can be discovered scientifically. Philosophical dualisms, then, constituted the source of *social* confusion or contradiction, existing because this fundamental essense of unity has *appeared* only "transcendentally"; hence, not only were the empirical and human world characterized with a certain fictitious quality, but human be-ing itself had been alienated from its moorings in nature. Dewey felt that these bifurcations in the way we thought, had and were separating people from grasping the positive evolutionary forces now propelling modernity. Science was good philosophy for Dewey because it stripped away the metaphysical or ideological blinders which created dualisms and reunited thought with experience. This presupposition of a basic unity—nature—supported and epistemologically legitimated the further conceptual argument for a "scientific praxis." Dewey's "naturalistic logic" was a philosophical attempt to link the evolutionary perspective, the "postulate of continuity,"[21] as he called it, with a social theory.

In also premising continuity in human be-ing, he required an epistemological theory that could account for both thinking and doing, one that situated the individual within a continuum of temporal/spatial sequences and could explain how the habits of existence were brought to the forefront of consciousness. Habits were the proper units of behavior (and analysis) because they are the consolidation and integration of the organism's repeated (and implicitly, at a minimum, accepted as pragmatically true) efforts for continuing some activity. Dewey stated that

> the basic characteristic of habit is that every experience enacted and undergone modifies the one who acts and undergoes, while this modification affects, whether we wish it or not, the quality of subsequent experiences.[22]

When a situation could not be immediately grasped, the organism's desire to solve a concrete problem resulted in thinking-doing (experience). It was clear to Dewey that thinking was inherently related to the needs and desires of the organism and necessary for all problem-solving activity. On the basis of one's own experience, one's own possibilities, the organism thought. This implicit pedagogical dimension, when carried into the human realm, was central to Dewey's basic sense of praxis and the social key to the realization of a progressively democratic society.

The context of experience, that is, the parameters in which the individual interacts, what Dewey referred to as "objective conditions," obviously was equally important to Dewey's theory.[23] Experience was the interaction of a living being with its physical and social environment.[24] Society, the pole of "objective conditions" we are concerned with, he further argued, was organically/functionally related to subjects who adapted to (after having established) the historical-developmental variables (culture), thus securing the success of both (survival). The interaction of self and society actually constituted a conduit and was the basis of "personality" (attitudes, interests, desires) and culture (institutions, art). Experience was a "starting point," a "method for dealing with nature," a disclosure of nature, how human beings understood their reality.[25] While he wanted to reject the idealistic implications of "consciousness," as a given starting point—he said, it is but "a symbol, an anatomy whose life is in natural and social operations"[26]—he also maintained that "every *new* idea, every conception of things differing from that authorized by current belief must have its origin in an individual";[27] the individual is the "pivot."[28] Thinking is original discovery; it is the world being clarified by the subject. The individual as a being-in-the-world, as one who thinks, "denotes the source of change in institutions and customs."[29] Hence, the capacity of the individual, as a "centered organization of energies identify[ing] itself with a belief or sentiment of independent and external origination,"[30] to affect change (praxis) was enhanced by a method that facilitated "distinctive ways of experiencing natural objects."[31]

One final example of Dewey's interactional posturing with the concept of experience was stated (philosophically) in *A Common Faith* (1934). Here the movement from appearance to reality and from the real to the ideal was explained as experiencing. As he described the process,

> the ideal itself has its roots in natural conditions; it emerges when the imagination idealizes existence by laying hold of the possibilities offered to thought and action. There are values, goods, actually realized upon a natural basis—the goods of human association, of art and knowledge. The idealizing imagination seizes upon the most precious things found in the climacteric moments of experience and projects them. . . . There is at least enough impulse toward justice, kindliness, and order so that if it were mobilized for action, not expecting abrupt and complete transformation to occur, the disorder, cruelty, and oppression that exist would be reduced.[32]

He carved out a space between both the empiricist and idealist positions (what may pass for a definition of pragmatism) which could highlight the *individuals* propelling society, assuming and accepting functional roles in the continuous evolution of human be-ing. In so doing, the "transaction" (the term he later used to designate his praxis), rather than either the subject (idealism) or the object (realism), became the primary focus of social analysis. Integration (or happiness) was the desirable outcome of this synthesis, and

> since this end can be attained only by the coordination and integration of the various human tendencies and of their consequences in the external world, the end so conceived is not merely an ideal for an individual or a group of individuals but for society as a whole.[33]

Experience was seen as the bridge, the means by which organisms adapted to their environment, a concept which for Dewey was fundamental to the role of education in harmonizing the self-society relationship.

In putting forth a rational-empirical model of human be-ing, as we have seen, Dewey used categories of nature rather than metaphysics, instincts rather than "soul" which he thought more accurately situated the tasks and the means itself of problem-solving. The result of this functional analysis of "experience and nature" was to *familiarize* the "natural." In Dewey's educational writings his concern was clearly towards the functionality of (modern) commonsense life. Learning was the process of becoming aware of the essential unity of human be-ing. And if, as Dewey stated in *Problems of Men*, "the school is the essential distributing agency for whatever values and purposes any social group cherishes,"[34] then the competencies to be developed were to be pragmatically selected and organized from the historical reality of the American enterprise.

The functionalistic linkage at the core of Dewey's concept of experience idealistically collapses the duality of subject and object (self-society) because it leaves in place the materialized conditions. The individual's attitude—so often confused because of dualistic conceptions—was the problem. Education needed to create practices which could continuously *unify* the individual with the functional prerogatives of the progressively modern state. But if Dewey's emphasis upon functions or norms *excluded* the ideological dimension of power in the ordering of social reality, then his interactionalism reveals itself as an instrumentally laden theory far removed from the transformation of the social world (in contrast to Giddens' analysis). If "role" is the basic unit of socialization, and it is through roles that tasks in society are allocated, policies and institutions made to enforce them, and pedagogical programs created to enhance them, then, as Giddens argues, role "betrays a particular, and deficient view of society according to which stability and the 'ordered regulation of expectations' are natural, and to which change is foreign."[35] Experience simply cannot be understood as completely natural. In Karel Kosik's terms:

> experiencing the workaday life naively and uncritically, as though it were the natural human environment . . . a particular historical form of the everyday is considered the natural and immutable basis for all human coexistence. . . . To behold the truth of the alientated everyday, one has to maintain a certain distance from it.[36]

A consequence of Dewey's naturalism is the gross deproblematization of the concrete and a psychologicalization of history. He pragmatically based his educational theory on the "functions" observable in the social world, the importance of scientific method, and a necessary "re-thinking" of the "important things" (in Dewey's words). Naturalization dictated the boundaries of Dewey's pedagogical reform, one which I do not think can reach the situations of crisis existing both in society and in the classroom. Paradoxically, liberal reformers tend to perpetuate a kind of stasis which undermines the transformative capacity of an experiential-based pedagogy.

Social reform was formulated, then, largely as a philosophical collapsing of dualisms. This instrumental means actually exposed an "idealistic current" within pragmatism wherein the concrete "problems" of social reality were resolved by establishing practical (scientific) differences. Gramsci in the late twenties (and Marx even earlier) has critiqued the "utopic" quality of this maneuver.[37] Functioning (successfully) in society was ultimately a matter of will, perceiving the essential unity of the world, overcoming irrational habits and poorly managed institutions (the new individualism). Philosophy's business was to expose "the doctrines which seem to justify this separation and which certainly obstruct the formation of measures and policies by means of which science and technology (the application of science) would perform a more humane and liberal office."[38] "Reconstruction . . . is strictly an intellectual work."[39] Consequently, experience tended to remain "subjective"; in the individual's interaction with a materialized world, change (or Dewey's favorite concept, growth) would always be an individual development with *potentially* social repercussions. Freedom would occur as we recognized the limit of our personal power, adjusting to the "natural process of living" and its "rules."[40] With a naturalistic metaphysic he could not account for the fact that the "individual" is *already* socialized, that the "individual" forms of consciousness have a historical specificity. The "self" of experience, this core with which Dewey seemed to be left, remained clouded (as any metaphysical posture does); more importantly, it tended as well to camouflage the ideological construction of consciousness. Subjectivity was not seen as an effect, but as a biological cause.

As we have seen, American democracy referred to a context wherein "the subjects' relation to meaning within the total available or potential universe of meanings is produced—i.e., subjectivity depends upon a social location within the ideological space of the social formation."[41] The ideological hegemony of liberal democracy and scientific rationality, with which Dewey would have us integrate, prescribed the limits of his awareness and the "necessity of pragmatism." Gonzalez maintains that Dewey in his pragmatic best was "tightrope walking his way between individualism and social cooperation; the welfare of the individual is supreme, yet it cannot be separated from the welfare of a single capitalist enterprise."[42] We may interact with an institution (the system of structures) by walking away from it (rejection), apathetically, by conforming to it or, ideologically, by glorifying it. All of which leave the institution as it is. The inefficacy of the experience concept for a *social* theory of praxis lies with Dewey's reluctance to conceptualize it in its personal *and* political forms. I have been arguing that liberalism and the taken-for-granted praxis of experience is bankrupt today, that to whatever extent it has liberated individuals in the past it has reached a moment of crisis in the nuclear era. At best, the "objective conditions" of late capitalism seem capable only of generating what Wolfe refers to as a "narcissistic democracy," where the "structure of choices . . . increasingly forces people to uphold their self-interest at the risk of undermining society, or to work to preserve society at the risk of sacrificing private need."[43]

Dewey's progressivism (along with the contemporary attempts to resuscitate its spirit, even seen as a counter to the surge of neo-conservatism) somewhat benignly appealed to a trust in the advances of scientific thinking and economic expansion, with the consequences that people tended to "voluntarily refuse to raise larger questions about the meaning of growth and security."[44] For similar reasons, his functional and pragmatic analysis seems an inadequate accompaniment to a concept of school experience. The implicit concern running through this book—should education question the everyday?—does not surface in Dewey's approach. The paradox of liberal reform, of course, is in its stated response to that question. In his regard for education as "the fundamental method of social progress and reform,"[45] Dewey has seen the implicit quality of the public sphere in the school site. However, the experimental and democratic praxis of his pedagogy evaporates when the "everyday" has been naturalized and normalized.

> In the everyday, the activity and way of life are *transformed* into an instinctive, subconscious, unconscious and unreflected *mechanism* of acting and living: things, people, movements, tasks, environment, the world... *simply are there,* and are accepted as inventory, as components of a *known* world.[46]

A critical theory of education alternatively explores the pauses, the disruptions, the gaps, and the contradictions in history. The historical inquiry, which I refer to as the conceptualization, materialization, hegemony, and decomposition of ideology, is emphatically different from a disclosure of evolutionary phases progressively revealing human be-ing. The unprecedented era of nuclearization, I believe, exposes a "disruption" that is not easily assimilated by a functional analysis, nor without serious contradictions for liberal democracy. It is not simply a matter of acquiring a rhythm, a set of habits that allow one to adapt to the disruption (Victor Frankel's experience in a Nazi concentration camp is a testimony to the habits one can acquire), but rather a matter of locating the disruption within the "routine" conditions of the everyday within "normal" consciousness. Kosik poses the paradox:

> While the everyday appears as confidence, familiarity, proximity, as "home," History appears as the derailment, the disruption of the everyday, as the exceptional and the strange. This cleavage simultaneously splits reality into the *historicity* of History and *ahistoricity* of the everyday.[47]

Another of the educational issues of this book has been with how concrete social relations, not the function or roles prescriptive for a particular ideological organization, can be examined and, if necessary, transformed. If we are to take our cues from the imperatives given by the functioning of political economy, then obviously it is within those existing structures that our functionability is conditioned. It is from there that the choices which we select as our own are produced. Yes, "cooperation" is a desirable and fundamental human quality to nurture, but when it is *not* in evidence, *why* not? What inhibits it? In Dewey's concept of experience he asked us to develop activities which nourish the bonds of unification and identify and strengthen the role which each individual will take in society. His notion of growth as the movement from instinct to habit implied an "invisible hand" of evolution which upholds and guides the harmonious production of integrated individuals into society. The goals of both self and society are socially stable individuals, the natural, instinctual homeostasis characteristic of all organisms and environments. To service in a critical educational praxis, however, seems unlikely.

Dewey suffered from what I will call "the fallacy of ascendancy," which in the context of America, accepted and posited that the white, middle-class, bourgeois, Puritan-ethic, opportunity-knocks, science-as-power, growth values were "universal" in any progressive civilization. This fallacy was further reflected in the assumption that the advance of consciousness must go through the discourses of the master, the elites, the technocrats, scientists, industrialists, and intellectuals. As such, the ongoing paradox of the Enlightenment, American-style—secure the freedom of the middle class and you have secured democracy—remained an undialectical certainty. The empirical analysis and methodology of naturalism and scientific rationality were assigned by Dewey as the fundamental means (shared by positivism) for advancing human society. A specific activity was required to expose the conflicts of thought which are the source of error. Science was that activity which removed the scales from our eyes. This was the methodological basis of experience, too, which enabled us to see the connectedness of things. But in so doing, he and science no longer could voice the protests of exclusion, the victims, those left untouched by the progress of science. Instead of revealing meanings, to paraphrase a view of Martin Jay, science had become nothing more than a tool of the dominant forces in society.[48] While Dewey considerably expanded the scope of experience for a pedagogical foundation, the boundaries of school experience could examine no more than the "prevalence of consensual as opposed to conflictual views of societal development [with] the tendency to exclude real conflicts in present-day society as well as their explicit appearance in the student's own subjective and existential life."[49]

The replacement of one god for another, however, may not be enough, and the totality gained by Dewey's evolutionary model unfortunately sacrificed the concreteness of social reality. By retaining an Aristotelian analysis where the whole predominates and is logically prior to the parts, he accepted the empirical and pragmatic efficacy of a system from which the particular elements took their cues. The priority of function in this outlook clouded the possibility of friction/conflict and the ideological ordering of societies by power configurations. His concept of experience, therefore, was severely restricted by the scope of his philosophical lens.

It is not outlandish to suggest that the situation of schooling today is (significantly) a result of a massive retreat from the schools, an acceptance of their impotence to affect change by education, the *felt-contradictoriness of experience.* The desires of the social system, being what they are today, the manufacturing of those desires by elements external to the individual (student), and the conditioning of values nearly exclusively by the system's need to consume, leave the school as a twelve-year rite of passage, a certificate of qualification for a job somewhere down the line. It is no surprise that the corporations and the interests of business typically show the greatest concern towards the schools, and it is their bauble of a vocational and financial future which continues to be the wellspring of value and the source of paradox in the schools.

Here we are at the juncture of a transformational praxis and where the separation from Dewey's concept of experience becomes most acute. The educational praxis to which I am speaking situates the everyday functions in the larger ideological contexts, where the consequences of power are felt, where the concrete conditions of daily life are politicized. Science and technology, work and family, nation and community do not exist as pre-ordained realities. To regard scientific method, for example, as the growth of human rationality at best reveals only one aspect of human be-ing; it prescribes both what it is looking for and how to find it; it does not sufficiently address who controls the products of science nor how its consequences by virtue of that control "actually enter into human life."[50] As Raymond Geuss argues, individuals

> can't be freed from their coercive social institutions as long as they retain the ideological world-picture which legitimizes them, nor can they get rid of their ideological world-picture as long as their basic coercive social institutions render it immune to free discussion and criticism.[51]

Social institutions and the structures they foster (themselves heavily ideological) are not natural phenomena, but the result of people acting within the boundaries of freedom and confinement. Scientific-experiential praxis yields power but not critical consciousness.

Dewey's social theory is interesting, perhaps even vital, yet its tendency to mystify is no less incredible. In taking into account the subjective, voluntary, willful aspects of agency and the reflective potential to disclose muddleheadedness in oneself and in others, Dewey established an educational theory that captures the positive and progressive potential available to classroom work. In a theory of praxis, it is important to avoid, as Dewey did, any account of socialization that presumes the individual is 1) a product determined by environment or culture; 2) a product of historical or material forces. But no less important, I claim, we must also avoid 3) any account "which takes subjectivity for granted, as an inherent characteristic of human beings, not in need of explication."[52] In avoiding 1) and 2) Dewey's concept of experience slipped into overly-indulging 3), thereby exposing the two serious flaws of the concept: its failure to account for the dialectical and ideological tensions of human be-ing; and, the implicit reassertion of dualistic epistemology of subject and object, which privatized the individual and depoliticized the social. Of course, I am not maintaining that it was Dewey's intention to create an epistemological notion that did address transformative rather than reform practices, but that it is the absence of that possibility that significantly invalidates further mining of Dewey's work today.

A concrete dialectic, as I have been using the term, does not grasp totality as ready made because it does not define it organically, as somehow prepossessing its own unification; rather, the genesis and development of totality are components of its very determination.[53] Praxis is engaged in the division of totalities (at first) rather than in confirming a priori unity. Unification resolves dichotomies at the ideal level, but the concrete contradictions remain. Epistemologically, praxis is inverse to Dewey's direction in experience. What experience and reform cannot do, I believe an educational praxis can. I sketch such a notion in the last section.

Praxis

The praxis notion being built conceptually borrows from a number of perspectives outside the United States; in particular, Gramsci, Kosik, the Praxis School, Freire, and Giddens provide the underpinnings.[54] I have found that part of the theoretical difficulty in outlining a theory of praxis which can service the ideologically sedimented school practices in this country can be lessened with an analysis outside the American hermeneutic. Also to be gained is a dialectic of the ideas and implications of American neo-pragmatism, neo-liberalism, and educational reform practices which have begun to emerge during the intense conservative climate of the post-Vietnam years. Eventually, of course, we need to return to native soil and see what sort of hybrid will respond here. Henry Giroux has achieved this to some extent in his collaboration with Freire, as have William Bean Kennedy and Ira Shor.[55] Several curriculum projects referred to in this book also indicate the contexts for American educational praxis focused on social justice.[56]

In general terms, much of the praxis concept has already been hinted at in the above section and in the main ideas of this book. Before we go on, it may be helpful to summarize these points:

1) the materialized quality of the social world is always politicized in which social relations, social hierarchies, issues of power, and knowledge itself are contestable;

2) material change includes theoretical reorientation, which is to say that praxis refers not only to action but to the *depth, context,* and *purpose* of action;

3) consequently, praxis is fundamentally ideological insofar as it includes consciousness and our own intervention in and/or reproduction of structure, institutions, etc.;

4) a critical-dialectical (rather than scientific) method/ inquiry into the historically sedimented and politicized world;

5) emancipation (rather than competency);

6) transformative practices (rather than reformative), i.e., engagement towards more equitable relations (rather than maintaining existing relations);

7) some notion of agency which bridges subject-object duality (e.g. Giddens' theory of structuration) without necessarily requiring a unification;

8) the explication of moral values or emancipatory premises (rather than pragmatic socialized functions) for decision making.

This last section will elaborate on these points, briefly synthesizing the praxis notion.

In his *Prison Notebooks* Gramsci develops the view that "everyone is a philosopher," i.e., each of us has "a specific conception of the world."[57] As Gramsci says:

> The starting-point of critical elaboration is the consciousness of what one really is, and is "knowing thyself" as a product of the historical process to date which has deposited in you an infinity of traces, without leaving an inventory.[58]

In other words, Gramsci is proposing in a "revolutionary" (pedagogical) way that in starting from personal-individual conceptualizations and experiences, one can be drawn to the sedimented concepts that have been preserved, to the ideas, doctrines, values, and morals that have been maintained, full circle to what has often come to be regarded as commonsense, second nature, or practical consciousness (the philosophical). These ideas, for example, the organization and hierarchy of the family, of authority, of the democratic, of schooling, which have been materialized in structures and institutions fortified by custom and tradition, ritual and practice, force and repression, become the ground and context of all inquiry (the political). I believe that our "spontaneous philosophies," as he calls these beginnings, initiates an educational agenda with decidedly more transformational potential than the behavioristic source of Dewey's experience. The relationship of the personal to the philosophical and political—the dialectics of be-ing—can (and should) become the fundamental concern for pedagogical theory.[59] Our experience is intimately conditioned by the philosophical and political materializations of the everyday. Rather than exploring "self" in its relation to a "given" (experiencing-the-natural), Gramsci begins with the more critical insight that the given—in its social manifestations of philosophy and politics—is always a fabrication. However, such a premise does not mean that we are "introducing from scratch" an ad hoc method of inquiry,

> but of renovating and making "critical" an already existing activity. It must then be a criticism of the philosophy of the intellectuals out of which the history of philosophy developed and which. . . can be considered as marking the "high points" of progress made by common sense.[60]

Hence, praxis begins in a criticism of commonsense, what Dewey seems to have largely taken for granted in his concept of experience. This is not to say that our experience and commonsense are completely determined by historical and ideological categories, nor that Dewey's experiential method cannot illuminate important dimensions of human be-ing. As Rachel Sharp notes, we may also see that

> elements spontaneously generated, residual elements handed down intergenerationally (even though the conditions which produced them by now may have disappeared) and borrowings from inter-class contact, [are] intersected and moulded by the operation of hegemony into some kind of contradictory unit.[61]

Therein, (simply) we can see the empirical basis for the variety of populist movements, activism, strikes, demonstrations, and other forms of popular resistance to hegemonic constructs. But when the relation between commonsense and power/knowledge is seen as a political arrangement, then another fundamental factor of praxis—the intervention into social (material) reality is illuminated. Gramsci writes:

> Critical understanding of self takes place therefore through a struggle of political "hegemonies" and of opposing directions, first in the ethical field and then in

that of politics proper, in order to arrive at the working out at a higher level of one's own conception of reality.[62]

In addition to Gramsci, Kosik has prompted much of my thinking on this point. He, along with the Praxis School thinkers have considerably expanded the praxis concept. If I may collectively group this Eastern European perspective for a moment, I take their fundamental agenda to 1) distinguish the context of praxis from its orthodox interpretations in socialism; and 2) to infuse the praxis concept with recognizable values and characteristics while distinguishing it from its equally slanted "scientific" moorings. In this respect, David Crocker explains, "its members [Praxis School] have sought to develop a critical social theory by which they can understand contemporary societies and confront social dilemmas."[63]

Kosik, for example, characterizes the critical and dialectical features of "praxis" in its attention to the distinction between the "concrete" and the "pseudoconcrete." In our everyday encounters with our surroundings (experience), we often accept the phenomenal as the real. Dewey's habit-based psychology maintained that human beings revealed themselves in their behavior, in the ways they habitually respond to their environment. Behavior is phenomenal; nothing is (or need be) mysterious about it (thanks to science) because it is always external, always exposed. The "immediate utilitarian praxis" which allows us to get on in the world, to retain familiarity with our environment, and to more easily manipulate the circumstances in our lives, while in no way unimportant or unnecessary, "does not provide [us] with a *comprehension* of things and of reality."[64] What is formed in this praxis, Kosik continues,

> is both a particular material environment of the historical individual, and the spiritual atmosphere in which the superficial shape of realty comes to be fixed as the world of fictitious intimacy, familiarity and confidence within which man moves about "naturally" and with which he has his daily dealings.[65]

Hence, certain structural configurations of domination, hierarchy, and stratification, such as those which may order teacher-student, administrator-teacher, or school-society relations, appear as the behavior of good or bad, rational or irrational individuals. A "scientific praxis" leaves structures *pedagogically* uncontested, i.e., how power has hidden itself in social reality. Structures which infiltrate, for example, as the "second sex," or the "student as nigger," or "might as right" exist irrespective of the individual's ignorance, acceptance, rejection and/or transcendence of them. Dialectically, the focus of praxis towards such structures more recoverable in a social justice inquiry clearly engages the concrete while better able to expose the pseudo-concrete. Kosik states that "to capture the phenomenon of a certain thing is to investigate and describe how the thing manifests itself in that phenomenon but also how it hides in it."[66]

These structures and those I have alluded to as the context for a social justice pedagogy are maintained and upheld through our institutions and their systemization throughout our everyday lives. They profoundly condition how we experience "objective conditions." Praxis commences neither in the abstract object, in some historicist idea of a finished world, or an evolutionary progressing world in which our present status is a phase of development, nor with an abstract subject, in the existentialist-phenomenologist tendency which grants sole legitimacy to an autonomous subject. Rather, praxis is here presented as the social and practical activity emergent from confrontations with the concrete, the order of power, and those objective conditions.

What Dewey advocated was indeed a transactional epistemology which could counter a positivist-empiricist-materialist position and a "banking knowledge" pedagogy. In a progressive age, imbued with the progressive spirit of a middle-class man, Dewey put forth an educational point of view vastly superior to the "tradition." He also admirably described the "consciousness" side in its relationship with the social/environmental pole without overly indulging the self. This tactical positioning established the humanistic agenda of progressive reform. Presumably, the game of life had been organically and naturally set up; science had revealed it; psychology had shown us how best to play; education would give us the practice to play better. Dewey would not acknowledge that much about the game is not natural at all, that the game and the construction of the natural is the ideological terrain established in the progressive discourse of scientific enlightenment, and constituted by its relation to class, culture, custom, power. Ideas and beliefs are always a social product. The value of science for liberal reform is its assumption that a value-free, ideologically pure foundation to understand human be-ing is possible. In Kosik's analysis, the naturalist conception created a distorted idea of social reality, of human consciousness and of nature. It understood human consciousness exclusively as the biological function of the organism's adaption and of its orientation in an environment, characterized by two basic elements: impulse and reaction.[67]

But it is impossible to educate for empowerment towards social change with a pedagogy originating in a psychology of experience. What can be achieved is a well-adjusted, harmonious, accommodating individual who sees a role in society, an "organic union of individuals,"[68] and an agreement that everyone can have a role. This liberal dream has always accepted a hierarchical society where definite class divisions, "roles" in Dewey's functionalist lexicon—philosophers, guardians, workers, outcasts—prevail, each of whom constitutes an organic function. Dewey's intent, of course, was not to foster rigidity and elitist preservationism, but in grounding his theories and methods of investigation in the pseudoconcrete, he never challenged the claim of the few to control the many, nor the structural dictates of power.[69]

Schools receive their raison d'etre from the needs required of social functioning; it is not the schools which provide the impetus nor the source of these needs. The implicit elitism of the scientist, the industrialist, the technocrat, managerial and intellectual classes, and their consolidation of power while maintaining that their methods are accessible to all, cannot be a source of empowerment, of emancipatory practices, nor as sites where praxis is generated. Recall an analogous paradox in the shift of thinking from the remarks of Socrates and the accessibility of the philosophical path in the *Apology*, and Plato's pessimism in the *Statesman* and *Republic* about philosophy for the man in the agora.) Because Dewey regarded "improvement of the system" and the social spheres it serviced as the schools' central role, the corollary implication is that reform would similarly lie with the enlightened few to pull the reins and the "new individuals" to find their respective places.

Dewey's limited concept of the politicized nature of social reality unfortunately did not permit (in a pedagogical sense) student experience to confront the ideological parameters of personal experiences, neither how nor why dominant discourses socialized human be-ing. Consequently, his "new individuals" remained "disempowered" in the sense that they were unexposed and unaware of the contradictory strains within social relations. Experience, as we saw, does not address structural change; it cannot include the excluded; i.e., experience takes as its context the functional, along with the slow agenda inherent to the discourse of individual opportunity.

In Dewey's time perhaps the pretense existed that schools provided such outlets, escapes from second-class status (and there is no denying that they have positively affected many), but their function today as credentializing institutions where one's badge of completion is the ticket into the system of consumption, allows little inquiry into democracy, little development of intelligence, let alone critical thought, and ironically, less real choice.

The problem is complex and to a large extent nearly out of the hands of the schools. Even with a "radicalizing" of the curriculum (potentially about all a "social justice" focus can hope to implement in the short run), and a refocusing upon the lived culture, the contents and impact of a media-structured consciousness (by the age of eighteen, children will have spent more time watching television than in the classroom) and the now-overt individualism it seeks to reproduce, would still confuse and bewilder students. Whether schools and educational praxis can initiate a transformational agenda which takes these paradoxes as central is hardly a certainty. Indeed, as Herbert Kohl claims, the schooling situation at this time may only tolerate "expos[ing] our students to the biases of texts in all subjects, as well as in the structure, management, and financing of schools."[70]

I suppose that the paradox that confronted Dewey and liberalism may have been in the *logistics of transformation*. While the bulk of my arguments have contended that the educational reform is out of touch in a nuclearized world, I am not sure that Dewey did not purposely channel his progressivism in ways that would minimize radical transformation, an orientation C. Wright Mills found reproduces "a kind of perennial mugwump."[71] Real institutional transformation for Dewey could only be envisioned as cataclysmic, singular, disruptive, unnecessary, political, risky, dangerous, or violent. Dewey's concept of experience sought to maintain a lengthy, piecemeal, preservationist method of inquiry which took its cue from what was given to it from existing patterns. Insofar as it permitted individuals to reassess their relationship to their "environment," Dewey's experience was a social theory of gradual individual change favoring the already-advantaged.

Nonetheless, what I am trying to conceive with the praxis notion is a dialectically posed mode of learning that better situates learning possibilities in an agency of social responsibility. The idealistic implications of a nonmaterialized notion of praxis (such as Dewey's "experience") generally focuses upon the acting subject within a public sphere. While we find (in varying degrees) a humanist position, which in the relative absence of such acting today is not unwelcome, experience was not conceived transformationally but "representationally"; i.e., it left to the actor the choice of participation, while the complexes of power were left largely untouched.[72]

Praxis offers in its theoretical construction to extend Dewey's interactionalism by abandoning the naturalism that grounds experience. An alternative social theory to the functional ideas of nature and naturalist epistemology, as set forth by Giddens, for example, attends to relations of power, of conflict in society, institutional analysis, differentiated and stratified aspects of society. Here the attention fixes on the more objectified characteristics of society, while not succumbing to determinism. Instead of assuming the organic naturalness of the relation between individual and society, as a basis for praxis, Giddens describes a more illuminating approach which implies a praxis that supercedes Dewey's "experience," and forms the basis for a critical pedagogy. Human beings are neither to be understood nor treated as passive objects, nor as wholly free subjects.[73] The interaction of subject and object, each side impacting and being impacted by the other, as we have seen, was central to the Deweyan notion of experience. What Giddens' work approaches which Dewey's did not, however, is this analysis of structure and the politicized nature of action.

Examining structures involves a recognition of knowledges about how things are done, said, and written; the social practices organized through those knowledges; and the capabilities that the production of those practices presupposes. Structures penetrate below the surface of appearances[74] and constitute the level at which an analysis may more completely investigate. This is not to assign an ontological status to structure. Structures are not things; they do not exist in space-time except in the moments of their constitution in social systems (institutions). Structure has a "virtual existence";[75] it is both static and dynamic; both enabling and constraining. As Giddens states:

the same structural characteristics participate in the subject (agent) as in the object (social sphere) [and] form personality and society simultaneously but in neither case exhaustively.... Structure is not a barrier to action but essentially involved in its production.[76]

In my understanding of "structure," as a category of social analysis, its value becomes apparent when it acquires specificity. I have alluded to the structures of race, gender, class, our relation with the ecosphere, and the modes in which we resolve our interpersonal conflicts as a working context not only for understanding self and society, but for establishing radical democratic spheres. As educators we draw upon the rules, generalizations, and commonsense interpretations of race, gender, personhood, success, etc., in the production of our work, our speech, and our culture, but not mechanistically, robotically. In following the "rules" or even in rejecting them, we reconstitute those structures of our everyday lives through our acceptance of the unintended consequences of our acts. So, for example, when the liberal decries racists, we are pleased with the humanism of the view; nevertheless, by accepting the functional necessity of an underclass in capitalism (domestic or foreign), an unintended corroboration in the reproduction of the condition the liberal finds appalling is secured. The slowness of social change, I think, can be attributed to a theory of action (Dewey's experience) in which the focus is not upon structure but agency, i.e., upon the subject's intentionality and not upon the structures which condition and determine choice. Institutions or collectives do indeed result from human agency; they are constituted by and transformed by activity; but "they are the outcome of action only in so far as they are also involved recursively as the medium of its production."[77] By locating intentionality ultimately in the subject, whose motives, attitudes, and interests emerge biologically, Dewey underestimated the significance of structures in shaping human consciousness.

Praxis poses, as a *method* of inquiry, a context for learning, a challenge to the status of existing roles, the organization of schools, and the normative legitimacy of their prescription. By reversing the focus of inquiry from a psychology of experience to a dialectic of the concrete, educators begin a learning process that not only emerges from the personal and the experiential and infuses real empowerment in individuals, but also takes the

further step to examine the structural, institutional, conse-
quential, and ideological terrain of their lived culture. This is
praxis. Role prescriptions, even while buttressed by their
normative content as stabilized and habituated social forms, are
probed, investigated, and studied as interpretations. All social
positions and social conditions—homelessness, ghettoization,
blight, poverty, teenage pregnancy, the arms race, pollution,
chauvinism, and their antitheses—within social systems "are
'power positions' in the sense that they are integrated within
reproduced relations of autonomy and dependence; *contestation*
of role prescriptions is a characteristic feature of power struggles
in society."[78] Praxis, insofar as ideology is the terrain of the
everyday, inquires into the very assumptions that the world has
been organized justly and declared natural by the prescribers,
the "identity" of the prescribers themselves, and the sites from
which social change can be made effective. Dewey regarded
socialization as the adaptation by and adoption of the child to
the roles required in a modern society. The emotional prepar-
ation/development of the child as a learning objective was stated
as a natural process of integration into society. One is
assimilated into the society at the levels that each personal
endowment will tolerate. As we probe not the functions that
facilitate the "forward movement" of society, but the increasing
illiteracy in America, the mortality rate, the suicides of American
youth, the general lack of attention to school facilities, the
depressed wages of teachers, the bureaucratization of schools
and the disempowerment of educators, along with the social
phenomena of daily violence in the streets, a pervasive
psychopathology roaming everyday life, and the increasing
impoverishment of people to derive some sort of meaning from
their situations, the question arises: why are we educating to
conform to existing society?

The pedagogical issues, thus, become: how does the
development process into the everyday become integrated with
the historical, i.e., where are the entries from the personal to the
political? What criteria do educators consider in the
organization of a historical/personal agenda? Can educational
practice in American schools even begin a praxis in this sense?

While in no way offering a "syllabus" for educational praxis,
I have instead contrasted the premises of liberal reform which
only asks, "how can my experience allow me to adapt?" with a
praxis which attends to the materialized world. The difference

between "experience" and "praxis" is the difference between interaction and transformation, between pragmatic and radical. By extracting the ideal and the functional from the concrete and the personal, Dewey could not dislodge the alienating components operative in schooling and learning. The child ultimately remains inattentive to the abstracted values of American society because they are not grasped in their immediacy, nor examined in their contradictoriness. How, for example, is American intervention in Latin America and our support of authoritarian regimes so that corporate interests and American economic well-being may be secured reconciled with "democracy"?[79] How is the existence of black ghettoization justified with the slogans of "equal opportunity" and the "land of the free"?[80] How is the nuclear arsenal we maintain commensurate with the fact of some 125 wars since the end of World War Two?[81] Why is it that simultaneously we hear of economic growth, more millionaires, new products, advances in technology *and* the dramatic increases in homelessness, in poverty, in violent and senseless acts? With universal public education why is there an increase in unwed mothers and teenage pregnancies? Why do educators unquestioningly think that their efforts to prepare students to take their places in society by refraining from history's contradictions is but a hit-or-miss enterprise? How many times have you said or heard "if I only reach one or two kids every term I will feel satisfied"?

Praxis is a dialectical activity of objectifying the materialized world in order to become a subject in it. In disclosing and uncovering the independent structure of the world, one's experience in the world also acquires definition. "It involves not practical activity as opposed to theorizing; it is the determination of human being as the process of forming reality."[82] As such, an explicit moral quality—what I have identified as social justice— significantly defines school activity. As Dewey realized, schoolwork must take on immediate relevancy in young persons' lives for school to be effective, education to occur. An educational praxis requires this quality both as a means and an end by which other forms of activity can be critiqued/evaluated. Thus it illuminates and accentuates some forms of activity rather than others. This point is very much in keeping with Dewey's experiential continuum and his pedagogic intervention against mis-educative experience.[83] When experience is clearly involved along issues of social justice, educational priorities forcefully capture the personal/political connection. Self-reflection is part of praxis. Praxis is the intercession of agency into structure. Kosik isolates the distinction precisely: "Man transcends conditions not *primarily* in his consciousness and intentions, in his ideal project, but in his praxis."[84]

Praxis, as a more critically focused activity, does not regard "experience" as natural, or at least not as an all-inclusive interpretation of human be-ing, but rather, as Marcuse has stated, from the perception that "the world is unfree; that is to say man and nature exist in conditions of alienation, exist as 'other than they are'."[85] Praxis, then, is fundamentally concerned with emancipatory action, a notion, as Giroux explains, that

> penetrates the world of everyday life with critical concepts that link the pre-conceptual, the ritualized experiences and the routine practices of daily existence with forms of reflection that reveal their objective and social roots.[86]

This can no more be denied to young people—at that time when questions and doubt appear—than it can be to adults. An educational praxis requires an explicit politicalization of the classroom and school in order to empower, not simply expand, experience. Part of its emphasis, consequently, lies with overcoming "idealist illusions and pipe dreams of an eventual humanistic education for mankind without the necessary transformation of an oppressed and unjust world."[87] Unfortunately, as H. Svi Shapiro notes, educational praxis in contemporary schooling is hardly common.

> There is no discussion of the existential nature of teaching and learning in the present culture—the meaningfulness and purpose of what it is that is learned or intended to be learned; there is not concern with the "hidden curriculum" which is now clearly established as a profoundly influential dimension of schooling; there is no attempt to engage the issue of education for citizenship. . . . Nor is there any discussion of the perversions of education that are induced by the bureaucratic, credentializing functions of schooling or the hierarchical, frequently despotic manner by which schools are typically governed.[88]

Praxis is the activity of transforming the structures of consciousness; hence, it is concerned with identifying the history and materialization of structures which condition human be-ing. An educational praxis must supercede an instrumentalism, even at the risk of becoming alternative and directed. As I have been developing the term, *social justice* focuses upon and designates certain structures which condition any understanding of social reality. A praxis of social justice, then, is the activity that seeks to transform the structures of racism, sexism, violence, and class division. Social justice maintains that the abolition of such structures, or at least the reduction of their efficacy as determinants of human be-ing, will dialectically also address and pose counter-structures which can foster autonomy, empowerment, and social responsibility.

It is not my intention to blame the condition of American schooling/culture on the pedagogical efforts of Dewey and liberal reform, for they have advanced an agenda which *in its classroom procedures* has much to emulate. Yet, it has been my strong contention that the educational praxis I have been sketching vastly reorients perspectives to the concrete conditions of their lives and begins a process wherein students/learners become socially empowered.

Epilogue

It is impossible to think of transformation, of education for
transformation, without thinking how to mobilize and how to
organize power—political power. If you want to transform the
world, you have to fight power in order to get it. But for me, the
question today in the end of this century is not just to get power,
but to reinvent power.

—Paulo Freire, *Pedagogies for the Non-Poor*

This book has been concerned entirely with ideology. In one
respect this concern is positioned within the huge discourse of
school reform; how learning may be enhanced, how teaching can
improve, what values guide us. I have argued that we discover
the world ideologically; i.e., we always find ourselves in a world
not of our making, and often not of our liking. We are always
positioned by existing discourses of the good, the bad, and the
ugly. Our relation to the world, then, is always both a personal
and political identification. The project of education and school
practice historically has interceded in this process by pointing
out pitfalls and wrong turns and by offering advice. When we
locate these projects in the context of socialization—how we
define ourselves and our social reality—their relationship to the
larger, more overtly ideological spheres conditioning us can also
be revealed.

The constructed-ness of social reality appeals and dispels;
we are drawn to its "naturalness" and repelled by its cruelty.
As educators we take a stance towards it and try to disclose the
multiplicity of attachments which are constantly claiming our
allegiance. I have tried to show that social reality is dialectical;
it is the tension that frames the world in contradictory terms,
the shadows that conceal but also keep us in the dark. A
dialectical analysis as well as a dialectical epistemology are
central.

Our appropriation of the terms for defining the world, of
course, is ideological as well. The respective positions of the
reform and radical camps, which I have been discussing in this
book, offer to engage students, to accommodate them, to motivate
them as well as to situate them in the larger world. Each holds
out to young people a vision and the provisions one needs to
carry in searching for it. My argument has claimed (in short) that

the liberal and progressive praxis of John Dewey and the model
of reform—existentially and philosophically—today no longer
possess a vision, nor the means to realize an appointed agenda.
Ultimately, the methods and analysis, for all reform's rhetorical
posturing, leave us no exit from the "circle of certainty" inherited
from the Enlightenment.

In another important respect this book is a prolegomenon
to a genealogy of social justice. I have tried to clear the terrain
for "a new philosophy"[1] generating from concerns which
historically have been excluded and marginalized by the
structures of power and the power of structures. Social justice,
insofar as it is grounded in the concrete realities which position
each of us as subject and object, affords us a perspective from
which the paradoxes of our lived world are more sharply
disclosed. An analysis of social justice allows us to "demyth-
ologize" the ideological construction of human be-ing. By
stripping away the blocks of power, which I have argued reside
in Dewey's pillars of science, democracy, experience, and the
natural, and which camouflage the conditions of racism, sexism,
classism, and violence, we confront more explicitly (and with
greater trepidation) what Milan Kundera refers to as "the planet
of inexperience."[2] I do not think that Dewey faced this terrain;
hence, he is caught in a web of paradox which forces him to
backpedal in the past and leapfrog into the future while leaving
the present in perpetual *potentia*.

I have tried to show that Dewey's pedagogical agenda,
resting in the absence of a dialectical grasp of the concrete,
fosters neither a full democratic society nor a critical consciousness. The relations of power which have produced, sustained,
and legitimated the organization of social reality in the discourse
of liberal democracy have been presented as "how things have
always been and ought to be [and] acquire a timelessness...
[whereby] the social order is seen as a natural one."[3] More than
simply a difference in perspective, a radical pedagogy, one which
draws from and is nurtured by emancipatory (rather than
competency) concerns, addresses the structural conditions which
persistently have accompanied the "evolutionary" advances of
science and democracy. While these have created change—
progress, if you must—they have also limited it, defined how far
and to what extent freedom would be practiced. By claiming that
scientific method—experience—reveals human be-ing as
"natural," as a history of evolving relations with the environ-

ment, we are offered a world which, indeed, appears on the surface where we all have equal opportunity to view it, but which shows us no depth. Such a praxis makes several assumptions which, I have tried to show, no longer investigate the "situation of humanity." Do "surfaces" reveal be-ing? Does "method" alone ameliorate social reality? Does each of us have access to the dominant discourses of knowledge and power? Even to the degree that many people (at least in the liberal democracies of the world) have tapped into them, what is the nature of the mastery gained, the control exercised? The great insight of Foucault is his contention that power, "this enigmatic thing . . . which is at once visible and invisible, present and hidden"[4] should engage us in pedagogical archaeology: "to force the institutionalized networks of information to listen, to produce names, to point the finger of accusation, to find targets."[5] We are learning when we get our hands dirty.

Dewey clearly saw a relation of democracy and education and the ground which the school, as an institution in a democracy, could till. However, as my remarks suggest, unless an educational praxis "reinvents power"—which his pragmatism ultimately would not allow—learning and its contexts remain a hit-or-miss venture. Heller addresses this theme of power from her understanding of radical democracy:

> The total realisation of democracy is identical with the abolition of all domination. It therefore involves an equal distribution of power, for that presupposes that *every person* disposes over the material goods and people of the society; it presupposes that there is no sphere over which or in which people cannot control. In a society free of domination *all people* decide.[6]

Unfortunately, the structure of power, universalized in the conditions of nuclearization, is well-entrenched pedagogically in the organization of school practices as well. Those who currently control the production of power/knowledge are, of course, the least likely to see the need for, let alone initiate, structural change. I cannot fault Dewey for his "progressivism" in promoting "a new order of conceptions leading to new modes of practice."[7] He clearly sought to deconstruct the dichotomy of power exercised in the typical classroom. He explored a vital educational ground between Plato and Rousseau and in this mediation was actually ahead of his time. However, he remains to be recovered. The time is not now. A generation of American rebels have only begun to plumb the depths to which the nuclearization of humanity extends. We need to see that in Dewey's (and reform's) experimental attitude where "anticipation is . . . more primary than recollection, projection than summoning of the past, the projective than the retrospective"[8] we have come to be increasingly mesmerized by the superficial, the fleeting, the impersonal, and the ephemeral. Materially speaking, we are following the modus operandi of planned obsolescence.

While not blind to Dewey's "failure to be radical,"[9] Richard Bernstein seems typical of those who find in Dewey a voice for present time. Bernstein believes that all the reasons I have argued in this book for *not* resurrecting Dewey, are outweighed by the perspicacious and forceful quality of his pragmatic praxis.[10] Undeniably as important as the checks-and-balances activity is, it does not sufficiently empower us to deal with the huge paradoxes of the post-nuclear world. If we are to reinvent power we require a transformational praxis which encourages us to look through the nuclear terror.

Notes

Preface

1. Henry A. Giroux, "Beyond the Limits of Radical Education Reform: Toward a Critical Theory of Education," *The Journal of Curriculum Theorizing* 2:1 (1980): 22.

2. Raymond Williams, "Base and Superstructure in Marxist Cultural Theory," in *Problems in Materialism and Culture* (London: Verso, 1980), 38.

3. Karel Kosik, *Dialectics of the Concrete: A Study on Problems of Man and World,* Boston Studies in the Philosophy of Science, vol. LII (Dordrecht, Holland: D. Reidel Publishing Company, 1976), 4.

4. Herbert Marcuse, *Reason and Revolution: Hegel and the Rise of Social Theory* (New York: Oxford University Press, 1941; repr., Boston: Beacon Press, 1960), ix.

5. I use the term *human be-ing* throughout the book to refer to both consciousness and the materially constructed dimensions of human beings.

6. John Dewey, "Introduction: The Problems of Men and the Present State of Philosophy," in *Problems of Men* (New York: Philosophical Library, 1946), 16.

7. Dewey, *Liberalism and Social Action* (New York: G.P. Putnam's Sons, 1935), 65. I find ironic the most recent usurpation of "critical" language in a statement of Procter and Gamble President John Pepper and presented by the National Alliance of Business. I am struck by a similar connotation which I find motivated Dewey's pedagogical insights: "We need *systemic* change. We have a school system that in many ways was designed for a totally different work place and set of social conditions-30 and 40 years ago. Today the world has changed dramatically, but we haven't restructured our education and youth support system." In An Advertising Supplement to *The New York Times Magazine,* September 20, 1987.

8. A representative statement, expressed in numerous ways, may help to keep us on track: "The crisis in contemporary culture, the confusions and conflicts in it, arise from a division

of authority. Scientific inquiry seems to tell one thing, and traditional beliefs about end and ideals that have authority over conduct tell us something quite different." John Dewey, *The Quest for Certainty: A Study of the Relation of Knowledge and Action* (New York: Minton, Balch and Company, 1929), 43-4.

9. Russell Jacoby, *Social Amnesia: A Critique of Conformist Psychology from Adler to Laing* (Boston: Beacon Press, 1975), 68.

10. Stanley Aronowitz, *Science as Power: Discourse and Ideology in Modern Society* (Minneapolis: University of Minnesota Press, 1988), 12.

11. An interesting book, recently published, which also posits that a reclamation project of Dewey has been underway since the publication of Richard Rorty's *Philosophy and the Mirror of Nature* (1979), poses as its theme the primacy of "aesthetic experience" at the nucleus of Dewey's philosophy. Unfortunately, this argument avoids the politicized and ideological positioning of Dewey's work. See Thomas M. Alexander, *John Dewey's Theory of Art, Experience and Nature: The Horizons of Feeling* (Albany: SUNY Press, 1987).

12. George Novack, *Pragmatism versus Marxism: An Appraisal of John Dewey's Philosophy* (New York: Pathfinder Press, 1975), 230.

13. C. Wright Mills, *Sociology and Pragmatism: The Higher Learning in America,* ed. with an introduction by Irving Louis Horowitz (New York: Oxford University Press, 1964), 417.

Introduction

1. See David Purpel, *The Moral and Spiritual Crisis in Education: A Curriculum for Justice and Compassion in Education* (Granby, MA: Bergin and Garvey, 1989) on this last point.

2. Ralph Waldo Emerson, in "The Fortune of the Republic," went on to say: "Let us realize that this country, the last found, is the great charity of God to the human race." In *Works* vol. XI (Boston: Houghton, Mifflin and Co., 1883), 421. Historian Sacvan Bercovitch refers to the particular form of vision in this country as the "American Jeremiad." Bercovitch states, "To be American for our classical writers was by definition to be radical—to turn against the past, to defy the status quo and

become an agent of change. And at the same time to be radical as an American was to transmute the revolutionary impulse in some basic sense by spiritualizing it (as in *Walden*), by diffusing or deflecting it (as in *Leaves of Grass*), by translating it into a choice between blasphemy and regeneration (as in *Moby-Dick*), or most generally by accommodating it to society (as in "The Fortune of the Republic")." In *The American Jeremiad* (Madison: The University of Wisconsin Press, 1978), 203. Dewey's vision, I would argue, was similarly conditioned.

3. John Dewey, "Science and Society," in *Philosophy and Civilization* (Gloucester, MA: Peter Smith, 1968), 330.

4. Ibid.

5. I preserve the Marxian connotation of "radical" which has come to characterize social, political, and philosophical critiques of modernity, liberal democracy, and latent idealism. While I am quite sympathetic with the recent nuances which some "post-liberal" thinkers have assigned to the concept of radical, abandoning the concept does not seem necessary. See C.A. Bowers, *Elements of a Post-Liberal Theory of Education* (New York: Teachers College Press, 1987) and Neil Postman, *Teaching as a Conserving Activity* (New York: Delacorte Press, 1979) and *Conscientious Objections* (New York: Alfred A. Knopf and Co., 1988).

6. Walter Feinberg, *Reason and Rhetoric: The Intellectual Foundations of 20th Century Liberal Educational Policy* (New York: John Wiley and Sons, 1975), 14.

7. Samuel Bowles and Herbert Gintis, *Schooling in Capitalist America: Educational Reform and the Contradictions of Economic Life* (New York: Basic Books, 1976, 1977), 49. This text remains the classic pronouncement of the role of schooling in the processes and relations of production and power. While a critique of their "radical functionalism" is appropriate (see Sherry Gorelick, "Undermining Hierarchy: Problems of Schooling in Capitalist America," *Monthly Review* 29:5 (1977): 20–36, the fundamental contention of the book is that the "roots of inequality in the United States are to be found in the class structure and the system of sexual and racial power relationships" (85). In important respects, however, *Schooling in Capitalist America* provides an "orientation" for educational praxis.

8. See Bowles and Gintis, *Schooling in Capitalist America*, 164–179.

9. See National Alliance of Business, "Our Youth: Our Future," in an Advertising Supplement to the *New York Times Magazine* September 20, 1987. For a fuller development of the intervention of business into schools, see the work of Joel Spring, *Education and the Rise of the Corporate State* (Boston: Beacon Press, 1972), *The Sorting Machine Revisited: National Educational Policy Since 1945*, updated ed. (White Plains, NY: Longman, 1989), *Conflict of Interests: The Politics of American Education* (White Plains, NY: Longman, 1988).

10. Horace Mann, "Fifth Annual Report of the Secretary of State Board of Education, 1842"; quoted in Bowles and Gintis, *Schooling in Capitalist America*, 164.

11. Bowles and Gintis, *Schooling in Capitalist America*, 23.

12. John Dewey, *Democracy and Education: An Introduction to the Philosophy of Education* (New York: Macmillan Co., 1916; repr., The Free Press, 1944), 326.

13. Horace Mann, *Republic and the School: Horace Mann on the Education of Free Men*, Classics in Education, No. 1, ed. Lawrence A. Cremin (New York: Bureau of Publications, Teachers College, Columbia University, 1957), 84; quoted in Clarence J. Karier, *Man, Society, and Education* (Glenview, IL: Scott, Foresman and Co., 1967), 61; see Bowles and Gintis, *Schooling in Capitalist America*, ch. 2.

14. Attempts to explain Dewey within narrow categories, while illuminating aspects of his thought (often buried in congratulatory praise), are indecisive. For example, a text which I have found helpful is reductionistic, nonetheless, in its condemnation of Dewey; see Gilbert G. Gonzalez, *Progressive Education: A Marxist Interpretation* (Minneapolis: Marxist Educational Press, 1982) for the view of Dewey as a lackey of capitalism. On the other hand, it is simplistic to assimilate Dewey with Marx; see Salvatore D'urso, "Can Dewey Be Marx's Educational-Philosophical Representative?," *Educational Philosophy and Theory* 12:2 (1980): 21–35 for the view that Dewey is "compatible" with Marx. In the latter vein see the early work of American philosopher Sidney Hook.

15. Dewey, *Liberalism and Social Action*, 30–1.

16. Dewey, *Individualism Old and New* (New York: Capricorn Books, 1929, 1930, 1962), 171.

17. Michel Foucault, "The Eye of Power," in *Power/Knowledge: Selected Interviews and Other Writings 1972–1977,* ed. Colin Gordon, trans. Colin Gordon et al. (New York: Pantheon Books, 1980), 155.

18. See Michel Foucault, *Discipline and Punish: The Birth of the Prison,* trans. Alan Sheridan (New York: Vintage Books, 1979), especially Part Three.

19. Dewey, "Class Struggle and the Democratic Way," *The Social Frontier* 2:8 (1936): 241.

20. Dewey, "Reconstruction as Seen Twenty-five Years Later," in *Reconstruction in Philosophy,* (New York: Henry Holt and Co., 1920; repr., Boston: Beacon Press, 1948), xxi; xxxvi; xxxv.

21. Dewey, *Liberalism and Social Action,* 50.

22. John Dewey and Evelyn Dewey, *Schools of Tomorrow* (New York: E.P. Dutton and Co., 1915, 1943, 1962), 58. For a different perspective, see the brief remarks in William Appleman Williams, *America in a Changing World: A History of the United States in the Twentieth Century* (New York: Harper and Row, 1978), 120–1; Lloyd C. Gardner, *Imperial America: American Foreign Policy Since 1898* (New York: Harcourt Brace Jovanovich, 1976), 47–53; Howard K. Beale, *Theodore Roosevelt and the Rise of America to World Power* (New York: Collier Books, 1956), 101–8; Albert K. Weinberg, *Manifest Destiny: A Study of Nationalist Expansionism in American History* (Chicago: Quadrangle Books, 1935, 1963), chapter eleven; Howard C. Hill, "The Taking of Panama," in Williams, ed. *The Shaping of American Diplomacy: Readings and Documents in American Foreign Relations,* vol. 1, 2nd ed. (Chicago: Rand McNally, 1970), 441–6. Williams lists 111 incidences of American intervention (excluding declared wars) from 1829 to 1919. See *Empire as a Way of Life* (New York: Oxford University Press, 1980).

23. See Stanley Aronowitz and Henry A. Giroux, *Education Under Siege: The Conservative, Liberal and Radical Debate Over Schooling* (South Hadley, MA: Bergin and Garvey, 1985), 186; chs. 8 and 9.

24. *Education for Democracy: A Statement of Principles* (Washington, DC: Education for Democracy Project, 1987), 14, sponsored in part by the AFT and endorsed by Albert Shanker, William Bennett, Chester E. Finn, and Diane Ravitch among others.

25. Barbara Finkelstein refers to the slew of publications which followed *A Nation at Risk: The Imperative for Educational Reform* by the National Commission on Excellence in Education (Washington, DC: Government Printing Office, 1983) in "Education and the Retreat from Democracy in the United States, 1979–198?," *Teachers College Record* 86:2 (1984): 275–282. She finds that the "education reform movement sweeping across the United States . . . merits close attention because it reveals a retreat from democracy" (275). Also mentioned: *A Threat to Excellence: The Preliminary Report of the Commission on Higher Education and the Economy of New England* (New England Board of Higher Education, 1982); *Action for Excellence: A Comprehensive Plan to Improve Our Nation's Schools* (Task Force on Education for Economic Growth, Education Commission of the States, 1983); *Making the Grade: Report of the Twentieth Century Fund Task Force on Federal Elementary and Secondary Education Policy* (New York: The Twentieth Century Fund, 1983); in the same issue see Maxine Greene, " 'Excellence', Meanings, and Multiplicity" for an alternative conception of excellence.

26. See Alexander, *John Dewey's Theory of Art, Experience and Nature*; Ralph W. Sleeper, *The Necessity of Pragmatism* (New Haven: Yale University Press, 1986); James M. Wallace, "The Assault on Public Education: A Deweyan Response," *Phi Delta Kappan* 64:1 (1982): 57–8; Jerome A. Popp, "If You See John Dewey, Tell Him We Did It," *Educational Theory* 37:2 (1987): 145–152; pieces of Richard Rorty's and Richard J. Bernstein's work; and from a more critical perspective, Henry A. Giroux and Peter McLaren, "Teacher Education and the Politics of Engagement: The Case for Democratic Schooling," *Harvard Educational Review* 56:3 (1986): 213–238.

27. Response to my paper, "Dewey, History and Praxis" presented at a Teachers College Columbia University forum, October, 1988.

28. See Walter Feinberg, "The Conflict Between Intelligence and Community in Dewey's Educational Philosophy," *Educational Theory* 19:3 (1969): 236–249. The critical question, Feinberg asks, is whether Dewey believed that "all values are to be determined by the method of evaluation, which is the application of the method of intelligence to the problems of human values, or whether the method itself ultimately rests upon an assumed set of values which determine its proper direction and use" (237). See Dewey, *Liberalism and Social Action*: "The crisis in liberalism is connected with failure to develop and lay hold of an adequate conception of intelligence" (44).

29. Giroux and McLaren, "Teacher Education and the Politics of Engagement," 238.

30. Michael Apple, *Ideology and Curriculum* (London: Routledge and Kegan Paul, 1979), 2.

31. The reader may wish to contrast the crisis concept which I appropriate from Karl-Otto Apel, "The Situation of Humanity as an Ethical Problem," trans. David Roberts *Praxis International* 4:3 (1984) and Jürgen Habermas' *Legitimation Crisis,* trans. Thomas McCarthy (Boston: Beacon Press, 1973, 1975) along with the analysis of peace researcher Betty Reardon's *Sexism and the War System* (New York: Teachers College Press, 1985) against the 1975 conclusions of the Trilateral Commission, Michael Crozier, Samuel P. Huntington, and Joji Watanuki, *The Crisis of Democracy: Report on the Governability of Democracies to the Trilateral Commission* (New York, 1975).

32. Joel Kovel, *Against the State of Nuclear Terror* (Boston: South End Press, 1983), 4.

33. Apel, "The Situation of Humanity as an Ethical Problem," 250.

34. Robin Luckham, "Myths and Realities of Security," in *Toward Nuclear Disarmament and Global Security: A Search for Alternatives,* ed. Burns H. Weston (Boulder: Westview Press, 1984), 160.

35. The literature in this field is enormous. A one-volume work which substantiates and expands my use of nuclearization to convey the organization of contemporary social life by economic and military priorities is Burns H. Weston, ed., *Toward Nuclear Disarmament and Global Security: A Search for Alternatives*

(Boulder: Westview Press, 1984); also, Reardon, *Sexism and the War System.*

36. Stanley Aronowitz, "Politics and Higher Education in the 1980s," in *Curriculum and Instruction: Alternatives in Education* eds. Henry A. Giroux, Anthony Penna, William Pinar (Berkeley: McCutchan Publishing Corp., 1981), 462.

37. Dewey, *Liberalism and Social Action,* 31.

38. See William B. Stanley, "The Radical Reconstructionist Rationale for Social Education" *Theory and Research in Social Education* 8:4 and 9:1 (1981). Brameld stated in 1936 that "scientific method, despite its glorification, becomes an apologist for inaction, when it cautiously weighs all possibilities *ad infinitum.*" Theodore Brameld, "The Role of Philosophy in a Changing World," *Kadelpian Review* (January 1936); quoted in Stanley, 63-4.

39. Dewey, *Liberalism and Social Action,* 74.

40. Mark Poster, *Foucault, Marxism and History: Mode of Production versus Mode of Information* (Oxford: Polity Press, 1984), 16.

41. Ibid.

42. Dewey, *Democracy and Education,* iii.

43. William Bean Kennedy, "A Radical Challenge to Inherited Educational Patterns," *Religious Education* 74:5 (1979): 491-2.

44. Ramon Sanchez, *Schooling American Society: A Democratic Ideology* (Syracuse: Syracuse University Press, 1976), 15.

45. For my understanding of "ideology" I have found the following works to be most helpful: Antonio Gramsci, *Selections from the Prison Notebooks,* ed. and trans. Quinton Hoare and G.N. Smith (New York: International Publishers, 1971); the excellent collection of essays edited by Chantal Mouffe, *Gramsci and Marxist Theory* (London: Routledge and Kegan Paul, 1979); Karel Kosik, *Dialectics of the Concrete*; much of Michael Apple's work, particularly, *Ideology and Curriculum* and *Education and Power* (London: Routledge and Kegan Paul, 1982; repr., Boston: Ark Paperbacks, 1985); Goran Therborn, *The Ideology of Power and the Power of Ideology* (London: Verso, 1980); Rachel Sharp,

Knowledge, Ideology and the Politics of Schooling: Towards a Marxist Analysis of Education (London: Routledge and Kegan Paul, 1980).

46. C.B. Macpherson's work was quite helpful in grasping a sense of liberalism; see *The Political Theory of Possessive Individualism: Hobbes to Locke* (London: Oxford University Press, 1962); also, Peter Bachrach, *The Theory of Democratic Elitism* (Washington, DC: University Press of America, 1980). In distinguishing the pattern of modernity and the roots of crisis the following works were among those consulted: Lucien Goldmann, *The Philosophy of the Enlightenment: The Christian Burgess and the Enlightenment,* trans. Henry Maas (Cambridge: MIT Press, 1973); Max Horkheimer and Theodor Adorno, *Dialectic of Enlightenment,* trans. John Cumming (New York: Continuum, 1972); Michel Foucault, *The Order of Things: An Archaeology of the Human Sciences* (New York: Random House, 1970); Morris Berman, *The Reenchantment of the World* (Ithaca: Cornell University Press, 1981); Jonathan Schell, *The Fate of the Earth* (New York: Avon, 1982); "Special Issue on Critiques of the Enlightenment" *New German Critique* 41 (Sp/Sum 1987); and Aronowitz, *Science as Power.*

47. Sharp, *Knowledge,* 106.

48. Anthony Giddens, *The Constitution of Society: Outline of the Theory of Structuration* (Berkeley: University of California Press, 1984), 16.

49. In the *Prison Notebooks,* Gramsci refers to "common-sense" as "a generic form of thought common to a particular period and a particular environment...it holds together a specific social group, it influences moral conduct and the direction of the will" (330, 333).

50. Williams, "Base and Superstructure in Marxist Cultural Theory," 38.

51. Mouffe, "Hegemony and Ideology in Gramsci," in *Gramsci and Marxist Theory,* 186.

52. Dewey, *Individualism Old and New,* 146. In *Freedom and Culture* (New York: G.P. Putnam's Sons, 1939) Dewey acknowledged the *aberrational* ideological dimension while implying the *veracity* of scientific inquiry: "The story of the way in which ideas put forth about the makeup of human nature,

ideas supposed to be the results of psychological inquiry, have
been in fact only reflections of practical measures that different
groups, classes, factions wished to see continued in existence or
newly adopted, so that what passed as psychology was a branch
of political science" (29).

53. On the issue of language, see Dale Spender, *Man Made
Language* (London: Routledge and Kegan Paul, 1980); Jean
Grimshaw, *Philosophy and Feminist Thinking* (Minneapolis:
University of Minnesota Press, 1986).

54. Therborn, *Ideology of Power,* 80.

55. Ibid., 83.

56. See Peter Berger, *Pyramids of Sacrifice: Political Ethics
and Social Change* (New York: Basic Books, 1975) especially ch.
4, for this limited analysis of ideology applied to a critique of
Paulo Freire.

57. Therborn, *The Ideology of Power,* 78.

58. Apple, *Education and Power,* 15.

59. Jefferson, *Crusade Against Ignorance: Thomas Jefferson
on Education* (New York: Teachers College Press, 1961), 94;
quoted in Sanchez, *Schooling American Society,* 72. See Dewey's
"Introduction," in *The Living Thoughts of Thomas Jefferson*
(London: Cassell and Company, 1941, 1946).

60. As C.A. Bowers recently speculated in "The Dialectic of
Nihilism and the State: Implications for an Emancipatory Theory
of Education," *Educational Theory* 36:3 (1986): 228.

61. For the psychodynamic impact of nuclearization, an
inquiry could begin with the following: Nicholas Humphrey,
"Four Minutes to Midnight," *The Listener* 106 (October 29, 1981);
Robert Jay Lifton and Richard Falk, *Indefensible Weapons: The
Political and Psychological Case Against Nuclearism* (New York:
Basic Books, 1982); Lifton, *The Broken Connection* (New York:
Simon and Schuster, 1979); Kovel, *Nuclear Terror*; David
Goldman and William Greenberg, "Preparing for Nuclear War:
The Psychological Effects," *The American Journal of
Orthopsychiatry* 52:4 (1982); Sibylle Escalona, "Children's
Responses to the Nuclear War Threat," *Children* 10:4 (1963);
Escalona, "Growing Up with the Threat of Nuclear War: Some
Indirect Effects on Personality and Development," *AJOP* 52:4

(1982); Escalona, "Children and the Threat of Nuclear War," in *Behavioral Science and Human Survival,* ed. Milton Schwebel (Palo Alto: Science and Behavior Books, 1965); Milton Schwebel, "Effects of the Nuclear War Threat on Children and Teenagers: Implications for Professionals," *AJOP* 52:4 (1982); Schwebel, "Nuclear Cold War: Student Opinion of Professional Responsibility," in *Behavioral Science and Human Survival*; Schwebel and Schwebel, "Children's Reactions to the Threat of Nuclear Plant Accidents," *AJOP* 51:2 (1981); W.R. Beardslee and J. Mack, "The Impact on Children and Adolescents of Nuclear Developments," in *Psychosocial Aspects of Nuclear Developments* (Washington, DC: American Psychiatric Association, 1982); Mack, "Resistances to Knowing in the Nuclear Age," *Harvard Educational Review* 54:3 (1984); Mack, "Psychosocial Aspects of the Nuclear Arms Race," *Bulletin of the Atomic Scientists* 37 (April 1981); L. Goodman, J. Mack, W. Beardslee, R. Snow, "The Threat of Nuclear War and Nuclear Arms Race: Adolescent Experience and Perceptions," *Political Psycholgy* 4:3 (1983); *Boston Globe* Survey, October 29, 1981.

62. See, for example, *Problems of Men,* Part I.

63. Dewey, *Problems of Men,* 58.

64. Talcott Parsons, "Evolutionary Universals in Society," *American Sociological Review* 29:3 (1964): 339–57. See Dewey's essay "Democracy and Human Nature," in *Freedom and Culture.*

65. Todd Gitlin, "Televison's Screens: Hegemony in Transition," in *Cultural and Economic Reproduction in Education: Essays on Class, Ideology and the State,* ed. Michael Apple (London: Routledge and Kegan Paul, 1982), 203; also, Ariel Dorfman, *The Empire's Old Clothes: What the Lone Ranger, Babar, and Other Innocent Heroes Do to our Minds* (New York: Pantheon Books, 1983).

66. Sanchez, *Schooling American Society,* 10.

67. Charles Frankel, "John Dewey's Social Philosophy," in *New Studies in the Philosophy of John Dewey,* ed. Steven M. Cahn (Hanover: The University Press of New England, 1977), 26.

68. Sanchez, *Schooling American Society,* 8.

69. Paul Buhle, *Marxism in the USA: Remapping the History of the American Left* (London: Verso, 1987), 16.

70. John Locke, *An Essay Concerning Human Understanding* (Oxford: Clarendon Press, 1894) and *Two Treatises on Government,* ed. Thomas I. Cook (New York: Hafner Press, 1947, 1974); John Stuart Mill, *On Liberty* (Indianapolis: Bobbs-Merrill Company, 1956); John Rawls, *A Theory of Justice* (Cambridge: Harvard University Press, 1971); Bruce Ackerman, *Social Justice in the Liberal State* (New Haven: Yale University Press, 1980); see also, David Miller, *Social Justice* (Oxford: Clarendon Press, 1976).

71. Robert Lichtman, "The Facade of Equality in Liberal Democratic Theory" *Socialist Revolution* 1:1 (1970), 87.

72. Kai Nielson, "Capitalism, Socialism and Justice: Reflections on Rawls' Theory of Justice" *Social Praxis* 7:3/4 (1980), 259.

73. John Thompson, *Studies in the Theory of Ideology* (Berkeley: University of California Press, 1984), 144.

74. Stanley Aronowitz, *The Crisis in Historical Materialism: Class, Politics and Culture in Marxist Theory* (South Hadley, MA: J.F. Bergin, 1981), 77.

75. Sanchez, 30; here he introduces the notion of the "generalization of labor" as a basic principle in an ideology of education; see ch. 8.

76. *Aporia* is the wisdom gained from knowing that you do not know. See Plato's *Apology*; also, I regard Socrates as existentially and socially distinct from Plato and the formalization of philosophy.

77. See Paulo Freire, *Pedagogy of the Oppressed,* trans. Myra Bergman Ramos (New York: Seabury Press, 1970); *The Politics of Education: Culture, Power, and Liberation,* trans. Donaldo Macedo (South Hadley, MA: Bergin and Garvey, 1985).

78. See William Bean Kennedy, "Highlander Praxis: Learning with Myles Horton," *Teachers College Record* 83:1 (1981) and the bibliography, 118-9.

79. Myles Horton, "What is Liberating Education? A Conversation with Myles Horton," interview by Bingham Graves in *Radical Teacher* (1979).

80. Freire, *Pedagogy of the Oppressed,* 68-9.

81. Aronowitz and Giroux, *Education Under Siege*, 131–2.

82. Fred R. Dallmayr, *Polis and Praxis: Exercises in Contemporary Political Theory* (Cambridge: MIT Press, 1984), 8.

83. Giroux, *Theory and Resistance in Education: A Pedagogy for the Opposition* (South Hadley, MA: Bergin and Garvey, 1983), 116.

84. Agnes Heller, *Radical Philosophy*, trans. James Wickham (Oxford: Basil Blackwell, 1984), 40.

85. Ibid., 150.

86. Richard Rorty, "Solidarity or Objectivity?" in *Post-Analytic Philosophy*, eds. John Rajchman and Cornel West (New York: Columbia University, 1985), 15.

87. Michael Harrington, *The Politics at God's Funeral: The Spiritual Crisis of Western Civilization* (New York: Penguin Books, 1983), 201.

88. Like Hegel, Dewey believed that the great theme of the Enlightenment was the victory being achieved in the transformation of religion and metaphysics.

89. Thompson, *Studies in the Theory of Ideology*, 148–9.

90. Anthony Giddens, *Profiles and Critiques in Social Theory* (London: Macmillan Press Ltd., 1982), 29.

91. See Walter Kaufmann, *Nietzsche: Philosopher, Psychologist, Antichrist* (New York: Vintage Books, 1968), 82–93 for the subtleness of the dialectical concept.

92. Giroux, *Ideology, Culture, and the Process of Schooling* (Philadelphia: Temple University Press, 1981), 114–15.

93. An excellent book which sees a complementarity in joining the radical (Marx) and the reform (George Herbert Mead) is *Dilemmas of Schooling: Teaching and Social Change* (New York: Methuen, 1981) by Ann and Harold Berlak.

94. Couze Venn, "The Subject of Psychology," in Julian Henriques et al., *Changing the Subject: Psychology, Social Regulation and Subjectivity* (New York: Methuen, 1984), 150.

Part I

1. See Dewey, *The Public and Its Problems* (New York: Henry Holt and Company, 1927; repr., Chicago: Swallow Press, 1954), chapter three.

2. Dewey, "Intelligence and Morals," in *The Influence of Darwin on Philosophy And Other Essays in Contemporary Thought* (New York: Henry Holt and Co., 1910; repr., Bloomington: Indiana University Press, 1965), 59.

3. Dewey, "Consciousness and Experience," in *Influence of Darwin*, 267; see Part Two of this book as well.

4. Dewey, "Intelligence and Morals," 60 (italics mine).

5. Dewey, *The Public and Its Problems*, 85 (italics mine).

6. Ibid., 208.

7. Dewey, *Problems of Men*, 40.

8. Dewey, "Creative Democracy—The Task Before Us," quoted in Richard J. Bernstein, *John Dewey* (New York: Washington Square Press, 1966), 184. Dewey was well aware in 1938, e.g., of the "racial intolerance" in his own country that reflected how far democracy still had to go. "The facts," he stated in *Freedom and Culture*, "bring out in sharp outline that as yet the full conditions... for a completely democratic experience have not existed" (73).

9. Dewey, *Problems of Men*, 37.

10. Dewey, *The Public and Its Problems*, 143.

11. Ibid., 153.

12. Ibid., 149.

13. Nancy S. Love, in the opening chapter of a recent book writes that "the problem of modernity" involves three interdependent historical developments: the Enlightenment, or "the ascendancy of scientific reason over religion," the French Revolution, or the ascendancy "of contractual over status relations," and the industrial revolution, or the ascendancy "of modern industry over feudal production." Unlike Marx and Nietzsche, who are the study of her book, Dewey was more inclined to accept those developments. In *Marx, Nietzsche, and Modernity* (New York: Columbia University Press, 1986), 1.

14. Charles Frankel, "John Dewey's Social Philosophy," 22. "Paideia," as Mortimer Adler's work stresses, refers to a common cultural background from which learning draws in the formation of the intelligent citizen.

15. Ibid., 23, 26.

16. Alan Wolfe, "Inauthentic Democracy: A Critique of Public Life in Modern Liberal Society," *Studies in Political Economy* 21 (1986), 60.

17. Ibid., 69.

18. Dewey, *Democracy and Education,* 97.

19. See Rorty, "Solidarity or Objectivity?" 3-19.

20. Ibid., 7.

21. Ibid., 12.

22. Dewey, *Liberalism and Social Action,* 3, 57 respectively.

23. Richard Rorty, *Consequences of Pragmatism: Essays 1972-1980* (Minneapolis: University of Minnesota Press, 1982), 160-5.

24. Ibid., 167.

25. Max Horkheimer, *Eclipse of Reason* (New York: Oxford University Press, 1947; repr., New York: Continuum, 1974), 97.

26. Rorty, *Consequences,* 166.

27. Ibid, 173.

28. Rorty, "Solidarity or Objectivity?" 7.

29. Ibid., 11-12 (italics mine).

30. Dewey, *Freedom and Culture,* 70-1.

31. Dewey, *Problems of Men,* 57.

32. Williams, "Base and Superstructure in Marxist Cultural Theory," 39.

33. Rorty, "Solidarity or Objectivity?" 11.

34. A recent paper of mine has pursued this objection to pragmatic solutions in regard to Dewey's position on war. "Holding Up War: The Reform Approach of John Dewey" (unpubl.).

35. Cornel West, "The Politics of American Neo-Pragmatism," in *Post-Analytic Philosophy,* 267; also, recently published but too late to consider, is West's *The American Evasion of Philosophy: A Genealogy of Pragmatism* (Madison: The University of Wisconsin Press, 1989), esp. ch. 5.

36. Dewey, *Democracy and Education,* 83.

37. Dewey, *Liberalism and Social Action,* 7.

38. Dewey, *Democracy and Education,* 87.

39. Dewey, *Liberalism and Social Action,* 26.

40. Ibid., 34.

41. C.B. Macpherson, "Politics: Post-Liberal-Democracy?" in *Ideology in Social Science: Readings in Critical Social Theory,* ed. Robin Blackburn (New York: Pantheon Books, 1972), 19.

42. Ibid., 20. Also see, Macpherson, *Democratic Theory: Essays in Retrieval* (Oxford: Clarendon Press, 1973).

43. Dewey, *Individualism Old and New,* 118. See Buhle's *Marxism in the USA,* ch. one, for another perspective of the "spirit."

44. While I am not in complete agreement with their conclusions, a significant body of literature exists which finds Dewey's reformism to be a handmaid to a growing capitalist bureaucratic state. See Gabriel Kolko, *The Triumph of Conservatism: A Reinterpretation of American History, 1900–1916* (Chicago: Quadrangle Books, 1967); Clarence J. Karier, *Shaping the American Educational State* (New York: The Free Press, 1975); Madan Sarup, *Marxism and Education* (London: Routledge and Kegan Paul, 1978).

45. Macpherson, "Politics," 21, 22-3 respectively.

46. Dewey, *Freedom and Culture,* 126.

47. Ibid., 128. Two recent books have accented this religious-humanist background in Dewey. See Robert M. Crunden, *Ministers of Reform: The Progressives' Achievement in American Civilization, 1889-1920* (New York: Basic Books, 1982); Bruce Kuklick, *Churchmen and Philosophers: From Jonathan Edwards to John Dewey* (New Haven: Yale University Press, 1985).

48. Ibid., 164-5.

49. Dewey, *Liberalism and Social Action*, 173.

50. In an introduction to *The Living Thoughts of Thomas Jefferson*, Dewey glossed over the "selective purpose" of Jefferson's schooling in a democracy (13) wherein the rubbish would be raked annually for the twenty best geniuses (115).

51. Julian Henriques et al., *Changing the Subject*, 23.

52. Dewey, *Liberalism and Social Action*, 52 (italics mine).

53. Dewey, *Problems of Men,* 140.

54. Rorty, "Solidarity or Objectivity?" 16.

55. Ibid., 11.

56. Ibid.

57. In addition to the works of Rorty already cited, see his *Philosophy and the Mirror of Nature* (Princeton: Princeton University Press, 1979), Part Three; Dewey's essay "Democracy and America" in *Freedom and Culture* and his "Introduction" to *The Living Thoughts of Thomas Jefferson.*

58. Kant stated in the opening paragraph of "What is Enlightenment?" that it referred to the "release from self-incurred tutelage. Tutelage is man's inability to make use of his understanding without direction from another.... Have courage to use your own reason!—that is the motto of enlightenment." Immanuel Kant, *Critique of Practical Reason and Other Writings in Moral Philosophy,* trans. and ed. Lewis White Beck (Chicago: University of Chicago Press, 1949), 286.

59. William Ryan's little classic, *Blaming the Victim* (New York: Pantheon, 1971; rev. 1976) casts this paradox perfectly. While Dewey's prose and behavior suggest a genuine humanitarianism, his analysis ultimately inhibits it.

60. Venn, "The Subject of Psychology," 132-3; see my remarks, 18–24 in "Introduction."

61. See Foucault, "The Ethic of Care for the Self as a Practice of Freedom: An Interview with Michel Foucault on January 20, 1984," interview by Raul Fornet-Betancourt et al, trans. J.D. Gauthier, *Philosophy and Social Criticism* 12:2/3 (1987); also, Foucault's *Order of Things.*

62. In his essay, "Ideology and Ideological State Apparatuses," Louis Althusser designates the far-reaching pull of hegemony in the conditions and organization of everyday life: the religious, the educational, the family, the legal, the political, the trade union, communications, and the cultural. In *Lenin and Philosophy and Other Essays,* trans. Ben Brewster (New York: Monthly Review Press, 1971), 127-186.

63. Venn, "The Subject of Psychology," 151.

64. Poster, *Foucault, Marxism and History,* 86.

65. Michel Foucault, "What is Enlightenment?" in *The Foucault Reader,* ed. Paul Rabinow (New York: Pantheon Books, 1984), 32-50.

66. David R. Hiley, "Foucault and the Question of Enlightenment," *Philosophy and Social Criticism* 11:1 (1985): 74-5. In using Foucault to establish my point with respect to the construction of the subject, I am aware that even with my expanded notion of ideology a Foucauldian may find the association objectionable. Foucault finds the traditional concept of ideology to be problematic, a notion that one cannot use without circumspection. But the notion of hegemony which I have employed clearly addresses what Poster has referred to as the "extra-epistemological ground." That is, the ideological terrain examines how everyday practices are constituted; it is not limited solely to its production by the dominant classes, nor is its expression primarily a "superstructure" to the mode of production. In *Foucault, Marxism and History,* 85.

67. Dewey, *Individualism Old and New,* 31.

68. Dewey, *The School and Society,* in *The Child and the Curriculum* and *The School and Society* (Chicago: University of Chicago Press, 1956), 12.

69. Dewey, *Individualism Old and New,* 16-7.

70. Ibid., 18.

71. Ibid., 53.

72. Ibid., 52. See Søren Kierkegaard, *The Present Age,* trans. Alexander Dru (New York: Harper and Row, 1962) written in 1848 for a comparable starting point.

73. Ibid., 17.

74. Ibid., 59.

75. Ibid., 52.

76. Ibid., 58.

77. Ibid., 82.

78. Ibid., 93.

79. Dewey, *Democracy and Education,* 98.

80. *Individualism Old and New,* 83.

81. Ibid., 69.

82. Kovel, *Nuclear Terror,* 103.

83. Dewey, *Liberalism and Social Action,* 25.

84. Hegel, Marx explains, in the *Economic and Philosophical Manuscripts,* "merely discovered an *abstract, logical* and speculative expression of the historical process, which is not yet the *real* history of man as a given subject, but only the history of the *act of creation,* of the *genesis of man."* In *Marx's Concept of Man,* ed. Erich Fromm (New York: Frederick Ungar, 1961, 1966), 172. "In effect," writes Raya Dunayevskaya, recently deceased Marxist scholar, "what Marx is now saying is that the total dichotomy between the philosophic world, where alienations are transcended, and the actual world, where they are as big as life, is proof enough that the philosophic world is bereft of practice, that existence does not enter the world of essence." In *Philosophy and Revolution: From Hegel to Sartre and from Marx to Mao,* 2nd ed. with new introduction (Atlantic Highlands, NJ: Humanities Press, 1982), 58. Dewey, in my reading, in fact creates a similar "dualism" to Hegel's—reason and reality—which he can, like Hegel, only pragmatically address. See Hegel's "Philosophical History," in *Philosophy of History,* trans. J.B. Sibree (New York: Willey Book Co., 1900), 8-79; and ch. 7 in Marcuse's *Reason and Revolution.*

85. See Louis Althusser, "Ideology and Ideological State Apparatuses." Althusser, however, assigns to "ideology" a far more determined quality/role in the interpellation process as well as regarding it in fundamental opposition to something like the "truth." Thus, he says, "it is not their real conditions of existence, their real word, that 'men' 'represent to themselves' in ideology, but above all it is their relation to those conditions

162NOTES

of existence which is represented to them there. It is this relation which is at the centre of every ideological, i.e. imaginary, representation of the real world." In *Lenin and Philosophy,* 164.

86. Mouffe, "Hegemony and Ideology," 171.

87. Ibid.

88. See, for example, Colin Greer, *The Great School Legend: A Revisionist Interpretation of American Public Education* (New York: Basic Books, 1972); Joel Spring *Education and the Rise of the Corporate State*; Michael Katz, *The Irony of Early School Reform* (Boston: Beacon Press, 1968); Giroux, *Theory and Resistance*; Madan Sarup, *Education, State and Crisis* (London: Routledge and Kegan Paul, 1982); Sharp, *Knowledge.*

89. Dewey, *Democracy and Education,* 38.

90. Dewey, *Problems of Men,* 42.

91. Dewey, *School and Society,* 8.

92. Tony Skillen, "Marxism and Morality," *Radical Philosophy* 8 (1974): 12.

93. Dewey, *Democracy and Education,* 3, 10 respectively.

94. See Robert Pattison, "On the Finn Syndrome and the Shakespeare Paradox," *The Nation* (May 30, 1987), where he refers to Dewey as "the father of educational formalism" (710); also see Morton G. White, *Social Thought in America: The Revolt Against Formalism* (Boston: Beacon Press, 1957).

95. Dewey, *Democracy and Education,* 73, 63, and 63 respectively.

96. Clarence J. Karier, "Liberal Ideology and the Quest for Orderly Change," in *Roots of Crisis: American Education in the Twentieth Century,* eds. Clarence J. Karier, Paul Violas, Joel Spring (Chicago: Rand McNally and Company, 1973), 97.

97. Dewey, *School and Society,* 9.

98. Dewey, *The Child and the Curriculum,* in *The Child and the Curriculum* and *The School and Society,* 12.

99. *Democracy and Education,* 16.

100. Ibid., 27.

101. Ibid., 51.

102. Ibid., 111; "statement" is italicized in text.

103. Ibid., 41.

104. Ibid., 56.

105. Ibid., 20, 21 respectively.

106. Ibid., 73.

107. Ibid., 2.

108. Ibid., 296.

109. Dewey, *Dewey on Education,* ed. Martin S. Dworkin (New York: Columbia University Press, 1959), 32; quoted in Karier, "Liberal Ideology," 89.

110. Sanchez, *Schooling American Society,* 84.

111. Karier, "Liberal Ideology," 91.

112. Dewey, *Democracy and Education,* 83, 86, 87 respectively.

113. Ibid., 99.

114. Ibid., 122.

115. Ibid., 256.

116. Ibid., 83.

117. Ibid., 98.

118. While I refer to Talcott Parsons in Part Two, and his debt to earlier social theorists, Durkheim and Weber, I have not unpacked their sociology. Nor during a cursory search of the Boydston bibliography of Dewey have I found any references to Parsons.

119. Dewey, *School and Society,* 24.

120. Sanchez, *Schooling American Society,* 81.

121. Ibid.

122. Karier, "Liberal Ideology," 93.

123. In using the concept of paradigm, I am making an analogy with Thomas S. Kuhn's analysis in *The Structure of Scientific Revolutions,* 2nd ed. (Chicago: University of Chicago

Press, 1962, 1970). With the faith in "democracy" and industrial development, Dewey believed (what Kuhn later was to say) that "the issue [at stake] is which paradigm should in the future guide research on problems... [and that one must] have faith that the new paradigm will succeed with the many large problems that confront it" (157-8). I believe that (typologically at least) a concern with the ideological elements of schooling is a common focus for both of us. However, I am contending that Dewey, alive for only a few years in the nuclear age, was seeing a nova. The "paradigm shift" to which Dewey spoke must be *radically* transformed.

124. Dewey, *Liberalism and Social Action,* 3; but read Dewey's essays published in the *New Republic* during World War One, "The Future of Pacifism" (July 28, 1917); "What Will America Fight For?" (August 18, 1917); "Conscription of Thought" (September 1, 1917); "In Explanation of Our Lapse" (November 3, 1917); "A New Social Science" (April 6, 1918).

125. See Williams, *America in a Changing World.* Dewey could write in 1948 that "the new movements in science and in the industrial and political conditions which have issued from it" set the course for a "new moral order." In "Reconstruction Twenty-five Years Later," xxxix. Needless, to say, I am not in agreement with Dewey on the potential of those "movements."

126. See, for example, *Freedom and Culture,* where he said "the future of democracy is allied with the spread of the scientific attitude" (148).

127. Brian Fay, "How People Change Themselves: The Relationship Between Critical Theory and its Audience," in *Political Theory and Praxis: New Perspectives,* ed. Terence Ball (Minneapolis: University of Minnesota Press, 1977), 204.

128. Herbert Marcuse, *One-Dimensional Man* (Boston: Beacon Press, 1964), 158.

129. Easlea, *Liberation and the Aims of Science: An Essay on Obstacles to the Building of a Beautiful World* (Totowa, NJ: Rowman and Littlefield, 1973), 249.

130. Galileo Galilei, *Discoveries and Opinions of Galileo,* ed. S. Drake (Garden City: Doubleday Anchor, 1957), 63; quoted in Easlea, *Liberation and the Aims of Science,* 249. In a recent and more comprehensive analysis, Aronowitz provides a detailed argument tracing the culpability of science in regimes of power,

or in his words, " to show that science is not free of historical and discursive presuppositions and that it has constituted itself as an autonomous power precisely through its convincing demonstration that it is free of such preconditions." In *Science as Power,* viii.

131. Dewey, *Experience and Education* (New York: Collier Books, 1938), 86.

132. Dewey, *Schools of Tomorrow,* 180.

133. *Experience and Education,* 80 and 81. My argument in this section is not unmindful of Dewey's rejoinder in 1948 to "those who hold natural science to be the *fons et origo* of the undeniably serious ills of the present." However, he clearly confirms his lifelong orientation in reiterating philosophy's task of more diligent criticism of science. In "Reconstruction Twenty-five Years Later," xxii-xxiii.

134. Karier, "Liberal Ideology," 103.

135. Ibid., 104.

136. Aronowitz, *Science as Power,* 317.

137. Here Paul Willis' *Learning to Labour* (New York: Columbia University Press, 1981) comes to mind.

138. In chapter six of *Logic: The Theory of Inquiry* (New York: Henry Holt and Co., 1938), Dewey developed these steps: 1) the antecedent condition of an indeterminate situation; 2) determining a problem; 3) determination of a problem and hypothetical solution; 4) reasoning and determining relevancy; 5) operationality of meanings. Facts are the meanings assigned in inquiry. As Dewey says, "they are selected and described... for a purpose, namely statement of the problem involved in such a way that its material both indicates a meaning relevant to resolution of the difficulty and serves to test its worth and validity" (113); 6) in distinguishing scientific inquiry from its shared steps with commonsense thinking, Dewey provided the clear orientation of scientific method. "In scientific inquiry... meanings are related to one another on the ground of their character *as* meanings, freed from direct reference to the concerns of a limited group" (115).

139. Dewey, "Afterword" (1946), in *The Public and Its Problems,* 229.

140. See Ursula K. LeGuin, *The Lathe of Heaven* (New York: Avon, 1971) for a chilling account of science "in the right hands."

141. It may be said that Dewey has a suit for every occasion. His substantial appeal lies in the capacity to speak to the basic concerns of many people. My position, which regards Dewey fully within a liberal ideological position, simply maintains that from that position Dewey is able to articulate some points and ignore others; this is the paradox to which I have been speaking and which I find interesting. Secondly, the argument which regards Dewey to be an "everyman" is itself ideologically invested and in keeping with a depoliticalization of issues. One example from his *Human Nature and Conduct: An Introduction to Social Psychology* (New York: Henry Holt and Co., 1922; repr., New York: Modern Library, 1957) reveals how benign the cloak of reform can be. He referred to the "maladjustment" of human environment in the context of work and suggested that "play" or recreation is the effective counter. His inquiry there simply took for granted that modern industrial life is brutish at times, alienating, disempowering, stratifying, but with a greater participation in "sport" individuals can be "humanized." See his argument in sec. 6 of Part II, 148-156.

142. Frankel's phrase with reference to Dewey's scientific method approach; see "John Dewey's Social Philosophy," 15.

143. Raymond Geuss, *The Idea of a Critical Theory: Habermas and the Frankfurt School* (New York: Cambridge University Press, 1981), 27.

144. Apple, "Curriculum as Ideological Selection," *Comparative Education Review* 20:2 (1976): 210-11.

145. See Geuss, *The Idea of a Critical Theory*; Freire, *Pedagogy of the Oppressed.*

146. See Brian Fay, *Social Theory and Political Practice* (London: George Allen and Unwin, 1975), esp. ch. 5.

147. Ibid., 96.

148. Apple, *Ideology and Curriculum,* 132.

149. Fay, *Social Theory,* 94.

150. Giddens, *Constitution of Society,* 17.

151. In addition to the recent pamphlet "Education for Democracy," the National Endowment for the Humanities recently published "American Memory: A Report on the Humanities in the Nation's Public Schools" which evokes similar reform needs.

152. See Dewey's description of the "social as a category" in *The Moral Writings of John Dewey,* ed. James Gouinlock (New York: Hafner Press, 1976), 41-47. For the original, see "Social as a Category" *Monist* 28 (1928) or in *The Later Works* vol. 3, "The Inclusive Philosophic Idea," 41-54.

153. Apple, *Ideology and Curriculum,* 15.

154. See Dewey, "The Influence of Darwinism on Philosophy," in *The Influence of Darwin,* 17-19.

155. T.H. Wilson, *The American Ideology: Science, Technology and Organization as Modes of Rationality in Advanced Industrial Societies* (London: Routledge and Kegan Paul, 1977), 16, 20, 8 respectively.

156. Bob Jessop, "Capitalism and Democracy: The Best Possible Shell?" in *Power and the State,* eds. Gary Littlejohn et al. (New York: St. Martin's Press, 1978), 13.

157. Most prominent in this regard is the work of William Appleman Williams; also see Buhle, *Marxism in the USA;* Michael Parenti, *Democracy for the Few,* 2nd ed. (New York: St. Martin's Press, 1977) and *Power and the Powerless* (New York: St. Martin's Press, n.d.); Kolko, *The Triumph of Conservatism;* Gar Alperovitz, *Atomic Diplomacy: Hiroshima and Potsdam,* rev. (New York: Penguin Books, 1985); Sanchez, *Schooling American Society.*

158. See Marx's distinction between "political" and "human" emancipation in "On the Jewish Question," in *Writings of the Young Marx on Philosophy and Society,* ed. and trans. Loyd D. Easton (Garden City: Doubleday and Co., 1967), 216-48.

159. Nielsen, "Capitalism, Socialism, and Justice," 259.

160. "Education for Democracy: A Statement of Principles" (Washington: AFT, 1987) is sponsored and produced by the American Federation of Teachers, the Educational Excellence Network and Freedom House to stand as "guidelines for strengthening the teaching of democratic values." It serves as

an example because of the status of its leadership, its explicit attention to American citizenship, and its obvious adherence to the Deweyan principles of a "progressive school." See Dewey, *Experience and Education.*

161. Ibid., 14.

162. Ibid., 7.

163. Ibid., 8.

164. Ibid.

165. Ibid., 14.

166. However, as much of the writing on "resistance theory" reveals, reproduction theories are not simple correspondence. Apple, for example, states in *Education and Power:* "Resistance, subversion of authority, working the system, creating diversions and enjoyment, building an informal group to counter the official activities of the school, all of these are specifically brought out by the school, though all of these are the exact opposite of what the administrators and teachers want" (101). Indeed, one of the main themes of my book has been that while the agenda in liberal theory is humanized, it nonetheless reinforces "the interpretation that systems of social relations are not meant to be confronted and critically analyzed, but rather resisted through these oppositional forms [or conformed to]. And in the rise of the forms themselves, indeed the meaning attached to them, the basic system of social relations . . . remains unaffected, unexamined. . . . As participants, as creators of those cultural forms, students are reproducing forms that will damn them to expressions of reaction but will not foster critical opposition." In Robert Everhart, *The In-Between Years: Student Life in a Junior High School* (Santa Barbara: Graduate School of Education, University of California, 1979) quoted in Apple, 107.

167. "Education for Democracy," 10.

168. Ibid., 9-10.

169. Dewey, *Schools of Tomorrow,* 58.

170. Gonzalez, *Progressive Education,* 104. The availability of curricular materials which pose a transformational praxis appropriate to any age level is vast. My own research in helping to prepare a peace education text several years ago confirmed

that "progressive" pedagogies were simply not making the full commitment to social and educational change. See Betty Reardon, ed., *Educating for Global Responsibility: Teacher-Designed Curricula for Peace Education, K-12* (New York: Teacher's College Press, 1988) including the listing of recommended curriculum material, bibliographies, and resource organizations, 169-184.

171. Foucault, "Truth and Power," in *Power/Knowledge,* 116.

172. I believe the source of that basis begins with Marx. While my own guide has been influenced by Marx's thesis that our being-in-the-world not only interprets the world as presented, but changes it, the recent development of a liberation theology has significantly expanded "the meaning of the transformation of this world and human action in history" (8). Gustavo Gutierrez, a leading spokesperson for liberation theology, provides a perspective drawing upon the politics of salvation in Christian history which nonetheless is prominently situated in a philosophical and social framework of Marxism. In *A Theology of Liberation: History, Politics, and Salvation,* trans. and ed. Sister Caridad Inda and John Eagleson (Maryknoll, NY: Orbis Books, 1973, 1988). This perspective, which in some important respects eluded Marx, may be seen arising *simultaneously* in the 19th century in the social gospel movement: the "kingdom of God" encompassed more than socio-political organization. See Charles Howard Hopkins, *The Rise of the Social Gospel in American Protestantism, 1865-1915* (New Haven: Yale University Press, 1940); Ronald C. White, Jr. and Hopkins, *The Social Gospel: Religion and Reform in Changing America* (Philadelphia: Temple University Press, 1976).

173. Zbigniew Pelczynski, "The Roots of Ideology in Hegel's Political Philosophy," in *Ideology and Politics,* ed. Maurice Cranston (Firenze, Italy: LeMonnier, 1980), 66.

174. See note one in Part Two.

175. Quoted in Bahro, *Building the Green Movement,* trans. Mary Tyler (Philadelphia: New Society Publishers, 1986), 98.

176. See Robert Aspeslagh, "Structures of Violence in Daily Life and Means to Overcome Them," *Gandhi Marg* 6:4/5 (1984).

177. Daniel C. Maguire, *A New American Justice: Ending the White Male Monopolies* (Garden City: Doubleday and Company, 1980), 96.

178. For example, see a recent article on redefining legal theory by women jurisprudents. Tamar Lewin, "Feminist Scholars Spurring a Rethinking of Law" *New York Times,* Sept. 30, 1988, B9.

179. Aspeslagh, "Structures of Violence in Daily Life," 226.

180. There is some basis for this concept in the discourse of "world order." Reardon has stated that "World order refers to academic inquiry, action, research, and education related to the pursuit of world order values and to the changes in the global system necessary to the fulfillment of those values," generally identified as equity, justice and human dignity. Betty Reardon, "Disarmament Education as World Order Inquiry," in *Education for Peace and Disarmament: Toward a Living World,* ed. Douglas Sloan (New York: Teachers College Press, 1983), 137. Also, Saul H. Mendlovitz, ed., *On the Creation of a Just World Order: Preferred Worlds for the 1990's* (New York: Free Press, 1975). For concrete curriculum examples see, for example, Reardon, *Educating for Global Responsibility.* The literature is enormous. One excellent publication which differentiates among specific concerns, provides bibliographical information, organizations, curriculum resources and provides a sense of alternatives is Barbara Wien, ed. *Peace and World Order Studies: A Curriculum Guide,* 4th ed., (New York: World Policy Institute, n.d.).

181. See Johan Galtung, *Essays in Peace Research* (The Hague/Paris: Mouton/UNESCO, 1968); Reardon, *Sexism and the War System;* Birgit Brock-Utne, *Educating for Peace: A Feminist Perspective* (New York: Pergamon Press, 1985) all of whom utilize the social justice concept.

182. Heller, *Radical Philosophy,* 144–45.

183. Foucault, *Power/Knowledge,* 93.

184. It is clear that I have "transfigured" the historically rooted concept of social justice implied in Marx's work by assigning to it a greater degree of inclusiveness. In *Marx's Social Ontology: Individuality and Community in Marx's Theory of Social Reality* (Cambridge: MIT Press, 1978), Carol C. Gould explains that for Marx "justice" is constituted by the nature of social relations which were (nearly) exclusively determined by the conditions of production. I would like to expand that basis, and less reductionistically, consider social relations through their formation by other configurations of power.

Part II

1. See Bowles and Gintis, *Schooling in Capitalist America*; Apple, *Ideology and Curriculum*; Apple and Weis, *Ideology and Practice in Schooling*; Philip Wexler, *The Sociology of Education: Beyond Equality* (Indianapolis: Bobbs-Merrill, 1977); Sharp, *Knowledge, Ideology and the Politics of Schooling*; Giroux, *Ideology, Culture and the Process of Schooling*, and *Theory and Resistance in Education*; Sarap, *Marxism and Education*. All of these are indebted to Michael Young's work which began in the early seventies and whose sociology of education, writes Sharp, is self-consciously moral, political and at odds with reformist approaches (76–86). See Young, ed. *Knowledge and Control: New Directions in the Sociology of Education* (London: Collier-Macmillan, 1971).

2. See Reardon, *Sexism and the War System*; Lydia Sargent, ed. *Women and Revolution: A Discussion of the Unhappy Marriage of Marxism and Feminism* (Boston: South End Press, 1981); Jane L. Thompson, *Learning Liberation: Women's Response to Men's Education* (London: Croom Helm, 1983); Marie Louise Janssen-Jurreit, *Sexism and the Male Monopoly on History and Thought,* trans. Verne Moberg (New York: Farrar Straus Giroux, 1982); Dale Spender, *Man Made Language* (London: Routledge and Kegan Paul, 1980); Jean Grimshaw, *Philosophy and Feminist Thinking* (Minneapolis: University of Minnesota Press, 1986); Seyla Benhabib and Drucilla Cornell, eds. *Feminism as Critique: On the Politics of Gender* (Minneapolis: University of Minnesota Press, 1987); Carol C. Gould and Marx W. Wartofsky, eds. *Women and Philosophy: Toward a Theory of Liberation* (New York: G.P. Putnam's Sons, 1976).

3. Several books which I have found helpful are James Jennings and Mel King, eds., *From Access to Power: Black Politics in Boston* (Cambridge: Schenkman Books, 1986); Manning Marable, *How Capitalism Underdeveloped Black America: Problems in Race, Political Economy and Society* (Boston: South End Press, 1983); Johnnella E. Butler, *Black Studies: Pedagogy and Revolution: A Study of Afro-American Studies and the Liberal Arts Tradition Through the Discipline of Afro-American Literature* (Washington: University Press of America, 1981); the secondary sources on W.E.B. DuBois, e.g., Gerald Horne, *Black and Red: W.E.B. DuBois and the Afro-American Response to the Cold War, 1944–1963* (Albany: State

University of New York Press, 1986) and Marable, *W.E.B. DuBois—Black Radical Democrat* (Boston: Twayne Publishers, 1986); Robert C. Allen, *Black Awakening in Capitalist America: An Analytic History* (Garden City: Anchor, 1983); Richard J. Meister, ed., *The Black Ghetto: Promised Land or Colony?* (Lexington, MA: D.C. Heath, 1972).

4. Andre Gorz, *Ecology as Politics,* trans. Patsy Vigderman and Jonathan Cloud (Boston: South End Press, 1980), 8; see also, Murray Bookchin, *The Modern Crisis* (Philadelphia: New Society Publishers, 1986); Bahro, *Building the Green Movement.*

5. Albert Memmi, *The Colonizer and the Colonized,* trans. Howard Greenfeld (Boston: Beacon Press, 1967, 1972); C.A.O. Van Nieuwenhuijze, *Development Begins at Home: Problems and Prospects of the Sociology of Development* (New York: Pergamon Press, 1982); P.N. Agarwala, *New International Economic Order: An Overview* (New York: Pergamon Press, 1983); Robin Burns, "Development Education as a Key to the Understanding of Social Processes and Problems," paper presented at "The Challenge of Pluralism" conference, Darling Downs Institute of Advanced Education (Toowoomba, Queensland, Australia, November 1978); James Botkin, *No Limits to Learning* (New York: Pergamon Press, 1979); Mahmood ul Hasan Butt, "Role and Rationale of Educational Aid in Developing Countries: An Impending Crisis of Confidence" *Proceedings of the First World Congress of Comparative Education Societies on the Role and Rationale for Educational Aid to Developing Countries* (Ottawa, Canada: 1970); William Paringer, "Assessing the North-South Dialogue: Implications Toward Fulfillment," unpublished paper (1985); also, Dinnis M. Ray, "The Role of Ideology in Development" *International Journal of Comparative Sociology* 11:4 (1970) for a functionalist account of ideology with which Dewey would not be in disagreement.

6. For example, Arthur E. Murphy, "Dewey's Epistemology and Metaphysics," in *The Philosophy of John Dewey,* ed. P.A. Schilpp (Evanston and Chicago: Tudor Publishing Co., 1939), 219; quoted in Rorty, "Dewey's Metaphysics," in Cahn, *New Studies,* 45.

7. Dewey, *Experience and Nature* (New York: Dover Publications, 1958), x. Later in this text he defines "metaphysics" as a "statement of the generic traits manifested by existences

of all kinds without regard to their differentiation into physical and mental" (412).

8. Dewey, *Democracy and Education,* 91.

9. Dewey,*The Quest for Certainty,* 196.

10. Ibid., 198.

11. Dewey, *Democracy and Education,* 115.

12. Dewey, *Schools of Tomorrow,* 102.

13. Arthur Danto, "Naturalism," in *The Encyclopedia of Philosophy,* vol. 5, ed. Paul Edwards (New York: Macmillan Publishing Company, 1967), 448. While he does not treat Dewey in his study of naturalism, see Paul F. Boller, Jr., *American Thought in Transition: The Impact of Evolutionary Naturalism, 1865–1900* (Chicago: Rand McNally, 1969) including the bibliographic essay.

14. John E. Smith, "John Dewey: Philosopher of Experience," in *John Dewey and the Experimental Spirit in Philosophy,* ed. Charles W. Hendel (New York: Liberal Arts Press, 1959), 108.

15. Henriques et al., *Changing the Subject,* 2.

16. Jürgen Habermas, *Theory and Practice* trans. John Viertel (Boston: Beacon Press, 1973), 108. On the concept of "natural" as it was deployed in Enlightenment discourse see Habermas, chs. 2 and 3. Dewey "extends" the concept of natural from its philosophical usage to its scientific-empirical applicability. He sets this up, for example, in the second chapter of *Democracy and Education.*

17. Dewey, *Human Nature and Conduct,* v.

18. Morton G. White, *The Origin of Dewey's Instrumentalism* (New York: Octagon Books, 1964). In his *Social Thought in America,* White states: "Instrumentalism is Dewey's doctrine which holds that ideas are plans of action, and not mirrors of reality; that dualisms of all kinds are fatal; that the method of intelligence is the best way of solving problems; and that philosophy ought to free itself from metaphysics and devote itself to social engineering" (7).

19. Dewey, "The Influence of Darwinism," 8–9.

20. Dewey, *Human Nature and Conduct,* 272.

21. Melvin C. Baker, *Foundations of John Dewey's Educational Theory* (New York: Kings Crown Press/Columbia University, 1955), 18.

22. Bertell Ollman, *Alienation: Marx's Conception of Man in Capitalist Society* (Cambridge: Cambridge University Press, 1971), 23.

23. George Herbert Mead, *The Works of George Herbert Mead, vol. 3, The Philosophy of the Act,* ed. Charles W. Morris (Chicago: University of Chicago Press, 1936); quoted in Ann Berlak and Harold Berlak, *Dilemmas of Schooling,* 113. See Dewey's *Experience and Nature* (23) for a similar sentiment.

24. For the background of this "duality," as well an excellent context in which to understand Dewey's thought, see E.A. Burtt, *The Metaphysical Foundations of Modern Physical Science* rev. (1924, 1932; repr., Garden City, NY: Doubleday and Co., 1954), esp. "Introduction."

25. Dewey, *Human Nature and Conduct,* 276.

26. Gonzalez, *Progressive Education,* 91.

27. Dewey, *School and Society,* 29.

28. Dewey, "My Pedagogic Creed," in *John Dewey, The Early Works, 1882–1898,* vol. 5: 1895–1898 (Carbondale, IL: Southern Illinois University Press, 1972), 85.

29. Gonzalez, *Progressive Education,* 92.

30. Dewey, *School and Society,* 24.

31. Gonzalez, *Progressive Education,* 95.

32. Dewey, *Individualism Old and New,* 36.

33. Dewey, *Logic,* 19.

34. George Santayana, "Dewey's Naturalistic Metaphysics," in *The Philosophy of John Dewey,* ed. P.A. Schilpp (Evanston and Chicago: Tudor Publishing Co., 1939), 245; quoted in Rorty, "Dewey's Metaphysics," 47.

35. See Dewey, *Mind* XI (1886): 154–73.

36. Dewey, *Experience and Nature,* 216.

37. Ibid., 237–8.

38. Anthony Smith, *The Concept of Social Change: A Critique of the Functionalist Theory of Social Change* (London: Routledge and Kegan Paul, 1973); in addition to sketching a sociological analysis of "functionalism," he poses the "nature" vs. "history" distinction which I will be drawing out below. Dewey made no bones about this interpretation freely using "function" throughout his writings. While I am not aware of a direct link between Dewey and the sociology of Durkheim, the similarities are striking. Durkheim had seen in the sociological enterprise the basis for unifying industrialized societies. "The object of this new 'organic' solidarity," writes T.H. Wilson, "is to combine the economic benefits of modern technology and organization with pre-industrial values." In *The American Ideology*, 2. While neither Smith nor Wilson cites Dewey, both outline the Durkheim/Parsons scheme to which Dewey ascribed. Also, the reader should check, Alvin W. Gouldner, *The Coming Crisis of Western Sociology* (New York: Basic Books, 1970), esp. ch. 11, "From Plato to Parsons: The Infrastructure of Conservative Social Theory," 412–446.

39. The reader also might wish to check Karl Mannheim's efforts along this line in *Man and Society in an Age of Reconstruction* (New York: Harcourt, Brace and Company, 1954), Part One, "Rational and Irrational Elements in Contemporary Society."

40. This notion of "history," to be developed below, borrows from Foucault's genealogical approach. He argues that the "events" or views which attract the historian cannot be separated from the circumstances (political, philosophical, cultural) surrounding the historical formations of power and knowledge; more importantly, revealed in the selection of the historical, is a clue to understanding of agency and social change.

41. A theme of Part One identified the two primary values in Dewey's social theory which contribute to the evolutionary progress of the race, viz., science and democracy. Gouldner points out that "functional sociology" from Plato to Parsons has stressed the role of shared values as central sources of social order and consequently places great emphasis upon early education and socialization. There should be no need to belabor why Dewey fits into this continuum. In *The Coming Crisis of Western Sociology*, 442.

42. See Dewey's mild rejoinder to Aristotle's *Politics* in *The Public and Its Problems.*

43. Dewey, *Democracy and Education,* 14.

44. Ibid., 10, 11, 13–4 respectively.

45. Giddens, *The Constitution of Society,* 296.

46. Ibid.

47. Dewey, *Individualism Old and New,* 86.

48. Ibid., 32.

49. Dewey, *School and Society,* 23–4.

50. Gouldner, *The Coming Crisis of Western Sociology,* 421.

51. Dewey, *The Public and Its Problems,* 140.

52. C. Wright Mills, for one, has critiqued the American functionalist assumption, and the conservative-liberal consensus that regarded modernity—scientific and economic complexity—as the context to which individuals must adapt. See Mills, *The Power Elite* (New York: Oxford University Press, 1956) and *The Sociological Imagination* (New York: Oxford University Press, 1959).

53. Dewey, *A Common Faith* (New Haven: Yale University Press, 1934), 16.

54. Dewey, *The Public and Its Problems,* 18.

55. Talcott Parsons, "Evolutionary Universals in Society," *American Sociological Review* 29:3 (1964). These are defined generally as "any organizational development sufficiently important to further evolution . . . [and] a complex of structures and associated processes the development of which so increases the long-run adaptive capacity of living systems" (339). Without delving too deeply into Parsons, one social phenomenon which he defines in this article, stratification, clearly exemplifies the functionalist view: "Stratification, therefore, is an essential condition of major advances in political effectiveness, because . . . it gives the advantaged elements a secure enough position that they can accept certain risks in undertaking collective leadership" (345).

56. See Habermas, *Theory and Practice,* ch. 2. Habermas writes: "Because in serving the interest of the private proprietors

the state does not serve the interests of society as a whole, it remains an instrument of domination.... Marx only has to confront the expectations of the liberal, Natural-law construction of bourgeois society with the developmental tendencies of this society itself in order to confront the bourgeois revolution polemically with its own concept" (111).

57. Aristotle, *Politics*, trans. Benjamin Jowett (Oxford: Oxford University Press, 1905), Book VII, 1324a, 5.

58. Dewey, *Schools of Tomorrow*, 26.

59. Dewey, *The Public and Its Problems*, 217.

60. See Frederick Engels, *Dialectics of Nature* (New York: International Publishers, 1940); Richard Levins and Richard Lewontin, *The Dialectical Biologist* (Cambridge: Harvard University Press, 1985).

61. Dewey, *Art as Experience* (New York: G.P. Putnam's Sons, 1934; repr., Perigee Books, 1980), 25.

62. Also, see Dewey, "Social Psychology," *Psychological Review* 1:4 (1894): 400–11.

63. See Gonzalez, *Progressive Education*, 88; also William James, *The Principles of Psychology*, authorized ed., vol. 2 (New York: Henry Holt and Co., 1890; repr., New York: Dover Publications, 1950), 403–441 for an inclusive listing.

64. Dewey, *Experience and Education*, 67–8.

65. Dewey, *School and Society*, 97.

66. Dewey, *Democracy and Education*, 46.

67. See Dewey, "My Pedagogic Creed" and Gonzalez, *Progressive Education*, ch. 4.

68. Dewey, *Democracy and Education*, 46.

69. Dewey, *Human Nature and Conduct*, 40–1.

70. Dewey, *Experience and Education*, 35.

71. In *Experience and Nature*, Dewey distinguished an "empirical" end from traditionally conceived metaphysical ones: "The in-viewness of ends is as much conditioned by antecedent natural conditions as is perception of *contemporary* objects external to the organism.... That is, natural processes must

have actually terminated in specifiable consequences, which give those processes definition and character . . . [and] *only* as these objects are the consequence of prior reflection, deliberate choice and directed effort are they fulfillments, conclusions, completions, perfections" (102).

72. In *Art as Experience* Dewey explained, "An experience has a unity that gives it its name, *that* meal, that storm, that rupture of friendship. The existence of this unity is constituted by a single *quality* that pervades the entire experience in spite of the variation of its constituent parts" (37). See all of chapter three.

73. Dewey, *School and Society,* 29. In *Individualism Old and New,* Dewey's refrain was much more specific: "By accepting the corporate and industrial world in which we live," he wrote, "and by thus fulfilling the precondition for interaction with it, we, who are also parts of the moving present, create ourselves as we create an unknown future" (171).

74. Dewey, *Human Nature and Conduct,* 17.

75. See James, *The Principles of Psychology,* authorized ed., vol. 1 (New York: Henry Holt and Co., 1890; repr., New York: Dover Publications, 1950), 104–127.

76. Mead wrote in *The Philosophy of the Act* that "The individual and the society are selectively and causally determinative of the environment, and this determines the individual or the society—neither can be explained in terms of the other except as the other is determined by it" (153).

77. Zygmunt Bauman, *Culture as Praxis* (London: Routledge and Kegan Paul, 1973), 76–7.

78. Simone de Beauvoir, *The Second Sex,* trans. and ed. H.M. Parshley (New York: Random House, 1952), xxi–xxii; also, Alison Jaggar, *Feminist Politics and Human Nature* (Brighton, GB: Harvester Press, 1983).

79. The analogy I have in mind, which precedes a fuller analysis in the next chapter, is the relation of basic training to the activities of warfare. Here there is a developmental period where one thinks, acts, and prepares him/herself to be a soldier. Along the line certain qualities are extracted—teamwork, quick thinking, physical readiness, discipline, obedience, hierarchi-

calization, comradeship, emotional control—which can be nurtured and that will enhance one's performance (and increase the chances of survival) in the business that lies ahead. The structure of warfare, the context for the exercise of these qualities, like the structures upholding the modern industrial state, are taken for granted, their historical legitimacy accepted.

80. Dewey, *Experience and Education,* 67.

81. Gonzalez, *Progressive Education,* 92.

82. Valerie Walkerdine, "Developmental Psychology and the Child-Centred Pedagogy: The Insertion of Piaget into Early Education," in Henriques et al., *Changing the Subject,* 180.

83. Ibid., 164.

84. Ibid., 165.

85. Ibid., 190.

86. This knowledge of the natural world, discoverable by science, also identified existing social/intellectual problems as largely conceptual in nature, wrong thinking, if you will. Knowledge is to become naturalized; facts, as existing social phenomena, can be reassigned to conceptual arrangements subsuming the content or concrete in favor of the functional and procedural ideal. "Knowledge as a social category," Walkerdine explains, "is thereby marginalized in favour of knowledge as both individual production and competence, (hence the *reading* of children's responses to questions testing scientific and mathematical knowledge as evidence for the development of appropriate mental capacities)." In "Developmental Psychology," 171.

87. This phrase, which will be further unpacked in Part Three, refers to the coordinating of internally pluralistic but nonetheless shared instincts and the values identified with them upon which social unity is assumed dependent.

88. Wilson, *The American Ideology,* 178.

89. Walkerdine, "Developmental Psychology," 195.

90. See Ira Shor, *Culture Wars: School and Society in the Conservative Restoration, 1969–1984* (Boston: Routledge and Kegan Paul, 1986).

91. "Inquiry," as Dewey defined it in his *Logic,* "is the controlled or directed transformation of an indeterminate situation into one that is so determinate in its constituent distinctions and relations as to convert the elements of the original situation into a unified whole" (104–5).

92. Dewey compactly spells out the progressive pedagogy in *Experience and Education,* but his earlier works, *The School and Society, The Child and the Curriculum, Schools of Tomorrow,* and *Democracy and Education* should be consulted. The standard text for the progressive school movement is Lawrence A. Cremin, *The Transformation of the School: Progressivism in American Education 1876–1957* (New York: Random House, 1961, 1964); see also Rachel Sharp, *Education and Social Control: A Study in Progressive Primary Education* (London: Routledge and Kegan Paul, 1975) for an alternative view.

93. See Paul Violas, "Progressive Social Philosophy: Charles Horton Cooley and Edward Alsworth Ross," in Karier, *Roots of Crisis,* 40–65; also, David W. Noble, *The Paradox of Progressive Thought* (Minneapolis: University of Minnesota Press, 1958).

94. Ibid., 41–2.

95. Dewey, *School and Society,* 14.

96. Dewey, *Democracy and Education,* 4.

97. Cremin, *The Transformation of the School,* 122–3.

98. Dewey, *Individualism Old and New,* 18.

99. See both *A Common Faith* and *Art as Experience* for an elabortion of the unifying experience in religion and art respectively.

100. Smith, *The Concept of Social Change,* 41.

101. Dewey, *Individualism Old and New,* 36.

102. See Part One, "Individualism."

103. Dewey, *Individualism Old and New,* 31.

104. Ibid., 48.

105. Ibid., 36.

106. Ibid., 48.

107. Ibid., 53.

108. Ibid., 93.

109. Seymour Martin Lipset, *Political Man* (Garden City, NY: Doubleday, 1960) 319; Richard Hofstader, *The Age of Reform* (New York: Random House, 1955), 163-4; quoted in Normand Bernier and Jack Williams, *Beyond Beliefs: Ideological Foundations of American Education* (Englewood Cliffs: Prentice Hall, 1973), 303.

110. Dewey, *Individualism Old and New,* 171.

111. Dewey and Dewey, *Schools of Tomorrow,* 125-6.

112. Ibid., 180.

113. Ironically, the humanism of the progressive movement was perceived as potentially subversive, and certainly ineffectual by the dominant sociopolitical forces of realpolitik. In educational practice during the fifties, the child-centered agenda became a superfluity to cold war priorities, and the subtle humanizing potential of its premises and practices interfered with the functional-technocratic learning deemed necessary in the postwar world. The need to implement President Truman's challenge that education be the first line of defense ("Education is Our First Line of Defense," *School Life,* April 1, 1949), was perceived to be less likely in a progressive climate that sought "life adjustment."

114. While the general goals of Progressivism—social harmony, economic stability, growth, and the distancing from tradition—not undesirable by any means, were the concerns of progressive educators, some had also begun to see the contradictions that linked education to the capitalist state. Dewey became somewhat isolated from those who considered the unaffected segments of the progressive march of American society. While never specifically critiquing the ideological structures of racism, sexism, and violence that support the political economy in America, the social reconstructionists of the 1930s led by George Counts' ringing essay, "Dare the Schools Build a New Social Order?" significantly pushed past Dewey. In addition to Bowers, *The Progressive Educator and the Depression: The Radical Years,* and Stanley, "The Radical Reconstructionist Rationale for Social Education," see the volumes of *The Social Frontier* (1934-1939); for Dewey's

disagreement with the extreme social reconstructionist position, see "Can Education Share in Social Reconstruction?" *The Social Frontier* 1:1 (1934–5): 11–12; "Class Struggle and the Democratic Way," *The Social Frontier* 2:8 (1936): 241–2; "Education and Social Change," *The Social Frontier* 3 (1937–8): 237.

115. Wolfe, "Inauthentic Democracy," 61.

116. Ibid., 71. In addition to the incorporation of the individual into the categories of the industrial-military paradigm, another increasingly apparent affliction of this hegemony in the postnuclear era is the production of the atomistic, isolated, relativized individual whose own acts constitute the sole criteria of personal and social legitimacy. Robert Jay Lifton has called this condition in its particular associations with nuclearism "psychic numbing"; see Lifton, *The Broken Connection*; also, see Kovel's remarks contra Lifton and the "psychological explanation," but in sympathy with the diagnosis, in *Nuclear Terror,* ch. 1.

117. Gonzalez, *Progressive Education,* 29.

118. It is impossible to enter into here the "expansion of domination" that advanced capitalism has achieved. Mark Poster, in assessing Foucault's work, has stated "The form of domination characteristic of advanced capitalism is not exploitation, not alienation, not psychic repression, not anomie, not dysfunctional behavior. It is instead an [sic] new pattern of social control that is embedded in practice at many points in the social field and that constitutes a set of structures whose agency is at once everyone and no one." In Poster, *Foucault, Marxism and History,* 78.

119. Gonzalez, *Progressive Education,* 47.

120. See, for example the revisionist work of Greer, Karier, Spring, and Katz some of which is cited above, Part One, note 88; for a counter assessment of the schools, see Diane Ravitch, *The Revisionists Revised: A Critique of the Radical Attack on the Schools* (New York: Basic Books, 1978).

121. Feinberg, *Reason and Rhetoric,* 184.

122. Dewey, *Freedom and Culture,* 156.

123. Ibid., 168.

124. Rebecca Comay, "Interrupting the Conversation: Notes on Rorty" *Telos* 69 (1986): 125.

125. Gouldner, *The Coming Crisis of Western Sociology,* 107.

126. John L. Elias, *Conscientisation and Deschooling* (Philadelphia: Westminster Press, 1977), 136–7.

127. Dewey, "The Evolutionary Method as Applied to Morality," *Philosophical Review* 11:2 (1902): 121. In that essay he stated, "The essence of the experimental method I take to be control of the analysis of interpretation of any phenomenon by bringing to light the exact conditions, and the only conditions, which are involved in its coming to being" (107–8).

128. Keeping their vastly different lives in mind, it is nonetheless significant to see the outspoken opposition to war and technological sophistication which Albert Einstein, himself a liberal, and whose scientific methods and aims were instrumental in the making of atomic weapons, took after World War Two. See O. Nathan and H. Norden, eds., *Einstein on Peace* (New York: Schocken Books, 1968). Brian Easlea added an "Appendix" to his *Liberation and the Aims of Science* containing representative remarks of Einstein in the postwar period until his death in 1955; Dewey's remarks, on the other hand, in "Dualism and the Split Atom: Science and Morals in the Atomic Age," *The New Leader* (Nov 1945), and his 1948 "Introduction" to *Reconstruction in Philosophy* indicated no sign that a more critical inquiry might be in order.

129. Robert A. Woods and Albert J. Kennedy, eds. *Handbook of Settlements* (New York: Arno Press, 1911, 1970), 53.

130. Jane Addams, *Twenty Years at Hull House.* With Autobiographical Notes (New York: Macmillan Co., 1910), 237.

131. Comay, "Interrupting the Conversation," 126.

132. Feinberg, *Reason and Rhetoric,* 168–9.

133. Baker, *Foundations,* 67.

134. Dewey, *The Dewey School: The Laboratory School of the University of Chicago, 1896–1903,* ed. Katherine Camp Mayhew and Anna Camp Edwards (New York: Appleton-Century, 1936), 29–30; quoted in Karier, "Liberal Ideology," 97 (italics mine).

135. Feinberg, *Reason and Rhetoric,* 175.

184
NOTES

136. Dewey, *Logic,* 226, 234 respectively.

137. Ibid., 222.

138. Dewey stated this position explicitly: "Since the idea of history involves cumulative continuity of movement in a given direction toward stated outcomes, the fundamental conception that controls determination of subject-matter as historical is that of a *direction* of movement." In *Logic,* 234.

139. John L. Childs, "Social Assumptions and Education," review of *The Social Ideas of American Educators,* by Merle Curti, in *The Social Frontier* 2:4 (1936), 121–2.

140. Dewey, *Logic,* 227.

141. Wilson, *The American Ideology,* 47.

142. Dewey, *Logic,* 238.

143. Dewey, "My Pedagogic Creed," 85.

144. Gonzalez, *Progressive Education,* 92.

145. Charles A. Beard and William C. Bagley, *The History of the American People,* 2nd rev. ed. (New York: Macmillan Company, 1929); quoted in Feinberg, *Reason and Rhetoric,* 185.

146. Gonzalez, *Progressive Education,* 104.

147. Dewey, *Democracy and Education,* 309.

148. A similar disparity can be found in the conclusions of Hegel wherein the present order of things, the philosophical and political realization of freedom and democracy (respectively) exemplify the sine qua non of historical development. In fact, Hegel's vaunted dialectical analysis came crashing down (as subsequent events in German and European history were played out) as has Dewey's evolutionary or process model. I find Kojève's remark contra Hegel analogously addressing this sort of dialectic in Dewey. "He is content to observe and describe the dialectic which was effected throughout history, and he no longer needs to *make* a dialectic himself." Alexandre Kojève, *Introduction to the Reading of Hegel: Lectures on the* Phenomenology of Spirit, ed. Allan Bloom, trans. James H. Nichols, Jr. (Ithaca: Cornell University Press, 1969), 183. Rather than idealistic, however, Dewey promoted a "scientific" description of an empirical "Real." Which is to say that, for him,

a completion or unification of an ideal had been historically realized—democracy—which, while existentially unsatisfied, nevertheless clearly illuminated the new course of history. His sociological and psychological observations replaced Hegel's "Idea," but he still declared a philosophy of history based on the empirical significance of an incomplete and limited practice.

I am not suggesting that Dewey was historistic either. But in many places, as the statements from *Freedom and Culture* cited here seem to imply, "the democratic doctrine" called for "a faith based on ideas that are now intellectually credible and that are consonant with present economic conditions, which will inspire and direct action with something of the ardor once attached to things religious. . . . At the end as at the beginning the democratic method is as fundamentally simple and as immensely difficult as is the energetic, unflagging, unceasing creation of an ever-present new road upon which we can walk together" (164, 176). Just as Hegel had found the Prussia of his day congenial, Dewey idealized democratic America (as argued in Part One).

149. In *Democracy and Education* and *Schools of Tomorrow* Dewey advised training for occupations through schoolwork fitted to one's class and gender. Though I do not regard Dewey to be quite the reactionary that Gonzalez poses, his functionalist problem-solving would not necessarily find racist structures to be undemocratic if society functioned harmoniously.

150. See Gonzalez, *Progressive Education,* 101–4, and the works of the radical historians of education (Katz, Greer, Spring); also the research which Ravitch's counter-position brings to light. However, both the "radicals" and neo-conservatism are debating an issue which itself must be transformed. Liberal democracy was/is the challenge to external authority, the essence of the human struggle in the modern era for "happiness," or "free play." "Happiness" in this context has been (today more than ever) economically propelled. Without necessarily agreeing with Bookchin's entire social ecology thesis (see the essays in *The Modern Crisis*), I do find his argument to turn economics into culture, a market economy into a moral one, and efficiency into ethics to be central to the notion of social justice. Because it is derived concretely rather than functionally social justice begins in the recesses of democracy, in its forgotten streets.

151. Smith, *The Concept of Social Change,* 130.

152. Ibid., 151.

153. See Habermas, "History and Evolution."

154. Michel Foucault, *The Archaeology of Knowledge,* trans. A.M. Sheridan Smith (London: Tavistock Publications Ltd., 1972; repr., New York: Harper Colophon, 1976), 12.

155. Habermas, "History and Evolution," 14.

156. For an additional argument see H. Svi Shapiro, "Functionalism, the State, and Education: Towards a New Analysis" *Social Praxis* 8:3/4 (1981).

Part III

1. Certainly, modern and contemporary concepts differ from classical expressions. To give a full historical rendering of praxis is both beyond the scope of this book and unnecessary. Richard J. Bernstein's invaluable book, *Praxis and Action: Contemporary Philosophies of Human Activity* (Philadelphia: University of Pennslyvania Press, 1971), however, situates some of the historical and philosophical parameters of the term. For example, in his prefatory remarks Bernstein warns that we must not distort the shades of meaning originally assigned to the concept by Aristotle, one of which "signifies the disciplines and activities predominant in man's ethical and political life" (x). Furthermore, "praxis" clearly should not be defined as "practical," in any sense which eliminates or diffuses the dialectical quality inherent to acting and thinking. Praxis is *not* to be equated with commonsense. The standard text is Nicholas Lobkowicz, *Theory and Practice: History of a Concept from Aristotle to Marx* (Notre Dame: University of Notre Dame, 1967); see also, David A. Crocker, Praxis *and Democratic Socialism: The Critical Social Theory of Markovic and Stojanovic* (Atlantic Highlands, NJ: Humanities Press, 1983) especially 45–141; Bernstein, *Beyond Objectivism and Relativism: Science, Hermeneutics, and Praxis* (Philadelphia: University of Pennsylvania Press, 1983); Terence Ball, ed., *Political Theory and Praxis: New Perspectives* (Minneapolis: University of Minnesota Press, 1977).

2. Freire, *Pedagogy of the Oppressed,* 90–1.

3. Mihailo Markovic, "Historical Praxis as the Ground of Morality," in *Humanist Ethics: Dialogue on Basics,* ed. Morris B. Storer (Buffalo: Prometheus Books, 1980), 37.

4. I refer to the positivistic implications of historical materialism and scientific knowledge which many find in Marx's 19th century formulations, a "consciousness" of certainty, verifiability, and teleology which similarly (and obviously) had a hold of Dewey too. See Part One; also, Charles W. Mills, " 'Ideology' in Marx and Engels," *Philosophical Forum* 16:4 (1985) for a defense of ideology in Marx.

5. Karl Marx and Frederick Engels, *The German Ideology*, Parts One and Two, ed. and intro. R. Pascal (New York: International Publishers, 1947), 14–15.

6. Dewey did not address hierarchicalization along sex, race, the interpersonal, or psychoanalytically, but assessed social "distinctions" primarily along a functional division of labor. He weaved a pattern of society "as a loosely woven tissue of diverse groups" unconditionally elevating the concept of social over class and obliterating "the fundamentally different historical and economic factors which actually determine all the other manifestations of social activity in class formations." In Novack, *Marxism versus Pragmatism*, 204–5, but see all of ch. 10.

7. Foucault, *Archaeology of Knowledge*, 55.

8. Anthony Giddens, *Social Theory and Modern Sociology* (Stanford: Stanford University Press, 1987), 60. It is not possible to present the social theory of Giddens in this thesis, nor is it particularly necessary to the point I wish to make. The somewhat elliptical use of Giddens in this section only attempts to sharpen several obvious differences from the focus of Dewey's analysis. I have relied upon an admittedly incomplete reading of Giddens' works on a theory of structuration, in particular *Central Problems in Social Theory: Action, Structure and Contradiction in Social Analysis* (Berkeley: University of California Press, 1979); *The Constitution of Society*; also, John B. Thompson, *Studies in the Theory of Ideology* (Berkeley: University of California Press, 1984), 148–172, provides a brief summation of the theory while contending that Giddens' concept of structure, which is the basis of the theory, is insufficiently developed.

9. Giddens, *The Constitution of Society*, 2.

10. Ollman, *Alienation*, 57.

11. Giddens, *Central Problems*, 144.

12. Louise Kaplan has illuminated the work of psychoanalyst Margaret S. Mahler on differentiation during early childhood. While the toddler expects mother to be everywhere s/he pushes her away when she approaches. Kaplan describes the "oneness and separateness" as a "choreography—clinging and pushing away, shadowing and darting away, holding on and letting go." In *Oneness and Separateness: From Infant to Individual* (New York: Simon and Schuster, 1978), 191. Hegel, perhaps, produced the prototype of this dialectic in his analysis of "master and servant" in *The Phenomenology of the Spirit.* In depicting the struggle of consciousness in its egoistic and absolute polarities, the realization of the dependency of each on the other transforms the independence of each. Hegel maintained that relations are in a "constant process of conflict and interaction, which is at the basis of all movement and change." G.W.F. Hegel, *The Logic of Hegel,* trans. from *Encyclopedia of the Philosophical Sciences,* trans. William Wallace (London: Oxford University Press, 1873, 1892), 98. Freire conveys this movement in his critique of "the banking method." In its place, "dialogue" transforms "student" and "teacher." "The teacher is no longer merely the-one-who-teaches, but one who is himself taught in dialogue with the students, who in turn while being taught also teach. . . . In this process, arguments based on 'authority' are no longer valid; in order to function, authority must be *on the side of* freedom, not *against* it." In *Pedagogy of the Oppressed,* 67.

13. To enter into an account of the notion of "public sphere" would similarly take us too far afield. However, in obvious and general terms, it refers to the concrete capacity of persons to gather voluntarily to discuss and disclose social phenomena as it impacts and effects their individual and collective lives. In this respect, Maxine Greene advises "to lay particular stress on taking into account the actually lived world, where the search for meaning originates and where it finds its consummations" In " 'Excellence,' Meanings, and Multiplicity," 291. The organizational structure of such seems to me to always involve the dialectics of social justice.

14. Giroux, *Theory and Resistance,* 238–9.

15. Ibid., 239. See David Purpel, *The Moral and Spiritual Crisis in Education.*

16. Dewey, *Experience and Nature,* 398. See the source for the description in Marx and Engels, *The Holy Family or Critique of Critical Critique* (London: Lawrence and Wishart Ltd., 1957).

17. Bernstein, *John Dewey,* 45.

18. See Section "Scientific" in Part One. "Scientific praxis" is also part of the Marxian discourse; see V.I. Lenin, *Materialism and Empirio-Criticism: Critical Comments of a Reactionary Philosophy* (New York: International Publishers, 1927).

19. In "Ethics and Physical Science" (1887) Dewey wrote: "The present way of putting the question, that which makes it centre in human origin, nature, and development, is the outcome of the growth of physical science in general and of the theory of evolution in particular. Is man... the spiritual end... is his origin from God, that in his very life in nature he may yet find a way to make life divine and Godlike?" In *Early Works,* vol. 1, 205–6. In Dewey's early writings an explicit religiosity is evident. But right through *A Common Faith* Dewey sought to meld the religious in the secular as the cultural had become the natural.

20. Popper, "What is Dialectic?," *Mind* n.s. 49:196 (1940): 406, 407.

21. Dewey, *Logic,* 24; see chapter two for a fuller account of "naturalistic logic."

22. Dewey, *Experience and Education,* 35.

23. For the most part, Dewey used this notion, as he did in *Experience and Education,* to convey technological inventions and biological functions such as food, sleep, etc.

24. See Dewey, "The Need for a Recovery of Philosophy," in *Creative Intelligence: Essays in the Pragmatic Attitude* (New York: Henry Holt, 1917, 1945; repr., New York: Octagon Books, 1970), 3–69. This essay was of considerable help in understanding Dewey's notion of experience.

25. Dewey, *Experience and Nature,* 4a, 1 respectively.

26. Dewey, " 'Consciousness' and Experience," in *The Influence of Darwin,* 244.

27. Dewey, *Democracy and Education,* 296.

28. Ibid., 297; *Experience and Nature,* 211.

29. Dewey, *Experience and Nature,* 212.

30. Ibid., 233.

31. Ibid., 236.

32. Dewey, *A Common Faith*, 48, 47.

33. S.G. Sathaye, *Instrumentalism: A Methodological Exposition of the Philosophy of John Dewey* (Bombay, India: Popular Prakashan, 1972), 75.

34. Dewey, *Problems of Men*, 37.

35. Giddens, *Central Problems*, 116.

36. Kosik, *Dialectics of the Concrete*, 48-9. Kafka's "Metamorphosis" is a vivid account of the normalization of disruption/contradiction. The condition of Gregor Samsa is simply taken for granted.

37. See Gramsci, *Prison Notebooks*, 391, 407.

38. Dewey, *Problems of Men*, 14.

39. Dewey, "Reconstruction Twenty-five Years Later," xxxvi.

40. Dewey, *Logic*, 19.

41. Sharp, *Knowledge*, 107.

42. Gonzalez, *Progressive Education*, 98.

43. Wolfe, "Inauthentic Democracy," 78.

44. Ibid., 71. While there seemed to be a modification in his later writings from the psychological foundation sketched above and gleaned largely from his early work, Dewey nonetheless held fast to an organic functionalism. I have tried to balance *The School and Society, Democracy and Education, Schools of Tomorrow* with the collection of essays entitled *Problems of Men* and *Liberalism and Social Action*. Still, Dewey's theory of social action paled in design, scope, and practice even to his fellow reconstructionists. I do not believe it to be indiscriminate on my part to select the parts of Dewey's specifically pedagogical writings, albeit earlier and perhaps incomplete expressions, to build the critique against him. Writing as he does in *Problems of Men*, that science is still in its infancy, we can be relatively safe in assuming that his developmental basis and evolutionary models were not entirely a thing of his past.

45. Dewey, "Teachers and Labor," *The Social Frontier* 2:1 (1935): 8; quoted in Bowers, *The Progressive Educator*, 141.

46. Kosik, *Dialectics of the Concrete,* 43. Giddens offers a helpful concept, "practical consciousness," to describe "all the things which actors know tacitly about how to 'go on' in the contexts of social life without being able to give them discursive expression." In the *Constitution of Society,* 23. He describes how agents do behave without resorting to "naturalistic metaphysics" (Dewey), "internalized habits" (James), or "evolutionary universals" (Parsons). While Giddens does not draw out the pedagogical implications which a personal/political inquiry into practical consciousness evokes, the "routinized" character of activity associated with practical consciousness suggests the very organizational framework with which a pedagogy of social justice is concerned. "De-routinization" clearly illustrates the dialectical-critical educational praxis I have been advocating. See Giddens, *Central Problems.*

47. Ibid., 44.

48. Martin Jay, *The Dialectical Imagination: A History of the Frankfurt School and the Institute of Social Research, 1923–1950* (Boston: Little, Brown and Co., 1973), 263. This argument is completely developed by Aronowitz in *Science as Power.*

49. Magnus Haavelsrud, "On Inclusion and Exclusion," *Bulletin of Peace Proposals* 12:2 (1981): 107.

50. Dewey, *Problems of Men,* 31.

51. Geuss, *The Idea of a Critical Theory,* 60.

52. Giddens, *Central Problems,* 120.

53. See Kosik, *Dialectics of the Concrete,* 28–9. While Dewey is not altogether unaware that it is in "practice" that human beings prove the "truth," he does seem to forget Marx's next insight that while "men are products of circumstances and upbringing, and that, therefore, changed men are products of other circumstances and changed upbringing . . . it is men that change circumstances, and that the educator himself needs education. . . . The coincidence of the changing of circumstances and of human activity can be conceived and rationally understood only as *revolutionizing practice.*" Karl Marx, *Theses on Feuerbach,* in *Marx and Engels: Basic Writings on Politics and Philosophy,* ed. Lewis S. Feuer (Garden City: Anchor Books, 1959), 243–4.

54. In addition to the texts of these authors already referred to, the following have been most helpful in formulating a concept of educational praxis: Mihailo Markovic, *From Affluence to Praxis: Philosophy and Social Criticism* (Ann Arbor: University of Michigan Press, 1974); Dunayevskaya, *Philosophy and Revolution;* Gerson S. Sher, ed., *Marxist Humanism and Praxis* (Buffalo: Prometheus Books, 1978), chs. 1 and 4; Gould, *Marx's Social Ontology;* Jorge Larrain, *The Concept of Ideology* (Athens: University of Georgia Press, 1979).

55. For example, see Alice Frazer Evans, Robert A. Evans, and William Bean Kennedy, *Pedagogies for the Non-Poor* (Maryknoll, NY: Orbis Books, 1987); Ira Shor, *Critical Teaching and Everyday Life* (Boston: South End Press, 1980).

56. Additionally, Educators for Social Responsiblity is a national alliance of educators and parents working for nuclear arms reduction through school and community action and research.

57. Gramsci, *Prison Notebooks,* 323.

58. Ibid., 324.

59. Gramsci, as I mentioned in the Introduction, made explicit pedagogical suggestions. See *Prison Notebooks,* 24–43; also, an interesting secondary source is Harold Entwistle, *Antonio Gramsci: Conservative Schooling for Radical Politics* (London: Routledge and Kegan Paul, 1979).

60. Ibid., 330–1.

61. Sharp, *Knowledge,* 103.

62. Gramsci, *Prison Notebooks,* 333.

63. Crocker, Praxis *and Democratic Socialism,* 1. Along with Mihailo Markovic and Svetozar Stojanovic, the subjects of the book, Crocker refers also refers to the older and earlier member, Gajo Petrovic; see the introductory chapter for the origins and background of the *Praxis* group. Though not identified with *Praxis,* Jean Cohen's work, for example, is quite helpful for addressing some of these points. She offers the term "stratification" (contrast with Parson's usage) to replace "class" as a category of analysis, arguing that Marx's concern with the "social" fabric of a post-capitalist society was too immersed in "the logic and contradictions of a mode of production—the

capitalist economy." Cohen contends that a *"post-Marxist* approach to stratification should be able to *identify* the structural contradictions, crisis tendencies, and mechanisms of stratification within contemporary social systems; to *assess* the potentials for and of social movements without presupposing the primacy of either the economy or socioeconomic class struggles." In *Class and Civil Society: The Limits of Marxian Critical Theory* (Amherst: University of Massachusetts Press, 1982), 2, 195.

64. Kosik, *Dialectics of the Concrete,* 2.

65. Ibid.

66. Ibid., 3.

67. Ibid., 148.

68. Dewey, "My Pedagogic Creed," 86.

69. Milton Fisk's essay, "Dialectic and Ontology," in *Issues in Marxist Philosophy,* vol. 1, *Dialectics and Method,* eds. John Mepham and David-Hillel Ruben (Atlantic Highlands, NJ: Humanities Press, 1979), briefly alludes to a piece of this criticism. "Dewey knew there was a hierarchical division of labour in industry that required for its reproduction the inculcation of certain attitudes through the educational system. . . . His theory of reform through education required that his reform impulse . . . in numerous persons . . . could overturn the demands made on education by the hierarchical division of labour. He was considering the reform impulse and hierarchical division as isolated phenomena. . . . Yet both the reform impulse and the hierarchical division of labour are analytical components of the overall system of profit. Any connexion between them must be seen as sustained by that system" (124).

70. Herbert Kohl, "Can the Schools Build a New Social Order?" *Journal of Education* 162:3 (1980): 62.

71. Mills, *Sociology and Pragmatism,* 394.

72. Libertarian and humanist philosopher Paul Kurtz, in remarks responding to Markovic's essay "Historical Praxis as the Ground of Morality," explicitly assumes this anti-transformational and individualistic orientation of liberal reform. Addressing Markovic's notion of praxis, he asks, "Why not have a free society in which those who wish praxis *for themselves* can have it, but in which those who do not wish it are allowed to go

their own ways fulfilling any destiny that they may wish, however disparate it may be from the current utopian ideal defended by the intellectuals?" (54). It has been the fundamental premise of this thesis that such a position—idealistic and utopian—is entirely unsuitable to the vagaries of nuclearization.

73. Giddens, *Central Problems,* 150–1.

74. Ibid., 60.

75. Ibid., 63.

76. Ibid., 69–70.

77. Ibid., 95.

78. Ibid., 119 (italics mine).

79. Michael Klare's work has pointed out some irreconcilable facets of the spread of democracy. Why does it seem to be that American foreign interests are simultaneous to, as his *War Without End* (1972) depicts, a *structural* commitment by the United States to counterinsurgency exemplified by the fact that of the ten countries cited by Amnesty International with the poorest human rights record, "all have been *major recipients of U.S. arms and military assistance*"? In Klare and Cynthia Arnson, *Supplying Repression: U.S. Support for Authoritarian Regimes Abroad* (Washington, DC: Institute for Policy Studies, 1981), 4.

80. See, for example, Marable, *How Capitalism Underdeveloped Black America* which begins: "The most striking fact about American economic history and politics is the brutal and systemic underdevelopment of Black people" (1).

81. See Kovel, *Nuclear Terror*; Weston, *Toward Nuclear Disarmament*; "The New Arms Technology and What it Means," special issue *The Nation,* April 9, 1983; Jonathan Schell points out in *The Fate of the Earth* that 1.6 trillion dollars is to be spent on the military in the next four years; forty percent of research and development among all nations goes towards weapons; twenty-five percent of the world's scientists and engineers work on military projects.

82. Kosik, *Dialectics of the Concrete,* 137.

83. See Dewey, *Experience and Education.*

84. Kosik, *Dialectics of the Concrete*, 147.

85. Marcuse, *Reason and Revolution*, ix.

86. Giroux, *Ideology*, 114–5.

87. Freire, *Politics of Education*, 113.

88. H. Svi Shapiro, "Capitalism at Risk: The Political Economy of the Educational Reports of 1983," *Educational Theory* 35:1 (1985): 71.

Epilogue

1. Gramsci, *Prison Notebooks*, 424.

2. Milan Kundera, "Key Words, Problem Words, Words I Love," Book Review *New York Times*, March 6, 1988: 25.

3. Sharp, *Knowledge*, 109.

4. Foucault, "Intellectuals and Power," in *Language, Counter-Memory, Practice: Selected Essays and Interviews*, ed. and intro. Donald F. Bouchard, trans. Donald F. Bouchard and Sherry Simon (Ithaca: Cornell University Press, 1977), 213.

5. Ibid., 214.

6. Heller, *Radical Philosophy*, 157.

7. Dewey, *Experience and Education*, 5.

8. Dewey, "The Need for a Recovery of Philosophy"; quoted in Bernstein, *Praxis and Action*, 207.

9. Bernstein, *Praxis and Action*, 228.

10. Ibid., 229.

Bibliography

Addams, Jane. *Twenty Years at Hull House.* With Autobiographical Notes. New York: Macmillan Co., 1910.

Althusser, Louis. "Ideology and Ideological State Apparatuses." In *Lenin and Philosophy and Other Essays.* Trans. Ben Brewster. New York: Monthly Review Press, 1971.

Apel-Otto, Karl. "The Situation of Humanity as an Ethical Problem." Trans. David Roberts. *Praxis International* 4:3 (1984): 250–265.

Apple, Michael. "Curriculum as Ideological Selection." *Comparative Education Review* 20:2 (1976): 209–215.

———. *Education and Power.* London: Routledge and Kegan Paul, 1982; reprint, Boston: Ark Paperbacks, 1985.

———. *Ideology and Curriculum.* London: Routledge and Kegan Paul, 1979.

Aristotle. *Politics.* Trans. Benjamin Jowett. London: Oxford University Press, 1905.

Aronowitz, Stanley. *The Crisis in Historical Materialism: Class, Politics and Culture in Marxist Theory.* South Hadley, MA: J.F. Bergin, 1981.

———. "Politics and Higher Education in the 1980s." In *Curriculum and Instruction: Alternatives in Education,* ed. Henry A. Giroux, Anthony Penna, and William Pinar, 455–65. Berkeley: McCutchan Publishing, 1981.

———. *Science as Power: Discourse and Ideology in Modern Society.* Minneapolis: University of Minnesota Press, 1988.

Aronowitz, Stanley, and Henry A. Giroux. *Education Under Siege: The Conservative, Liberal and Radical Debate Over Schooling.* South Hadley, MA: Bergin and Garvey, 1985.

Aspeslagh, Robert. "Structures of Violence in Daily Life and Means to Overcome Them." *Gandhi Marg* 6:4/5 (1984): 224–236.

Baker, Melvin C. *Foundations of John Dewey's Educational Theory.* New York: Kings Crown Press/Columbia University, 1955.

Bauman, Zygmunt. *Culture as Praxis.* London: Routledge and Kegan Paul, 1973.

Beard, Charles, and William C. Bagley. *The History of the American People.* 2nd rev. ed. New York: Macmillan Co., 1929. Quoted in Walter Feinberg, *Reason and Rhetoric: The Intellectual Foundations of 20th Century Liberal Education Policy.* New York: John Wiley and Sons, 1975.

Bercovitch, Sacvan. *The American Jeremiad.* Madison: University of Wisconsin Press, 1978.

Berlak, Ann and Harold Berlak. *Dilemmas of Schooling: Teaching and Social Change.* New York: Methuen, 1981.

Berman, Morris. *The Reenchantment of the World.* Ithaca: Cornell University Press, 1981.

Bernier, Normand, and Jack Williams. *Beyond Beliefs: Ideological Foundations of American Education.* Englewood Cliffs: Prentice Hall, 1973.

Bernstein, Richard J. *John Dewey.* New York: Washington Square Press, 1966.

———. *Praxis and Action: Contemporary Philosophies of Human Activity.* Philadelphia: University of Pennsylvania Press, 1971.

Bowers, C.A. "The Dialectic of Nihilism and the State: Implications for an Emancipatory Theory of Education." *Educational Theory* 36:3 (1986): 225–232.

———. *The Progressive Educator and the Depression: The Radical Years.* New York: Random House, 1969.

Bowles, Samuel, and Herbert Gintis. *Schooling in Capitalist America: Educational Reform and the Contradictions of Economic Life.* New York: Basic Books, 1976, 1977.

Brameld, Theodore. "The Role of Philosophy in a Changing World." *Kadelpian Review* (January 1936). Quoted in William B. Stanley, "The Radical Reconstuctionist Rationale for Social Education." *Theory and Research in Social Education* 8:4 (1981): 55–79.

Buhle, Paul. *Marxism in the USA: Remapping the History of the American Left.* London: Verso, 1987.

Childs, John L. "Social Assumptions and Education." Review of *The Social Ideas of American Educators,* by Merle Curti. In *The Social Frontier* 2:4 (1936): 121–2.

Cohen, Jean. *Class and Civil Society: The Limits of Marxian Critical Theory.* Amherst: University of Massachusetts Press, 1982.

Comay, Rebecca. "Interrrupting the Conversation: Notes on Rorty." *Telos* 69 (1986): 119–130.

Cremin, Lawrence A. *The Transformation of the School: Progressivism in American Education, 1876-1957.* New York: Random House, 1961.

Crocker, David A. Praxis *and Democratic Socialism: The Critical Social Theory of Markovic and Stojanovic.* Atlantic Highlands, NJ: Humanities Press, 1983.

Dallmayr, Fred R. *Polis and Praxis: Exercises in Contemporary Political Theory.* Cambridge: MIT Press, 1984.

Danto, Arthur. "Naturalism." In *The Encyclopedia of Philosophy,* vol. 5, ed. Paul Edwards. New York: Macmillan Publishing Co., 1967.

de Beauvoir, Simone. *The Second Sex.* Trans. and ed. H.M. Parshley. New York: Random House, 1952.

Dewey, John. "Afterword." In *The Public and Its Problems.* New York: Henry Holt and Co., 1927; reprint, Chicago: Swallow Press, 1954.

———. *Art as Experience.* New York: G.P. Putnam's Sons, 1934; reprint, Perigee Books, 1980.

———. *The Child and the Curriculum.* In *The Child and the Curriculum* and *The School and Society.* Chicago: University of Chicago Press, 1956.

———. "Class Struggle and the Democratic Way." *The Social Frontier* 2:8 (1936): 241–2.

———. *A Common Faith.* New Haven: Yale University Press, 1934.

———. " 'Consciousness' and Experience." In *The Influence of Darwin on Philosophy and Other Essays.* New York: Henry Holt and Co., 1910; reprint, Bloomington: Indiana University Press, 1965.

———. "Creative Democracy—The Task Before Us." In *Classic American Philosophers,* ed. Max H. Fisch, 389–394. New York: Appleton-Century-Crofts, Inc., 1951. Quoted in Richard J. Bernstein, *John Dewey.* New York: Washington Square Press, 1966.

———. *Democracy and Education: An Introduction to the Philosophy of Education.* New York: Macmillan Co., 1916; reprint, New York: The Free Press, 1944.

———. *Dewey on Education.* Ed. Martin S. Dworkin, 32. New York: Columbia University Press, 1959. Quoted in Clarence J. Karier, "Liberal Ideology and Orderly Change." In *Roots of Crisis: American Education in the Twentieth Century,* ed. Clarence Karier, Paul Violas, Joel Spring, 84–107. Chicago: Rand McNally, 1973.

———. *The Dewey School: The Laboratory School of the University of Chicago 1896-1903.* Ed. Katherine Camp Mayhew and Anna Camp Edwards. New York: Appleton-Century, 1936.

———. "Ethics and Physical Science." In *John Dewey, The Early Works, 1882-1898,* vol. 1, 1882–1888, 205–226. Carbondale, IL: Southern Illinois University Press, 1972.

———. "The Evolutionary Method as Applied to Morality." *Philosophical Review* 11:2 (1902): 107–124.

———. *Experience and Education.* New York: Collier Books, 1938.

———. *Experience and Nature.* New York: Dover Publications, 1958.

———. *Freedom and Culture.* New York: G.P. Putnam's Sons, 1939.

———. *Human Nature and Conduct: An Introduction to Social Psychology.* New York: Henry Holt and Co., 1922; reprint, New York: Modern Library, 1957.

———. *Individualism Old and New.* New York: Capricorn Books, 1929, 1930, 1962.

———. "The Influence of Darwinism on Philosophy." In *The Influence of Darwin on Philosophy and Other Essays in Contemporary Thought.* New York: Henry Holt and Co., 1910; reprint, Bloomington: Indiana University Press, 1965.

————. "Intelligence and Morals." In *The Influence of Darwin on Philosophy and Other Essays in Contemporary Thought.* New York: Henry Holt and Co., 1910; reprint, Bloomington: Indiana University Press, 1965.

————. "Introduction." In *The Living Thoughts of Thomas Jefferson.* London: Cassell and Co., 1946.

————. "Introduction: The Problems of Men and the Present State of Philosophy." In *Problems of Men.* New York: Philosophical Library, 1946.

————. *Liberalism and Social Action.* New York: G.P. Putnam's Sons, 1935.

————. *Logic: The Theory of Inquiry.* New York: Henry Holt and Co., 1938.

————. "My Pedagogic Creed." In *John Dewey, The Early Works, 1882–1898,* vol. 5, 1895–1898, 84–95. Carbondale, IL: Southern Illinois University Press, 1972.

————. "The Need for a Recovery of Philosophy." Chapter in *Creative Intelligence: Essays in the Pragmatic Attitude.* New York: Henry Holt, 1917; reprint, New York: Octagon Books, 1970), 3–69.

————. *Philosophy and Civilization.* Gloucester, MA: Peter Smith, 1968.

————. *Problems of Men.* New York: Philosophical Library, 1946.

————. *The Public and Its Problems.* New York: Henry Holt and Co., 1927; reprint, Chicago: Swallow Press, 1954.

————. *The Quest for Certainty: A Study of the Relation of Knowledge and Action.* New York: Minton, Balch and Company, 1929.

————. *Reconstruction in Philosophy.* New York: Henry Holt and Co., 1920; reprint, Boston: Beacon Press, 1948.

————. "Reconstruction as Seen Twenty-five Years Later." Introduction to *Reconstruction in Philosophy.* New York: Henry Holt and Co., 1920; reprint, Boston: Beacon Press, 1948.

————. *The School and Society.* In *The Child and the Curriculum and The School and Society.* Chicago: University of Chicago Press, 1956.

———. "Social Psychology." *Psychological Review* 1:4 (1894): 400–11.

———. "Teachers and Labor." *The Social Frontier* 2:1 (1935). Quoted in C.A. Bowers, *The Progressive Educator and the Depression: The Radical Years.* New York: Random House, 1969.

Dewey, John and Evelyn Dewey. *Schools of Tomorrow.* New York: E.P. Dutton and Co., 1915, 1943, 1962.

Dorfman, Ariel. *The Empire's Old Clothes: What the Lone Ranger, Babar, and Other Innocent Heroes Do to our Minds.* New York: Pantheon Books, 1983.

Dunayevskaya, Raya. *Philosophy and Revolution: From Hegel to Sartre and from Marx to Mao.* Atlantic Highlands, NJ: Humanities Press, 1982.

Easlea, Brian. *Liberation and the Aims of Science: An Essay on Obstacles to the Building of a Beautiful World.* Totowa, NJ: Rowman and Littlefield, 1973.

Education for Democracy: A Statement of Principles. Washington, DC: Education for Democracy Project, 1987.

Elias, John L. *Conscientisation and Deschooling.* Philadelphia: Westminster Press, 1977.

Emerson, Ralph Waldo. "The Fortune of the Republic." In *Works*, vol. XI, 396–425. Boston: Houghton, Mifflin and Co., 1883.

Everhart, Robert. *The In-Between Years: Student Life in a Junior High School.* Santa Barbara: Graduate School of Education, University of California, 1979. Quoted in Michael Apple, *Education and Power.* London: Routledge and Kegan Paul, 1982; reprint, London: Ark Paperbacks, 1985.

Fay, Brian. "How People Change Themselves: The Relationship Between Critical Theory and Its Audience." In *Political Theory and Praxis: New Perspectives*, ed. Terence Ball, 200–233. Minneapolis: University of Minnesota Press, 1977.

———. *Social Theory and Political Practice.* London: George Allen and Unwin, 1975.

Feinberg, Walter, "The Conflict Between Intelligence and Community in Dewey's Educational Philosophy." *Educational Theory* 19:3 (1969): 236–248.

————. *Reason and Rhetoric: The Intellectual Foundations of 20th Century Liberal Education Policy.* New York: John Wiley and Sons, 1975.

Finkelstein, Barbara. "Education and the Retreat from Democracy in the United States, 1979–198?" *Teachers College Record* 86:2 (1984): 275–282.

Fisk, Milton. "Dialectic and Ontology." In *Issues in Marxist Philosophy.* Vol. 1, *Dialectics and Method,* ed. John Mepham and David-Hillel Ruben, 117–43. Atlantic Highlands, NJ: Humanities Press, 1979.

Foucault, Michel. *The Archaeology of Knowledge.* Trans. A.M. Sheridan Smith. London: Tavistock Publications Ltd., 1972; reprint, New York: Harper Colophon, 1976.

————. "Intellectuals and Power." In *Language, Counter-Memory, Practice: Selected Essays and Interviews.* Ed. and intro. Donald F. Bouchard. Trans. Donald F. Bouchard and Sherry Simon. Ithaca: Cornell University Press, 1977.

————. *The Order of Things: An Archaeology of the Human Sciences.* New York: Random House, 1970.

————. *Power/Knowledge: Selected Interviews and Other Writings 1972–1977.* Trans. Colin Gordon, Leo Marshall, John Mepham, Kate Soper and ed. Colin Gordon. New York: Pantheon Books, 1980.

Frankel, Charles. "John Dewey's Social Philosophy." In *New Studies in the Philosophy of John Dewey,* ed. Steven M. Cahn, 3–44. Hanover: University Press of New England, 1977.

Freire, Paulo. *Pedagogy of the Oppressed.* Trans. Myra Bergman Ramos. New York: Seabury Press, 1970.

————. *The Politics of Education: Culture, Power, and Liberation.* Trans. Donaldo Macedo. South Hadley, MA: Bergin and Garvey, 1985.

Galilei, Galileo. *Discoveries and Opinions of Galileo.* Ed. S. Drake, 63. Garden City: Doubleday Anchor, 1957. Quoted in Brian Easlea, *Liberation and the Aims of Science: An Essay on Obstacles to the Building of a Beautiful World.* Totowa, New Jersey: Rowman and Littlefield, 1973.

Geuss, Raymond. *The Idea of Critical Theory: Habermas and the Frankfurt School.* New York: Cambridge University Press, 1981.

Giddens, Anthony. *Central Problems in Social Theory: Action, Structure and Contradiction in Social Analysis.* Berkeley: University of California Press, 1979.

———. *The Constitution of Society: Outline of the Theory of Structuration.* Berkeley: University of California Press, 1984.

———. *Profiles and Critiques in Social Theory.* London: Macmillan Press Ltd., 1982.

———. *Social Theory and Modern Sociology.* Stanford: Stanford University Press, 1987.

Giroux, Henry A. "Beyond the Limits of Radical Educational Reform: Toward a Critical Theory of Education." *The Journal of Curriculum Theorizing* 2:1 (1980).

———. *Ideology, Culture, and the Process of Schooling.* Philadelphia: Temple University Press, 1981.

———. *Theory and Resistance in Education: A Pedagogy for the Opposition.* South Hadley, MA: Bergin and Garvey, 1983.

Giroux, Henry A. and Peter McLaren. "Teacher Education and the Politics of Engagement: The Case for Democratic Schooling." *Harvard Educational Review* 56:3 (1986): 213–238.

Gitlin, Todd. "Television's Screens: Hegemony in Transition." In *Cultural and Economic Reproduction in Education: Essays on Class, Ideology and the State,* ed. Michael Apple, 202–246. London: Routledge and Kegan Paul, 1982.

Goldmann, Lucien. *The Philosophy of the Enlightenment: The Christian Burgess and the Enlightenment.* Trans. Henry Maas. Cambridge: MIT Press, 1973.

Gonzalez, Gilbert G. *Progressive Education: A Marxist Interpretation.* Minneapolis: Marxist Educational Press, 1982.

Gould, Carol C. *Marx's Social Ontology: Individuality and Community in Marx's Theory of Social Reality.* Cambridge: MIT Press, 1978.

Gouldner, Alvin W. *The Coming Crisis of Western Sociology.* New York: Basic Books, 1970.

Gramsci, Antonio. *Selections from the Prison Notebooks.* Trans. and ed. Quinton Hoare and G. N. Smith. New York: International Publishers, 1971.

Greene, Maxine. "'Excellence,' Meanings, and Multiplicity." *Teachers College Record* 86:2 (1984): 283–297.

Gutierrez, Gustavo. *A Theology of Liberation: History, Politics, and Salvation.* Trans. and ed. Sister Caridad Inda and John Eagleson. Maryknoll, NY: Orbis Books, 1973, 1988.

Haavelsrud, Magnus. "On Inclusion and Exclusion." *Bulletin of Peace Proposals* 12:2 (1981): 105–114.

Habermas, Jürgen. "History and Evolution." *Telos* 39 (1979): 5–44.

———. *Theory and Practice.* Trans. John Viertel. Boston: Beacon Press, 1973.

Harrington, Michael. *The Politics at God's Funeral: The Spiritual Crisis of Western Civilization.* New York: Penguin Books, 1983.

Hegel, G.W.F. *The Logic of Hegel,* trans. from *Encyclopedia of the Philosophical Sciences.* Trans. William Wallace. London: Oxford University Press, 1873, 1892.

Heller, Agnes. *Radical Philosophy.* Trans. James Wickham. Oxford: Basil Blackwell, 1984.

Henriques, Julian, Wendy Hollway, Cathy Urwin, Couze Venn, and Valerie Walkerdine. *Changing the Subject: Psychology, Social Regulation and Subjectivity.* New York: Methuen, 1984.

Hiley, David R. "Foucault and the Question of Enlightenment." *Philosophy and Social Criticism* 11:1 (1985): 63–83.

Hofstader, Richard. *The Age of Reform.* New York: Random House, 1955.

Horkheimer, Max. *Eclipse of Reason.* New York: Oxford University Press, 1947; reprint, New York: Continuum, 1974.

Horkheimer, Max and Theodor Adorno. *Dialectic of Enlightenment.* Trans. John Cumming. New York: Continuum, 1972.

Horton, Myles. "What is Liberating Education? A Conversation with Myles Horton." Interview by Bingham Graves. *Radical Teacher* (1979).

Jacoby, Russell. *Social Amnesia: A Critique of Conformist Psychology from Adler to Laing.* Boston: Beacon Press, 1975.

Jay, Martin. *The Dialectical Imagination: A History of the Frankfurt School and the Institute of Social Research, 1923-1950.* Boston: Little, Brown and Co., 1973.

Jefferson, Thomas. *Crusade Against Ignorance: Thomas Jefferson on Education.* Ed. Gordon C. Lee, 83. New York: Teachers College Press, 1961. Quoted in Ramon Sanchez. *Schooling American Society: A Democratic Ideology.* Syracuse: Syracuse University Press, 1976.

Jessop, Bob. "Capitalism and Democracy: The Best Possible Shell?" In *Power and the State,* ed. Gary Littlejohn, Barry Smart, John Wakeford, Nira Yuval-Davis, 10-51. New York: St. Martin's Press, 1978.

Kant, Immanuel. *Critique of Practical Reason and Other Writings in Moral Philosophy.* Trans. and ed. Lewis White Beck. Chicago: University of Chicago Press, 1949.

Kaplan, Louise. *Oneness and Separateness: From Infant to Individual.* New York: Simon and Schuster, 1978.

Karier, Clarence J. "Liberal Ideology and the Quest For Orderly Change." In *Roots of Crisis: American Education in the Twentieth Century,* ed. Clarence Karier, Paul Violas, Joel Spring, 84-107. Chicago: Rand McNally, 1973.

Kennedy, William Bean. "A Radical Challenge to Inherited Educational Patterns." *Religious Education* 74:5 (1979): 491-95.

———. "Highlander Praxis: Learning with Myles Horton." *Teachers College Record* 83:1 (1981): 105-19.

Kierkegaard, Søren. *The Present Age.* Trans. Alexander Dru. New York: Harper and Row, 1962.

Klare, Michael and Cynthia Arnson. *Supplying Repression: U.S. Support for Authoritarian Regimes Abroad.* Washington, DC: Institute for Policy Studies, 1981.

Kohl, Herbert. "Can the Schools Build a New Social Order?" *Journal of Education* 162:3 (1980): 57-66.

Kojève, Alexandre. *Introduction to the Reading of Hegel: Lectures on the "Phenomenology of Spirit."* Ed. Allan Bloom. Trans. James H. Nichols, Jr. Ithaca: Cornell University Press, 1969.

Kosik, Karel. *Dialectics of the Concrete: A Study on Problems of Man and World.* Boston Studies in the Philosophy of Science, vol. LII. Dordrecht, Holland: D. Reidel Publishing Company, 1976.

Kovel, Joel. *Against the State of Nuclear Terror.* Boston: South End Press, 1983.

Kuhn, Thomas S. *The Structure of Scientific Revolutions,* 2nd ed. Chicago: University of Chicago Press, 1962, 1970.

Kundera, Milan. "Key Words, Problem Words, Words I Love." Book Review *New York Times,* March 6, 1988.

Kurtz, Paul. "Comment on Markovic Article." In *Humanist Ethics: Dialogue on Basics,* ed. Morris B. Storer, 51-54. Buffalo: Prometheus Books, 1980.

Lichtman, Robert. "The Facade of Equality in Liberal Democratic Theory." *Socialist Revolution* 1:1 (1970).

Lipset, Seymour Martin. *Political Man.* Garden City: Doubleday, 1960.

Love, Nancy S. *Marx, Nietzsche, and Modernity.* New York: Columbia University Press, 1986.

Luckham, Robin. "Myths and Realities of Security." In *Toward Nuclear Disarmament and Global Security: A Search for Alternatives,* ed. Burns H. Weston, 159-161. Boulder: Westview Press, 1984.

Macpherson, C. B. "Politics: Post-Liberal-Democracy?" In *Ideology in Social Science: Readings in Critical Social Theory,* ed. Robin Blackburn, 17-31. New York: Pantheon Books, 1972.

Maguire, Daniel C. *A New American Justice: Ending the White Male Monopolies.* Garden City: Doubleday and Company, 1980.

Mann, Horace. "Fifth Annual Report of the Secretary of State Board of Education, 1842." Quoted in Samuel Bowles and Herbert Gintis, *Schooling in Capitalist America: Educational Reform and the Contradiction of Economic Life.* New York: Basic Books, 1976, 1977.

———. *Republic and the School: Horace Mann on the Education of Free Men.* Classics in Education, No. 1. Ed. Lawrence A. Cremin. New York: Bureau of Publications, Teachers College, Columbia University, 1957. Quoted in Clarence J. Karier. *Man, Society, and Education.* Glenview, IL: Scott, Foresman and Co., 1967.

Marable, Manning. *How Capitalism Underdeveloped Black America: Problems in Race, Political Economy and Society.* Boston: South End Press, 1983.

Marcuse, Herbert. *One-Dimensional Man.* Boston: Beacon Press, 1964.

———. *Reason and Revolution: Hegel and the Rise of Social Theory.* New York: Oxford University Press, 1941; reprint, Boston: Beacon Press, 1960.

Markovic, Mihailo. "Historical Praxis as the Ground of Morality." In *Humanist Ethics: Dialogue on Basics,* ed. Morris B. Storer, 36-57. Buffalo: Prometheus Books, 1980.

Marx, Karl. *Economic and Philosophical Manuscripts.* Trans. T.B. Bottomore. In *Marx's Concept of Man,* ed. Erich Fromm, 85-196. New York: Frederick Ungar, 1961, 1966.

———. *Theses on Feuerbach.* In *Marx and Engels: Basic Writings on Politics and Philosophy,* ed. Lewis S. Feuer. Garden City: Anchor Books, 1959.

Marx, Karl and Frederick Engels. *The German Ideology.* Parts One and Two. Ed. R. Pascal. New York: International Publishers, 1947.

Mead, George Herbert. *The Works of George Herbert Mead.* Vol. 3, *The Philosophy of the Act.* Ed. Charles W. Morris. Chicago: University of Chicago Press, 1936. Quoted in Ann and Harold Berlak, *Dilemmas of Schooling: Teaching and Social Change,* New York: Methuen, 1981.

Mouffe, Chantal. "Hegemony and Ideology in Gramsci." In *Gramsci and Marxist Theory,* ed. Chantal Mouffe, 168-204. London: Routledge and Kegan Paul, 1979.

Murphy, Arthur E. "Dewey's Epistemology and Metaphysics." In *The Philosophy of John Dewey,* ed. P.A. Schilpp. Evanston and Chicago: Tudor Publishing Co., 1939. Quoted in Richard

Rorty, "Dewey's Metaphysics." In Steven M. Cahn, ed. *New Studies in the Philosophy of John Dewey.* Hanover: University Press of New England, 1977.

National Alliance of Business. "Our Youth: Our Future." An Advertising Supplement to the *New York Times Magazine* September 20, 1987.

Nielsen, Kai. "Capitalism, Socialism and Justice: Reflections on Rawls' Theory of Justice." *Social Praxis* 7:3/4 (1980): 253-277.

Norman, Richard. "Moral Philosophy Without Morality?" *Radical Philosophy* 6 (1973): 2-7.

Novack, George. *Pragmatism versus Marxism: An Appraisal of John Dewey's Philosophy.* New York: Pathfinder Press, 1975.

Ollman, Bertell. *Alienation: Marx's Conception of Man in Capitalist Society.* Cambridge: Cambridge University Press, 1971.

Parsons, Talcott. "Evolutionary Universals in Society." *American Sociological Review* 29:3 (1964): 339-357.

Pattison, Robert. "On the Finn Syndrome and the Shakespeare Paradox." *The Nation,* May 30, 1987: 710-20.

Pelczynski, Zbigniew. "The Roots of Ideology in Hegel's Political Philosophy." In *Ideology and Politics,* ed. Maurice Cranston, 65-73. Firenze, Italy: LeMonnier, 1980.

Popper, Karl. "What is Dialiectic?" *Mind* n.s. 49:196 (1940): 403-426.

Poster, Mark. *Foucault, Marxism and History: Mode of Production versus Mode of Information.* Oxford: Polity Press, 1984.

Purpel, David. *The Moral and Spiritual Crisis in Education: A Curriculum for Justice and Compassion in Education.* Granby, MA: Bergin and Garvey, 1989.

Reardon, Betty. "Disarmament Education as World Order Inquiry." In *Education for Peace and Disarmament: Toward a Living World,* ed. Douglas Sloan, 137-51. New York: Teachers College Press, 1983.

———. ed. *Educating for Global Responsibility: Teacher-Designed Curricula for Peace Education, K-12.* New York: Teachers College Press, 1988.

Rorty, Richard. *Consequences of Pragmatism: Essays 1972-1980.* Minneapolis: University of Minnesota Press, 1982.

―――. "Solidarity or Objectivity?" In *Post-Analytic Philosophy,* ed. John Rajchman and Cornel West, 3-19. New York: Columbia University Press, 1985.

Sanchez, Ramon. *Schooling American Society: A Democratic Ideology.* Syracuse: Syracuse University Press, 1976.

Santayana, George. "Dewey's Naturalistic Metaphysics." In *The Philosophy of John Dewey,* ed. P.A. Schilpp. Evanston and Chicago: Tudor Publishing Co., 1939. Quoted in Richard Rorty, "Dewey's Metaphysics." In Steven M. Cahn, ed. *New Studies in the Philosophy of John Dewey.* Hanover: University Press of New England, 1977.

Sathaye, S.G. *Instrumentalism: A Methodological Exposition of the Philosophy of John Dewey.* Bombay, India: Popular Prakashan, 1972.

Schell, Jonathan. *The Fate of the Earth.* New York: Avon, 1982.

Shapiro, H. Svi. "Capitalism at Risk: The Political Economy of the Educational Reports of 1983." *Educational Theory* 35:1 (1985): 57-72.

Sharp, Rachel. *Knowledge, Ideology and the Politics of Schooling: Towards a Marxist Analysis of Education.* London: Routledge and Kegan Paul, 1980.

Skillen, Tony. "Marxism and Morality." *Radical Philsophy* 8 (1974): 11-15.

Smith, Anthony. *The Concept of Social Change: A Critique of the Functionalist Theory of Social Change.* London: Routledge and Kegan Paul, 1973.

Smith, John E. "John Dewey: Philosopher of Experience." In *John Dewey and the Experimental Shift in Philosophy.* Ed. Charles W. Hendel. New York: Liberal Arts Press, 1959.

"Special Issue on Critiques of the Enlightenment." *New German Critique* 41 (Sp/Sum 1987).

Therborn, Goran. *The Ideology of Power and the Power of Ideology.*London: Verso, 1980.

Thompson, John B. *Studies in the Theory of Ideology.* Berkeley: University of California Press, 1984.

Venn, Couze. "The Subject of Psychology." In *Changing the Subject: Psychology, Social Regulation and Subjectivity,* ed. Julian Henriques, Wendy Hollway, Cathy Urwin, Couze Venn, and Valerie Walkerdine, 119-152. New York: Methuen, 1984.

Violas, Paul. "Progressive Social Philosophy: Charles Horton Cooley and Edward Alsworth Ross." In *Roots of Crisis: American Education in the Twentieth Century,* ed. Clarence Karier, Paul Violas, Joel Spring, 40-65. Chicago: Rand McNally, 1973.

Walkerdine, Valerie. "Developmental Psychology and the Child-Centred Pedagogy: The Insertion of Piaget into Early Education." In *Changing the Subject: Psychology, Social Regulation and Subjectivity,* ed. Julian Henriques, Wendy Hollway, Cathy Urwin, Couze Venn, and Valerie Walderdine, 153-202. New York: Methuen, 1984.

West, Cornel. "The Politics of American Neo-Pragmatism." In *Post-Analytic Philosophy,* ed. John Rajchman and Cornel West, 259-275. New York: Columbia University Press, 1985.

White, Morton G. *Social Thought in America: The Revolt Against Formalism.* Boston: Beacon Press, 1957.

Williams, Raymond. "Base and Superstructure in Marxist Cultural Theory." In *Problems in Materialism and Culture.* London: Verso, 1980.

Wilson, T.H. *The American Ideology: Science, Technology and Organization as Modes of Rationality in Advanced Industrial Societies.* London: Routledge and Kegan Paul, 1977.

Wolfe, Alan. "Inauthentic Democracy: A Critique of Public Life in Modern Liberal Society." *Studies in Political Economy* 21 (1986): 57-81.

Woods, Robert A. and Albert J. Kennedy, ed. *Handbook of Settlements.* New York: Arno Press, 1911, 1970.

Index